STUDIES ON THE HOLOCAUST IN HUNGARY

Edited by
RANDOLPH L. BRAHAM

SOCIAL SCIENCE MONOGRAPHS, BOULDER
AND
THE CSENGERI INSTITUTE FOR HOLOCAUST STUDIES
OF THE GRADUATE SCHOOL AND UNIVERSITY CENTER
OF THE CITY UNIVERSITY OF NEW YORK
DISTRIBUTED BY COLUMBIA UNIVERSITY PRESS

1990

EAST EUROPEAN MONOGRAPHS, NO. CCCI

Holocaust Studies Series

Randolph L. Braham, Editor
The Institute for Holocaust Studies
The Graduate School and University Center
The City University of New York

Previously published books in the Series:

Perspectives on the Holocaust, 1982
Contemporary Views on the Holocaust, 1983
Genocide and Retribution, 1983
The Hungarian Jewish Catastrophe: A Selected and Annoted Bibliography, 1984
Jewish Leadership During the Nazi Era: Patterns of Behavior in the Free World, 1985
The Holocaust in Hungary—Forty Years Later, 1985
The Origins of the Holocaust Christian Anti-Semitism, 1985
The Halutz Resistance in Hungary, 1942-1944, 1986
The Tragedy of Hungarian Jewry: Essays, Documents, Depositions, 1986
The Treatment of the Holocaust in Textbooks, 1987
The Psychological Perspectives of the Holocaust and of Its Aftermath, 1988
Reflections of the Holocaust in Art and Literature, 1990

The Holocaust Studies Series is published in cooperation with the Institute for Holocaust Studies. These books are outgrowths of lectures, conferences, and research projects sponsored by the Institute. It is the purpose of the Series to subject the events and circumstances of the Holocaust to scrutiny by a variety of academics who bring different scholarly disciplines to the study.

The first three books in the Series were published by
Kluwer-Nijhoff Publishing of Boston

ISBN 0-88033-198-4
Library of Congress Catalog Card Number 90-63584

Printed in the United States of America

Contents

INTRODUCTION

It is now generally recognized that the Holocaust in Hungary was unique in many respects. Although the Hungarian Jewish community of close to 800,000 was subjected to grave injustices, it survived the first four and a half years of World War II relatively intact. While their brethren in Nazi–dominated Europe were being eliminated under the Final Solution program, the Hungarian Jews continued to enjoy the physical protection of the aristocratic–conservative government of Miklós Kállay. They were, of course, not totally immune from the ravages of the National Socialist plague. An ally of the Third Reich, Hungary also adopted a number of anti–Jewish laws, depriving their citizens of the Jewish faith of their basic rights and drastically curtailing their livelihood. Moreover, the Jewish community suffered around 60,000 casualties as a result of several massacres and of the inhumane treatment to which many labor servicemen, especially those deployed in the Ukraine, were subjected. Nevertheless, the Jewish community as a whole continued to live in relative safety until the German occupation of Hungary on March 19, 1944.

It is an irony of history that this large community was to suffer perhaps the harshest blow in the Final Solution program. Since time was of the essence—the Soviet forces were rapidly advancing toward Hungary—the Nazis and their Hungarian accomplices decided to "solve" the Jewish question as swiftly as possible. Almost immediately after the occupation, the German–Hungarian dejewifiers began to implement the various phases in the Final Solution program. The Hungarian Jews were isolated, marked, expropriated, driven into ghettos, and deported within a record time. By July 9, 1944, close to 440,000 Jews were deported to Auschwitz, making the Hungarian countryside virtually *Judenrein*. By all historical accounts, this was by far the swiftest and most barbarous chapter of the Nazis' war against the Jews. And it happened on the eve of Allied victory, when the world already knew all the secrets of Auschwitz.

This volume—the thirteenth in the Holocaust Studies Series of the Emeric and Ilana Csengeri Institute for Holocaust Studies—is devoted to this tragic chapter of the Holocaust. It includes eight studies on various subjects that were left basically unexplored in the English historical literature. The first three essays are devoted to various aspects of rescue. The first is an in-depth interview with Reverend József Éliás, the former executive officer of the Good Shepherd Committee (*Jó Pásztor Bizottság*), the agency that was established under the auspicies of the Hungarian Reformed Church to help Jews converted to protestantism. Reverend Éliás has emerged as a major figure not only in the defense of the persecuted Jews during the Nazi era, but also in the postwar struggle against anti-Semitism. Conducted by Sándor Szenes, a well-known journalist and author, the interview provides new and exciting insights into the pre-war and wartime attitudes of church dignitaries, including Bishop László Ravasz, political figures, and resistance leaders. It also unravels some of the mysteries relating to the acquisition and distribution of the so-called Auschwitz Reports, revealing that the Hungarian political and church leaders had been familiar with the secrets of Auschwitz prior to the mass deportations that began on May 15, 1944. The second piece is by Dr. Uri Asaf, an Israeli scholar. It fills a void by providing succinct background information on a relatively large number of Hungarians who had the courage to swim against the Nazi ideological tide by helping or rescuing their Jewish friends and neighbors, often at the risk of their own lives. These biographical notes were culled from survivors' testimonies, journalistic and historical accounts, and archival sources, including those of the Department for the Righteous at Yad Vashem in Jerusalem. Closely related to this topic is the third article in this collection. It provides an inspirational insight into the blissful activities of Sister Margit Slachta, the then head of the Society of Social Sisterhood, on behalf of several Jewish families who were deported from Csíkszereda soon after the Hungarian occupation of Northern Transylvania in September 1940. Her humanity and concern for the persecutees radiate from the letters that were selected and annotated for publication by Reverend Tamás Majsai, a prolific author and one of the most genuine representatives of contemporary Hungarian liberalism.

The next three essays deal with various aspects of persecution. The first study in this group is by Dr. Maria Schmidt, a well-known expert on the Holocaust in Hungary. It discusses certain aspects of the Jewish persecutions in Slovakia as reflected in the reports of several Hungarian regional police precincts. The study demonstrates, among other things, that the Hungarian authorities were accurately informed about the nature of the anti-Jewish drive in Slovakia—a Nazi-supported state with a relatively large number of Hungarian-speaking Jews. The study by Dr. Szabolcs Szita, an associate of the University of Pécs, offers new insights into the plight of the Jews of Hungary, especially those of Budapest, during the Szálasi era. In his thoroughly documented piece, Dr. Szita provides details on the camps that were set up along the Hungarian border with the Reich. The Jews—men and women of all ages—who were marched or taken there during that tragic period in Hungarian history were used as slave laborers for the building of fortifications ostensibly for the defense of Vienna. Dieter Vaupel of the University of Kassel provides a documented study on a relatively unknown camp—the Hessisch Lichtenau sub-camp of Buchenwald—that employed a large number of Hungarian Jewish women. The study provides details about the agony and fate of the Hungarian deportees who were employed in the sub-camp's munitions plant. Skillfully translated by Maida Pollock, a survivor of that camp, the study includes many succinct interviews with several survivors, perpetrators, and local onlookers.

Dr. Julia Szilágyi and her co-authors—Drs. István Cserne, Katalin Pető, and György Szöke—present their findings concerning the psychopathological symptoms suffered by second and third generation descendants of Hungarian Holocaust survivors. While partially focusing on the special Hungarian circumstances that may have played a role in the development and/or exacerbation of these symptoms, the conclusions of the authors dovetail to a large extent with the findings of their American colleagues as reflected in Volume 11 of this Series: *The Psychological Perspectives of the Holocaust and of Its Aftermath.*

The last piece is a contribution to the debate on the losses suffered by Hungarian Jewry. Most postwar studies in this area were based on the statistics compiled by the Statistical Department of the Hungarian Section of the World Jewish Congress (HSWJC) shortly after the end of World War II. Relying on detailed national, county, and local statistical data, HSWJC concluded that close to 570,000 Hungarian Jews were killed during the Nazi era. In recent years, however, several articles were published in Hungary, claiming that the number of casualties suffered by the Jewish community was only around 400,000. The succinct statistical-demographic study by Dr. László Varga, an associate of the Institute of History of the Hungarian Academy of Science, corroborates the findings of the HSWJC, concluding that "the Holocaust in Hungary claimed at least 550,000 Jewish lives."

The views expressed by the authors are theirs alone and do not necessarily reflect those of the editor or the Emeric and Ilana Csengeri Institute of Holocaust Studies.

The publication of this volume was made possible by the generous support of many people. I would like to express my thanks, first of all, to Ilana and Emeric Csengeri, the benefactors of the Institute, for their consistent moral and financial support. I am indebted to my many friends who worked—and continue to work—tirelessly toward advancing the causes of the Institute through their involvement in the Special Holocaust Fund campaign. I am especially thankful to Valerie and Frank Furth, Eva and Norman Gati, Doris and Louis Glick, Elizabeth and Jack Rosenthal, Marcel Sand, and Elizabeth and Ernest Zelig. Finally, I would like to express my gratitude to President Harold M. Proshansky and Dean Solomon Goldstein of the Graduate School and University Center of The City University of New York for their consistent support.

Randolph L. Braham
September 1990

"SAVING PEOPLE WAS OUR MAIN TASK . . ." AN INTERVIEW WITH REVEREND JÓZSEF ÉLIÁS

Sándor Szenes

I had heard about József Éliás, retired Protestant minister from Debrecen, and his well-known deeds in the early sixties when as a correspondent of *Népszabadság* [People's Freedom] in Hajdú-Bihar and Szabolocs-Szatmár counties, I lived in Debrecen for a couple of years. We got to know each other personally more than ten years ago during a difficult time for him, when he had been suspended by his church superiors, brought before a church court, and was trying to protect the values of his parish and himself. As part of my duties I followed his case and tried to be of help because I was convinced of his integrity.

His father was a smith, his mother a seamstress and there were four children in the family, which had been forced to move from Budapest to the country. He himself had to commute between their village home and a high school in the capital. This was the start of the road which led to the historically significant Academy of Protestant Theology in Pápa (*Pápai Református Teológiai Akadémia*) for four years of study. He graduated as a minister in 1941 and started his career as an assistant minister in the countryside. He was summoned to Budapest in 1942 by the leaders of his church. He started off as clerical secretary and later became the chairperson of a national Protestant committee which was concerned with theology, the safeguarding of its interests, and the rescuing of people.

Even in Debrecen few people know that he was the only recipient of a special international award. The international ecumenical organization, the International Hebrew Christian Alliance (IHCA), which regards as one of its main duties the eradication of racial and religious prejudice, decided to give an award and £800 to the Protestant minister who, during World War II, carried out the most successful rescue work in a German–occupied country. At the 1948 London Conference of the IHCA this award was given to József Éliás.

• *You were twenty–three when you started your theological studies in Pápa. It seems that you chose to be a minister somewhat later than usual. Why?*

• I regard being a minister as a calling which developed out of the kinds of religious experiences that are so individual that they are difficult to explain to others. If I had to choose again, I would again choose to be a Protestant minister, despite my knowing the kinds of things I would have to undergo during those decades. It is true I was a few years older than most of my fellow students in Pápa but I was not the only exception. We were divided not by age but, even in those years, by far more serious matters: there were secret and open members of the Arrow Cross and there were those attracted to the theological left who were anti–fascists. I was one of the latter. We soon woke up to the fact or simply realized that we would not have an idyllic, peaceful clerical life. We were half way through the course when World War II broke out, and when we emerged from the Academy as trained theologians in 1941, Hungary was already at war with the Soviet Union and a state of war had been declared with the United Kingdom and soon with the United States as well.

• *Where did you start to work as a minister?*

• I found myself in Cegléd as an assistant to Sándor Ceglédy, the leading minister. We had a strong parish of 17,000 souls and Ceglédy was a wonderful person. He was a professor of theology, a former teacher at the Academy in Pápa, a great polymath, a hardworking philanthropist and humanist. His sons also acquired fame as respected theologians and excellent linguists. His best friend was the rabbi of the town, a learned debating partner, and the whole Ceglédy family was proud of this friendship in those years when not many ministers dared to cultivate such relationships. There were promises of an ideal clerical working life for many years in this parish, but fate chose a more difficult road for me. In 1942, things happened to me which gave a different direction to my clerical career, as well as to my life. One of these big events was that in the summer of that year I was able to join an anti–fascist group which stood against the pro–German attitude of the time.

• *Where and how did this happen?*

• While in high school I had become a good friend of Dr. Géza Soós, secular President of the Soli Deo Gloria Protestant Student Association. When I was a student of theology in Pápa, our friendship developed in a special way. At that time we often met in Budapest in summer and, once he had placed his trust in me, Géza openly discussed his political views. If these views had become known to the leadership, Géza would not have been able to be the official president of the Protestant Student Association. In the summer of 1942, as our relationship became even closer and more trusting, new meaning was added to it.

• *What happened in that summer?*

• Géza invited me to Szilice, then a part of Hungary. The Protestant youth organization was using a former Czechoslovakian military police compound to hold a conference for the leaders of the Christian Youth Organization (*Keresztyén Ifjúsági Egyesület*), which was the international youth organization of the Protestant Church. Neither Géza nor I was a leader, but he could hold important meetings undisturbed here. On one evening during this conference Géza drew aside a few of us for a private talk. As I remember there were nine of us, all young men. Géza, who knew each one of us, started off the conversation by asking us whether we thought there was a possibility that the Germans would win the war. All of us answered in the negative and some of us even gave reasons for it. Géza Soós then explained to us that, starting with Gyula Gömbös, the whole government and the Regency had led the country into a doomed war on the side of German fascism by carrying out an irresponsible, nationally destructive policy. Having realized this, patriotic Hungarians, concerned about their nation, had started to organize opposition. This movement was trying to find and organize people regardless of their social standing and religious beliefs who wanted to free the country from Hitlerist oppression, danger from the Arrow Cross, all the social problems of the Horthy regime, and the destruction caused by the war. He said that he was speaking openly with us because he wanted and hoped that we would adopt this movement's goals, tasks, strict discipline, need for secrecy, and the accompanying dangers. As an answer to our questions, he admitted that the movement had not yet had any political results but they had had success in choosing people and had managed to put the majority of them into positions of trust. Géza must have been one of them, because he had been a judge in the Ministry of Justice and had just recently been appointed to a higher position in the Foreign Ministry. All of us present at this night-long discussion in Szilice, enthusiastically agreed to Géza's statements and declared ourselves ready to become part of and play a role in this opposition movement.

• *Did you know or guess who were the leaders of this movement?*

• First I knew only about Géza Soós and I trusted him without reservation. Later, in 1944, I learned that one of the leaders was Domokos Szent-Iványi, a counsellor at the Foreign Ministry, and a close colleague and confidant of Horthy's younger son, Miklós, Jr. Naturally, I did get into contact with those whom I believed or knew were members of the movement. Our rule, all the stronger for being unwritten, and made in order to protect our work and ourselves, was that whatever we didn't know couldn't be forced out of us, even by the cruelest torture. This meant that it was prohibited for us to talk loosely, we didn't want to know about things that didn't affect us directly, we didn't ask each other probing questions, and we didn't give each other irrelevant information. Of course I now know more about the movement.

• *In 1942, this movement called itself the "Teleki Group." This was the predecessor of the Hungarian Independence Movement Magyar Függetlenségi Mozgalom (MFM), which was established after the German occupation.*

• I only considered our activities from 1942 on as an opposition movement, and I'll refer to it this way in our interview. The rest, I think, is not my but the historians' task and I can only contribute to their work to the best of my knowledge and recollection.

• *We were talking about that discussion in Szilice when, upon Géza Soós's invitation, you joined the opposition movement.*

• In Szilice Géza talked to me privately as well. Looking toward the future, he said that he would be my superior and that I should be available, and when he had need of me, he would come looking for me. I didn't get any concrete task then. I returned to Cegléd and did what I had to do as assistant minister in our parish. Six months later, in summer 1942, the rector of the leading national body of our church, the Universal Convent (*Egyetemes Konvent*), Dr. László Ravasz, summoned me to Budapest. He appointed me as the clerical secretary of the Good Shepherd Committee (*Jó Pásztor Bizottság—JPB*). The Universal Convent had established this committee in order to protect the interest of those Christians who were of Jewish origin. The name originated from the biblical story of the "good shepherd" who "gave his life to his sheep." Thus the name explains the program, and it proved to be especially necessary in the years of the tragic war and the atrocities against the Jews. When I started this work, they had already passed the three anti-Jewish laws; they had done away with the equal legal status of Jews. Those citizens of proven Jewish status who could be called up for military service had already for two years been sent into forced labor. There were more than 800,000 Jewish citizens within the then national borders, and from this number approximately 100,000 had become Christian, Catholic and Protestant. This mass of people lived under an increasingly merciless oppression of political anti-Semitism, justified by theories of racial superiority and purity. With the increase in their legal, moral, and physical defenselessness, most of them lived in fear of their lives. These anti-Jewish laws had broken down the boundaries between those Jews who were Jewish by faith and those who were Christian by faith. Thus at the center of the JPB's work lay the increasingly difficult work of rescuing people, quite apart from the differences between them.

• *What were the antecedents and motives of the Church in establishing the Good Shepherd Committee?*

• There were direct and indirect antecedents. One of the indirect ones was the Hungarian Holy Cross Society (*Magyar Szent Kereszt Egyesület—MSZKE*) of Catholic converts. In early 1939, Baron Móric Kornfeld, a well-known industrial magnate and member of the Upper House, had initiated it and its work was financed by the Manfréd Weiss family. Later, on the suggestion of Kornfeld, the Catholic Bishopric, under the presidency of Count Gyula Zichy, Archbishop of Kalocsa, set up a secular and clerical committee to protect primarily the ethical concerns of Catholics of Jewish origin. Dr. József Cavallier, secular president of the committee, later became the chairperson of the National Social Policy Institute (*Országos Szociálpolitikai Intézet*). Within time, under his leadership, the committee and the institute became united. From the autumn of 1942, following the death of Archbishop Zichy, the Bishopric elected the Bishop of Györ, Baron Vilmos Apor, to lead the organization. As Ca- vallier's partner, the clerical leadership was given to József Jánosi, Jesuit priest. And thus the Protestant Church had already had an example of Christian–Jewish cooperation. A Protestant social organization with similar goals existed, namely, the Hungarian branch of the Evangelical Alliance (*Evangéliumi Szövetség*), but in practice it did hardly anything.

These were the indirect antecedents. Greater direct impact was provided by the following. Pál Balkányi was appointed as commander of a forced labor service unit. He was an elder of Albert Bereczky's congregation at Pozsonyi út, who after the war became Minister of Culture and later Bishop. He had shocking experiences in this unit. Encouraged by Bereczky, Balkányi wrote an article about it in *Protestant Future (Református Jövő)*, our most widely circulated paper. The right wing was outraged, but respected church people such as Károly Dobos, Dr. Ferenc Benkó, Andor Sebestyén, and others under the leadership of Bereczky went in deputation to László Ravasz and urged the immediate establishment of an official, active rescue service primarily in the interest of Jewish Protestants, but also of all other persecuted people. The Bishop first gave a non–committal answer, but by the middle of 1942 it was his suggestion which led to the establishment of the Good Shepherd Committee. On its own, the Bereczky deputation couldn't have had the deciding impact. I don't want to go into the details of that whole process, but the truth of the matter is that, after the failure of the *Blitzkrieg* against the Soviets, László Ravasz, who had previously agreed to the two anti–Jewish laws with intricate justifications, came to the point of suggesting that the Good Shepherd Committee should be set up.

People are accustomed to saying that there is a false church and a true church within the Church. As a servant of God and a servant of the Church I just want to mention that there was a truly spiritual Evangelical stream in the Church. There are occasions when the true church gains victory over the false church due to some outside circumstances or inner renewing. Something of this kind happened in 1942, at least insofar as the Good Shepherd Committee is concerned.

• *How did you, the 28–year–old assistant minister from Cegléd, come to be the clerical secretary of the Good Shepherd Committee?*

• Although the Bishop had the absolute right to place assistant ministers wherever he wanted, in this particular case he asked for my opinion, and approval in advance in view of the gravity of the situation, its political sensitivity, and the expected dangers. He sent Károly Dobos, a minister from Budapest, to me in Cegléd in order to inform me of the task and to ask me whether I would take it on. It had been Bereczky and Dobos who had drawn Ravasz's attention to me. I accepted the task, but not immediately and not easily.

• *Why?*

• When I knew more exactly what my work would be and under what conditions I would have to do it, I wrote in my diary: "The placing of this duty on me is akin to asking someone who had never before touched a piano to play the D-minor Piano Concerto by Mozart." That is why I hesitated. But I also learned that five ministers had already refused the task before it had been offered to me and this is why I accepted it. In addition, I understood that it was rather awkward for the whole Convent and its President-Bishop that, months after they had decided to start the work of the Good Shepherd Committee, they were still unable to find a clerical person who could take on the job. This gave me a sense of guilt and responsibility.

• *So you came to Budapest from Cegléd. How did the Good Shepherd Committee's work start?*

• I presented myself to Gyula Muraközy, minister at Kálvin Square, and president of the Good Shepherd Committee. He told me that I should have an interview with Bishop Ravasz before starting anything else.

• *How did that go?*

• It was an exceptional situation that, within half an hour of making the appointment via the secretary, Mrs. Eta Juszkó, I found myself very cordially received by the Bishop. I can tell you in detail what counsel I received from him in that meeting because, immediately afterward, I made notes of what the Biship had told me and also added my comments to them. Luckily, I still have these notes in my possession—they survived the stormy times. The Bishop began with two parables. The first one was about the galley-ships of Venice, which were so loaded with migrating birds that at one point one of them sank. "Think about this," he said, and went on with the second parable. Consider a boat in which there are nine people whose lives can be saved. Along comes a tenth person. If he were to get in as well, the boat would sink. On what mathematical principles should the leader of the boat make his decision?

• *Did the Bishop give solutions to these parables?*

• No. He trusted me to solve these problems and then added the following five things. First, I would find myself, as a result of my duties, in a very sensitive situation with regard to the state and the church, as though I were in a whirlpool. I would need to be aware of it but I would not be able to express it clearly. Second, while work in the JPB was regarded as a legal church task, it offered opportunities for extension into other areas. In order that the extended work not overstep the boundaries of legality, the church would inform the public by means of leaflets of the existence and aims of the JPB. Third, Gyula Muraközy, the chairman of the JPB, had received instructions to give me a free hand in the work. On the other hand, I should know that the church would be willing to take responsibility only for those activities that were mentioned on the leaflets and that were within the constitution of the JPB. Nevertheless, I should do what I thought was needed in the knowledge that I would have to take responsibility for it. The most that the church could do would be not to start proceedings against me. However, there was the possibility that even this could happen. Fourth, I should always keep in mind the two parables that he had told me. Fifth, what he could do in the interest of my work would be to allow me to use a rubber stamp on which would be written "Universal Convent of the Hungarian Protestant Church" (*Magyarországi Református Egyház Egyetemes Konventje*). This would provide a legal status and protection to the JPB. He couldn't provide office space in the Convent Center, nor financial help.

• *What was the commentary you made upon this counsel?*

• I'll tell you as it is written in my notes. The tension between state and church was not real. It probably just meant that the government had a grudge against him because he had not voted in favor of the Third anti-Jewish Law, the so-called Race Protection Law of 1941. Although not one Church leader had voted in favor of it, it had still been passed. On the whole though, there were far more agreements between state and church than disagreements. To the second and the third points I added the following: The Honorable Bishop Ravasz, with high Hungarian decorations, would obviously not be willing to enter into any conspiracy with an unknown little nobody like me, no matter what the issue was. Like many others, His Excellency had learned a great deal from Queen Elizabeth I of England about how to deal with pirate captains. He had hinted to me that I could do a lot more than what was contained in the official aims, and under a blanket of legality, underground activities could take place. If I were to succeed, he and others would be given the credit for it, but if I didn't succeed, I would not be able to count on him.

The parables involving the mathematics of rescuing people were a stroke of genius but in reality it came down to a "mathematics of death," so I could not really gain much in the way of ethics from Ravasz. The rubber stamp, the leaflets, and the officiality of the committee all helped a lot, but this help was compromised by the lack of office space and money. At the interview I had stated that I accepted everything but that I was not a magician and that I would need help to obtain at least a minimum of funding. The Bishop had said I was right and had promised help. The result was that the Bishop sent requests for money to the congregations, so after a while money started trickling in. Church money was in the hands of the National Land Credit Institute (*Országos Földhitel Intézet*), and it was here that JPB had an account into which the money was deposited. When a certain amount had accumulated, I was able to withdraw it. In order to do this, I had to submit an application to the Presidency of the Convent. To withdraw money, two signatures were required, those of László Ravasz and Dr. Jenő Balogh, retired Minister of Justice, who was the secular president of the Synod and the Convent. He lived on his property in Bönyrétalap, and rarely came to Budapest, so it was always a real adventure to get the two signatures. The first large donation was given by Baroness Edit Weiss, daughter, I think, of Manfréd Weiss. I have never met her in person, but once, near to the start of our work, she telephoned me and said that she had spoken to one of my friends and that she had arranged that 5,000 *Pengő* should be deposited into the JPB account. I assume that her donation came from her own funds—she was well-known for being charitable.

In one of his books, Zola writes that, by the second or the third generation in a wealthy family, there usually are one or two members who develop a social conscience and spend a part of their time and resources on charity work. Yet where was the money right after the interview with the Bishop? At that time, all that happened was that János Victor, minister of the Szabadság Square congregation, offered a part of his office building to JPB on a temporary basis, which meant in practice that I became second-assistant minister in this congregation. Later, due to the goodwill of one of our elders, we obtained an independent office at 5 Lázár Street. Here, too, I was able to procure a humble dwelling-space. My salary had to be collected from the Budapest congregations. At the start, in order to obtain stationery and other bare essentials, Gyula Muraközy lent us two hundred *Pengö* from the purse of the Kálvin Square congregation. The then-used clerical garments made it possible for me to survive on just two white shirts and half a dozen stiff collars. I had never been a great eater, and, what is more, I found that the more I got involved in things, the less time I had for food or sleep. Not long after I had arrived in Budapest, Géza Soós had called upon me, and from that time, that is December 1942, we were constantly in touch with each other. It was only the coming into power of the Szálasi clique which interrupted this contact. From the beginning then, my people-rescuing work in the Good Shepherd Committee became merged with my anti-fascist political activities in the opposition movement.

• *So now we are up to the end of 1942 which is when the work of JPB started. Let's digress now, and look into those events which had an impact on your work. The end of 1942, beginning of 1943, marked a turning-point in the history of the war. Stalingrad, the Battle of the Don, Africa—all of these were catastrophic defeats for the German, Italian, Hungarian, and Romanian armies. Could you provide a sketch of the viewpoint of the Protestant Church with regard to the war itself and the so-called Jewish question?*

• I am very glad that you have asked me this question, because I can base my answer on a document which has been known to me for forty years—from the spring of 1943 to be exact. I have not yet been able to talk about this document. It has never been published. Historical literature has not recognized it. I would now like to call attention to it.

• *What is this document?*

• It is a letter which was sent on March 22, 1943 by the Presidency of the Hungarian Protestant Church to W. A. Visser't Hooft, then Chairman of the World Council of Churches. The letter was signed by László Ravasz, the clerical President of the Convent, and the secular President, Jenő Balogh. I have, in my possession, the exact text, and its contents give an appropriate answer to both of your questions. I do, however, have to correct your choice of words, since it reflects the viewpoint not of the entire Church but only of *the inner leadership.* I will later explain the reason for this distinction. Let me add that I am happy to base my response on this letter, for thereby nobody can assume that, after all these decades, I am exaggerating or distorting the facts.

• *How did you acquire the text of this letter?*

• I didn't get it from those who wrote or signed it, because they regarded it as top secret. A while ago, I mentioned that, from the end of 1942, I had been constantly in touch with Géza Soós, who, in those time, often used to go to Switzerland on official business, and it was during one of these journeys that, probably on the orders of Ravasz, he got in touch with Visser't Hooft. The relationship between Geneva and the Hungarian Church had deteriorated since the beginning of the war. The Hungarian Church had received well–intentioned warnings and criticism from churches both of the warring and the neutral countries, because it had become a servant of those German–allied war policies pursued by the Hungarian government. Using the fight against Bolshevism as an excuse, Ravasz haughtily refused to pay attention to these sober, brotherly warnings. Following the great military defeats of the fascists, Ravasz was one who suggested that the relationships with the Western churches be patched up. So, Géza made contact with Visser't Hooft and brought a letter from him to the church leadership. Because he didn't agree with the response of the church's foreign affairs committee, Géza didn't want to take the letter to Switzerland with him on his next journey. However, Domokos Szent–Iványi suggested that he shouldn't reveal his opposition to Bishop Ravasz, so Géza worded his critique in German and gave this to Visser't Hooft together with the official church letter. Before he left, he had had an official copy made of the letter. It is this that I read, and in 1946 I even obtained it.

• *Didn't you consider it strange that he showed you such a secret letter?*

• No, I didn't. Rather, I thought that it was perfectly natural, because we didn't have political secrets from each other. Géza's trust might have been motivated by the fact that he knew that there had been a period when the intelligence and mental virtuosity of Ravasz had made an enormous impact on me. I find it very difficult to escape from the impact of high intelligence, and in those times I had not yet realized just how long–winded and full of sophisms were the Bishop's sermons, talks, and writings. Géza probably gave me the letter in order to save me from later disappointments. He might also have had the aim to make me realize that what the Bishop had told me as the clerical Secretary of the JPB, about rescuing Jews, was different from what he actually thought about the matter. Since we are on the subject, I have to tell you that by the spring of 1943 I had already ceased to be amazed by László Ravasz, and today I can state that I have long since overcome the need to pardon him, only because of his intelligence, for the terrible damage he caused through his anti-Semitism and enthusiasm for war, and not only in Protestant circles. It has become fashionable to reinstate Ravasz's fame—the centenary of his birth gave the opportunity for some to whitewash him. For all these reasons I feel the need to paint the true portrait of Ravasz.

• *How did the writers of the letter justify their participation in the war?*

• I can't read out the whole text, but I can reliably sum up its contents and also give direct quotations from it. The argument starts with the point of view that Trianon caused the nation and individual Hungarians to cling to Italy "*even when at that time Italian fascist politics showed many trends which were alien to Hungarian public opinion,*" and this was due to their life instincts being confronted by "*deathly dangers.*" Events "*swept Italy into the German camp . . . and this is how the Axis Alliance came into being.*" A positive result of this was that "*Hungary acquired more than forty thousand square kilometers of its old territories.*" When, in Serbia, "*the situation changed*" the life of our Hungarian nation "*became endangered. Hungary invaded Yugoslavia. Not considering those atrocities committed by a half-crazed soldier in Újvidék, Hungarian rule meant legal rights and life security to the population. Hungary's top leadership was determined to retain the neutrality of their country. The guarantor of this was Pál Teleki,*" who committed suicide because "*he could not safeguard his nation's neutrality. Then everyone was forced to realize that the powers of Fate were at work, and that these were greater than any human will and that the ability to change these was denied to individuals, groups, and the churches. This is how Hungary got involved in the war.*"

• *So, if I understand you correctly, the Hungarian leaders wanted the country to stay neutral, but due to fateful powers greater than human will, they entered the war.*

• Yes, this is what is written here.

• *What are these great fateful powers?*

• I can only provide you with quotes, not with explanations. But I'll continue now with the justifications for the war against the Soviets. In Hungary, as the authors put it, "*an invisible revolution had taken place underground and this had changed public opinion.*" The Swabians, feeling a "*kinship*" with Germany, retired and active soldiers, fascinated by the German army, the intelligentsia, longing for social changes, the petit bourgeoisie, and finally "*those strata of the industrial and agricultural workers which were saturated by communist ideology, suddenly found themselves united in the Hungarian National Socialist Movement. If, on June 27, 1941, after the bombing of Kassa, Hungary hadn't indicated its readiness to get involved in the war, the situation would have deteriorated and a revolution would have come knocking on the door. While order was maintained in Hungary, not everything would be lost even if the war were lost, but if this order were to be upset, nothing could be gained, even if the allies were victorious.*"

• *This is really a peculiar explanation.*

• That's putting it mildly. It had been written by the same László Ravasz who, on June 22, 1941, from the pulpit of the Kálvin Square Church—even broadcast on the radio—started to talk about the things that a man would have to do before being able to go on holiday. He wove into his sermon the following: "This morning, when the radio announced the outbreak of the German–Russian war, a lot of Hungarian people sighed with relief: some unfinished business has at last been seen to. The Russian threat was hanging over all of Europe like the sword of Damocles—at last we are getting rid of it." In May 1942, when the Second Hungarian Army set off on its doomed mission to the Don, Ravasz published an open letter to the "Hungarian soldiers on the road to war, fighting for the integrity of God's country, the Kingdom of Christ and thereby for the survival of our earthly homeland." At the meeting of the Convent, Jenő Balogh, secular President, thanked him for a "message which so wonderfully summed up the truth." I could quote many more of these propagandistic, stupefying, war–glorifying statements by representatives of the official clerical leadership, primarily by László Ravasz, but also by the clerical press.

This tone and way of thinking did not start to change until the end of 1943. The letter which had been sent to Geneva had accused the majority of the population, united in National–Socialism and threatening revolution, of forcing the Hungarian leadership, wanting to stay neutral, into war. However in November 1943, at the general assembly of the National Congregation of Protestant Ministers (*Országos Református Lelkészegyesület*), László Ravasz said the following: "It is a decisive element that Hungarian public opinion had always been dominated by a true longing for peace . . . from the point of view of their own survival and for the good of Europe." And he also added that, "there comes a moment when you may have to jump out of an airplane which is on fire, because this is the only way of surviving." The letter sent to Geneva was really nothing more than an attempt by the church leadership to justify itself and to make excuses for the Horthy clique. Neither did they omit praising themselves. They wrote that, "they were truly evangelical, clever as the snake and gentle as the dove."

• *What did they write about the Jewish question?*

• First, the authors stated that "*that revolution which had invisibly changed the souls of men had shown itself most clearly and most passionately in the struggles surrounding the Jewish question,*" and they followed this up by stating that in this question, the Christian churches "*followed the commands of their Heavenly Master.*"

• *The revolution which had changed the souls of men is again a reference to National Socialism, isn't it?*

• Yes, it is. Then the authors stated that "*despite all the romantic and naive slogans to the contrary, there was a Jewish question in general, and especially in Hungary.*" According to the authors, Jewry does have its own interests "*towards the surrounding world*" and in Hungary these had increased so much that they had "*invisibly*" taken over the control of economic life, public opinion, everyday social contact and public taste. As they wrote, Jewry "*had abandoned its ancient beliefs, these having faded from the hearts of men, and it had looked toward Christianity only as a means for assimilation and social masking. All of this had led to the situation in which Jewry had become the greatest societal power in Hungary. It was even greater than the churches. . . . It was so great, that it would be impossible even to attempt a societal struggle against it, and only the passing of a law, forced by revolutionary pressure, had been able to overcome it. This is how the first anti-Jewish law had come about.*" And because "*you can rarely run faster than a a revolution*" and because it turned out that "*the first anti-Jewish law was not strict enough by far*" it was followed by the second and the third. The first had been approved by the clerical representatives in the Upper House, the second had been passed after much debate by them, viewing it as "*the price they had to pay*" in order to protect the "*political stability of the country.*" The third was met with the "*greatest opposition of the church*" because it didn't recognize "*the power to change*" of Christianity when it came to marriage. The authors assured the addressee that "*the Church had taken over a new field of work, namely the special spiritual care of congregational members who were of Jewish origin*" and thus "*we have established the Good Shepherd Committee*" whose tasks have to be accomplished in such a way that "*the world shouldn't know about it*" or otherwise "*the work would be a failure.*" According to Christ, "*let the right hand not know what the left is doing.*"

I feel it would be unnecessary for me to assess and explain the views surrounding the Jewish question and the anti–Jewish laws. I do, however, make two points. One is that, of the clerical leaders of the traditional Hungarian churches, László Ravasz was the only one who had made a name for himself in Hungarian public life by writing anti–Semitic articles as early as in 1916–17, when he was a young theologian in Kolozsvár. At that time Endre Ady had written of him that "in the literary periodical of Calvinism, the most extreme anti–Semitic views are represented by a man by the name of László Ravasz, who should have known better." He represented not so much the theological, but rather the political anti–Semitism. Two decades later, when he was President–Bishop of the Hungarian Protestant Church, Ravasz proudly referred to these earlier articles in the Upper House debate on the anti–Jewish laws, saying that his viewpoint had not changed.

The other point I wish to make is that, of the Protestant Members of Parliament, Zoltán Szabó, professor of theology in Sárospatak, voted in favor of even the third anti–Jewish law with the approval of the Church leadership, and in connection with "Hungarian race–protection" he had even gone so far as to suggest that converted Jews should be isolated into a "separate type of church where they could passionately prove their faith in the assimilational purgatory."

• *What Szabó had only suggested had been put into practice in the German Evangelical Church.*

• It wasn't a secret in our Church that German Protestantism had tragically separated into the "German Christians," who fully cooperated with the Hitler ideology, and the "Church of Faith" which sharply condemned that ideology. We also knew that the leader of the Church of Faith, Martin Niemöller, and several hundred of his fellow–ministers, were in prisons or concentration camps. What is more, we learned that the German Evangelical Church Bureau had suggested in December 1941 that non–Aryan Christians should be placed in their own congregations. Szabó's suggestion in parliament had thus preceded by months that of the hateful Nazi Evangelical leaders.

In November 1941, at a general assembly of his congregation, Ravasz, in his Bishop's Report, had scoffed at the warnings of the Western churches with the following statements: "Constant and cruel is the lie that National Socialism is anti–God and not tolerant of other religions. We send a message to our brothers over the ocean that here, in the center of Europe, allied to the German Reich, and swept along by momentous ideological changes, we can feel and declare ourselves to be free, independent and undeniably Christian. . . . It's a cruel game that Satan plays with the world when he manages to bring people so far as to getting the Archbishop of Canterbury to pray for a Soviet victory."

I have already mentioned that, beside or in opposition to the evangelical trend in our church, there was another trend, the political one. This was the trend which served and helped in the pro–war policies and in the persecution of Jews. This trend cannot be equated with the Church as a whole, only with the leadership, and even then, only with a small clique of leaders. The church was really those two and a half million people of Protestant faith and the ministers living amongst them. The great majority of them were the poor peasants and impoverished masses of the Alföld, the Trans–Tisza region, and Northern Transylvania as well as manual workers of the small towns. Unfortunately, the anti–Semitism and pro–war policies of the leadership had affected some of them, but the souls of most of them had probably not been permanently poisoned. It's a pity that I cannot give you data on what was saved from the evangelical teaching according to which the Christian believer is against war, violence, and injustice toward other people, and on the numbers of people that did in fact cling to it.

• *Could you tell me who was included in the smaller circle of the church leadership which you are talking about?*

• In the first decade of this century, two great personalities had an important impact on Protestant ideology—Dezső Baltazár and László Ravasz. In many ways, they were worlds apart from each other. Baltazár was in favor of liberal theology and politics, against anti-Semitism, kept the social problems of simple people constantly in mind, and respected the traditional democracy of church life. The Horthy regime didn't want this. Until his death in 1936, he was the President of the Synod and the Convent, but he had already been pushed into the background. Ravasz led the Church always in accordance with the policies of the ever-changing governments and with the leader of the entire regime, Miklós Horthy. He had a personal, friendly, and advice-giving relationship with the Regent, himself of Protestant faith. He was a clever politician, in his own way a great personality, influential in clerical and public circles alike. He was surrounded by such secular leaders of the church who had important positions and a say in political life. These people were in the Synod and in the Convent, they were supervisors and chief supervisors of the smaller and larger divisions of the church, had the deciding vote in various committees, and influenced the clerical press too.

• *Can you give examples of a few?*

• From the end of the twenties until 1945, among others, the following had various secular positions in the church: Count István Bethlen, former Prime Minister, and one of the most significant political personalities of the regime; Kálmán Darányi, Prime Minister when the rearmament program was carried out; Andor Lázár, Minister of Justice in the Gömbös government; and András Tasnádi Nagy, Minister of Justice in the Imrédy government, and one of the formulators of the first anti-Jewish law. Later, as President of the House of Representatives, he supported even Szálasi. Ignác Darányi was supervisor of a church district and once Minister of Agriculture. Then there were Count József Teleki, Count József Dégenfeld, Captain István Horthy, brother of the Regent, and Baron László Vay, State Secretary. In the Upper House, the Church was represented by five bishops and five chief supervisors. There were some among even the latter who had the titles of 'Honorable' and 'His Excellency.' Naturally, theologians, leaders of the press, clerical members of Parliament, leaders of Protestant associations, and many others who belonged to the formal and informal leadership of the official, established church, and who could be influential because of their positions—all of these cooperated with the clerical and secular leaders. We are talking now about people with different ideologies, posts, and levels of participation and I wouldn't even be able to say of most of them that they were extremely right-wing. As a whole, however, they ensured that there was a continuous political impact by the regime on church life, and a continuous support by the church for the regime.

• *Let's carry on from where we left off. You started to work in the winter of 1942–43, a little more than a year before the German occupation of Hungary. What did the Good Shepherd Committee do during this time?*

• I can divide the work of the JPB into four periods, namely from its inception to the German occupation, from the German occupation to the coming into power of Szálasi, from the period of Arrow Cross power until the liberation, and finally, from the liberation until the time when the threat of famine was overcome. Including me, there were nineteen people who worked in our Lázár Street offices, and a lot of volunteers helped us too. As soon as the leaflet advertising our existence had been distributed, the immediate emergency tasks started to accumulate. Our first task was to make contact with other clerical organizations with similar aims, namely the Catholic Holy Cross Society and its leaders József Cavallier and Father Jánosi, and the Jewish community, represented by one of its leaders, Dr. István Földes. From the Evangelicals, it was Lajos Kemény and later Gábor Sztehló who helped us a great deal. I believe that, among certain people from the Hungarian churches and denominations, these difficult years were the first time that an ecumenical spirit and cooperation developed, not experienced before that time, and probably not again since.

• *What were these accumulating tasks?*

• As a result of the anti-Jewish laws and the discrimination against Jews, there was a lot of unemployment. Emergency cash could not offer a permanent solution; instead, we needed to provide them with work. The anti-Jewish laws brought up a lot of legal problems as well, which meant that we had to organize legal counselling and provide legal protection. Excellent lawyers helped us in our work, but it was well-known that in many cases it wasn't legal arguments that decided the outcome. We had to find the appropriate supporters inside the Ministry of Justice. Ministerial Secretary, Dr. István Bibó tried to provide us with this support.

The greatest problems were connected with those sent into forced labor service and their families. Jewish men between the ages of twenty and fifty were called up for forced labor. For those in poor financial circumstances, we had to find clothes, boots, blankets, and underwear. This became a matter of life and death in winter in Transylvania and from the autumn of 1942 at the Don. We needed donations of money and of clothes to be able to help. Members of the Arrow Cross always used to spread the lie that Jews were basking in their wealth. We experienced at close range that most of the Jewish families lived at the then average socioeconomic level, and that mass impoverishment had increased among them as a result of their being deprived of their rights. Both in the Ukraine and in Hungary, there was a high rate of deaths among the forced laborers, and many orphans, half-orphans, and widows. The Good Shepherd Committee set up an orphanage in Noszvaj, and from the beginning of 1944, this orphanage provided shelter not only for children, but also for soldiers and forced laborers on the run and those whom the police were looking for. We used to hear cries of help from internment camps in Garany, Ricse, Csörgő, and Budapest, and I used to visit all these camps together with a Catholic priest from Nagytétény. The sermons, Holy Communion, Confession, and spiritual discussion all provided us with good opportunities to exchange some words in private with the prisoners, whether they were of other faiths or atheists. In Garany, for example, there were a lot of atheistic political internees. Remembering well their complaints, we used to write our reports later at home. Via the contacts of József Cavallier we managed to rescue 83, mostly older internees, from prison. From the very beginning of the JPB work, we had an especially interesting action, that is, the collection of certificates of baptism.

• *How did you do this?*

• In those years, in order to get a job, most places required a certificate of baptism. These were later stored on file. By mobilizing our friends, we managed to get hold of a lot of them and sorted them out into groups according to age and sex. These were of great service to some people, even before the German occupation. When the Germans arrived, the value of these documents was immeasurable. They saved lives. We selected them with great care before assigning them to people, and they had to be examined as to their knowledge of the contents.

• *Did you receive requests for help from people of Jewish faith as well? After all, you were a committee for the Protestants of Jewish origin?*

• We never asked anyone for proof of religion. Neither did Cavallier and his group. When we were convinced of the needs of those who came to us, and we were able to help, we did so. Of course it is only natural that our brothers of Jewish origin found their way to us the easiest, at least at the beginning. Later, not only them.

• *In the first period of your work, that is from the beginning until the German occupation, what do you consider were the greatest successes?*

• First, we could bring news to the relatives of typhoid patients who were in military quarantine. Some time at the beginning of May 1943, I learned, I think from Géza Soós, that the defeated and scattered Hungarian Army at the Don had gathered up their soldiers and forced laborers and typhoid had spread among them. Those for whom there had still been hope had been brought home and were kept in isolation in a camp in the forest next to Rimaszombat. I traveled to this town and was met by Sándor Varga, later Protestant Bishop of Slovakia, at the station. To my surprise, he told me that he had been warned earlier that very morning by a detective that a false minister would come looking for him, asking about the quarantine, and that he shouldn't give him any information. Varga only vaguely knew the way to the camp so I followed the tracks of army vehicles through a little path in the wood. This was how I got to the camp. I was very happy that the camp commanders, who were medical officers, welcomed me and were ready to work with me. They provided me with a loudspeaker, thus enabling me to give the word of God to the whole camp. Afterward, on a little table outside the camp fences, I sat down to write the names of the patients and the addresses of their families. Only this was contained in the messages: XY was back home, well, under medical care, recovering, etc. When I returned to Budapest, my colleagues spent days writing and posting these message-cards to the relatives, who until then had known nothing about their loved ones, not even that they were not at the front anymore. This was the first real success of our work. A few days later, a police investigator came looking for me and questioned me about my source of knowledge concerning the location of the quarantine, why I had gone there, etc. He wasn't mean. He understood that we were doing the best for the ill soldiers, forced laborers and their worrying families. There were no unpleasant consequences from this. Another of our successes was, in cooperation with the Holy Cross Society developing a network of denominational representatives from the forced labor units.

• *What was this network and who were these representatives?*

• In the spring of 1943 we started to visit the forced labor service units which were stationed in Hungary. I represented JPB most of the time, together with a representative of the MSZKE. By the nature of these visits we had sermons, but what was more important was to find out who needed what sort of help and in what situations their families found themselves. Our most important concern was to find out how the officers and guards treated them, but we always did this with great care to ensure that our informants did not get into trouble.

• *There was a time when the Családi Lap, a family magazine, under the editorship of Jenő Lévai, undertook similar tasks.*

• Lévai was arrested and his paper banned approximately at the same time as we started this work. Following our visits, we soon had such a network of informants that JPB and the MSZKE were able to send reports of detailed information to the Ministry of Defense about the situation in each of the forced labor service units. General Gusztáv Hennyey, later Foreign Minister in the Lakatos government, was at that time head of the personnel department of the Ministry of Defense and he was responsible for the forced labor service units, while Colonel Ede Gátföldi was the officer in charge of forced labor matters. We sent our reports to them and I have to admit that both Hennyey and Gátföldi handled these complaints about the cruelty of the officers and guards with much goodwill, and sometimes with genuine compassion. They couldn't do much, for matters did not depend solely on them. A decision had to be made at the Ministry—they either had to prohibit our visits or legalize this network of informants. It is the latter that came to pass. In the official gazette of the Ministry of Defense, they published the regulations concerning the work of what they called "denominational company representatives."

• *What did this mean?*

• It meant that forced laborers of different denominations, with the approval of their captains, were allowed to appoint company representatives from among themselves, who, also with the approval of the captains, could turn to the charitable services of their denominations for help for their fellow soldiers and families. There was, therefore, a legalized network from which we gained, besides the requests for help, a lot of other information too. Our third important success was the campaign for the collection of boots during the winter of 1943–44.

• *Boot collection?*

• No. We had obtained information from Gyergyóholló and other Transylvanian camps that there had been a lot of frostbite of the foot because the boots of the laborers had become worn out. These laborers had to provide themselves with clothing. From the army they only received caps.

• *Later the regulations of the Sztójay government even did away with that.*

• Boots at that time were precious items. You couldn't buy them in shops, and on the black market, 200 *Pengö* was the starting price for a good pair. This was too much for a lot of families. We had to help. I went to the Ministry of Defense in search of the person in charge of supplying boots. Zoltán Kodály was also there on some charitable errand, tapping his feet in the cold at the front door. The next time I met him was in the waiting room of Sándor Szilágyi, Counsellor in the Ministry of the Interior, where he was again trying to help somebody. After much difficulty, I at last got to some or other honorable colonel of the Ministry of Defense and said that I had come to ask for the provision of boots for forced laborers. I had to listen to a long tirade against the Jews, something in the style of a front page article in the Arrow Cross publication *Virradat* [Dawn], but I persisted, nicely yet stubbornly with my request, until he wrote out an order for a thousand pairs of boots from one of the military stores at 25 *Pengő* per pair. This was like a dream come true. It only dawned on me when I was outside in the street that we only had 5,000 *Pengő* in our account. Where were we to get 20,000 more to pay for the boots? In this kind of situation one simply walks around aimlessly, lost in thought, and suddenly I found myself at the home of Lajos Kemény, Evangelical Dean of Budapest. He was a reticent man, yet quick to make decisions and with a warm heart, a wholehearted supporter of our work. I informed him of the problem and, putting on his coat, he said to me: "Come with me." We went to Tihamér Fabinyi who was a good friend of Kemény's.

• *Fabinyi was Minister of Finance in the Gömbös and Darányi governments, wasn't he?*

• When we went to see him, he was President of the Association of Savings and Commercial Banks (*Takarékpénztárak és Bankok Egyesülete—TEBE*). Lajos Kemény had a weekend house somewhere near Budapest and he asked for a mortgage of 20,000 *Pengö* from Fabinyi on this. In a couple of hours, he was able to withdraw the money.

Having obtained the boots, our next question was where to put them. Our brother in God András Keken helped us. We were enabled to store them in a building of the Evangelical Church at Deák Square. Lajos Kemény and I decided that we would sell the boots for 35 instead of 25 *Pengö* a pair so that we could donate every fourth pair for those who couldn't afford that much. We had already collected enough blankets and other warm clothing, so we gave these away for nothing with the boots. Within a short time we had distributed or posted the thousand clothing parcels and Lajos Kemény was also soon able to pay back the money. So, these and similar actions were our successes in the first period of our work. Putting it rather pathetically, these were mere drops of goodness in the ocean of suffering, but believe me, there was suffering. We didn't know yet what was awaiting us. Only two days after the Germans occupied the country, on March 21, 1944, I had my first taste of what was to come.

• *What happened?*

• I was awakened early in the morning by a loud ringing of the bell in my small room in Lázár Street. "Two gentlemen" from the Gestapo and two Hungarian policemen were standing at my door together with the caretaker's wife, who was wailing and questioning why they wanted to take away the minister who hadn't done any harm to anybody. The Gestapo people checked up on my identity as a minister, the policemen all the while explaining and later making it clear that it wasn't me they were looking for, but the owner of the house, a Freemason, who was on the list of those to be arrested. The poor soul, luckily, had already been dead for two years. The Germans were a bit irritated and shook my hand upon departing. One cannot always choose who one is to shake hands with.

• *Thus a new and even more difficult phase of your work started. Let's call to mind, from the mass of events in the life of the Good Shepherd Committee in 1944, that one when you received the Auschwitz Report for translation and delivery.*

• This happened either in the last days of April or the first days of May in 1944—my memory is not clear enough to give you the exact date—but I repeat that it was one of the days in late–April or early–May, when Géza Soós called upon me for our usual rendezvous. He had warned me in advance that it would be longer than usual, because he had important things to tell me.

• *What was the usual format of these meetings?*

• On each occasion we arranged the place, that is the park, square or café, of the next meeting. When Géza had anything of importance to tell me, he had only to say the date and time. We never met at his office in the Foreign Ministry, neither in the JPB office in Lázár Street, and I didn't call him by phone because we suspected that his telephone was bugged.

• *What was the procedure if it was you who wanted a meeting?*

• Then I called István Bognár, joint President of the Soli Deo Gloria and Géza's colleague in the student association, at home, and he passed on my message to Géza. István was a teacher and unfortunately he didn't live to see the liberation. Later I learned that he had been a member or supporter of the illegal Communist Party.

• *Well then, Géza called you. Where did you meet and what was the purpose?*

• As far as I can remember, we met in the Múzeum Café. Géza, an energetic but cool–tempered man, was on this occasion, bristling with excitement. I felt that he had something very significant to share. I was right. He said that a secret prisoners' organization, working in a German concentration camp in Poland, by the name of Auschwitz, had managed to rescue, in a miraculous way, two young Slovakian Jews and had given them the task to spread the news about what was happening in Auschwitz. Once they were in a place of safety, the fugitives gave an extended description, complete with drawings, of Auschwitz. By calling this a report, they wished to emphasize its validity and authenticity. One member of our opposition movement, who was living in the Slovakian border territories, received a

German-language copy of this report directly from these fugitives. The messenger from these border areas had arrived with this copy in the early hours of that morning. The leaders of the movement had decided that the tasks concerning this report would be given to me.

• *What were these tasks?*

• First of all, I needed to make a quick, clear, and exact translation of the text from German into Hungarian. Second, six Hungarian copies had to be typed. Third, five of these had to be delivered to people designated by Géza in a way that they shouldn't even suspect from where the text had come and how it had got to them. Fourth, the sixth copy and the original had to be returned to Géza in a way that would be worked out later. Fifth, and finally, the copies were not to be typed on the JPB's typewriters. During our conversation—I can almost picture the scene right now—there was an empty chair between us on which we had placed our bags and, imperceptibly, Géza slipped the report into my bag. When he gave a list of the addresses, first the clerical leaders of highest standing, he added that government officials were not to know that the report was in our hands. They didn't need to be informed because, as Géza emphasized, most of the cabinet ministers, from the Regent down, knew about Auschwitz and its role anyway. The opposition movement wanted primarily to inform the leaders of the clergy so that the government could not mislead them and so that they could press the government and the Regent to ward off the tragedy facing the Jews. Géza added that the movement would have the capability to forward the report to Hungarians and other important people in Switzerland. He finally placed on my heart the fact that everybody whom I was to involve in this action, whether translator or deliverer, had to be not only loyal, but also suitable and trustworthy in all respects. We discussed who the deliverers could be and we decided that we were going to ask one of our most loyal, intelligent, and experienced colleagues, Mária Székely, to do the translation. She was known at the JPB simply as Marcsi. In 1945, she became the wife of the recently deceased surgeon, Dr. László Küllői-Rhorer, and besides being a translator and interpreter, she was also a mother and grandmother.

• *Had your people in the JPB known anything about Auschwitz before that?*

• When I received the report I had already known almost everything that was important. My colleagues, I think, had known only the ever–spreading, yet unverifiable rumors concerning the German camps.

• *From what sources had you known almost everything?*

• On the first Wednesday following the occupation of the country by the Germans, József Cavallier asked me to visit him in his Múzeum Street offices of the MSZKE. On arriving, he told me on the basis of confidential information, probably of Vatican origin, which he had heard at the Papal Nunciature in Budapest, the entire German schedule concerning Hungarian Jewry. This schedule, as was the case in all other countries, started with the deprivation of their civil rights, compulsory wearing of the Yellow Star, followed by the ghettoization and the transit camps, and finally deportation, gas chambers, and crematoriums. Cavallier, who had come from an old French Catholic family, and I were in a truly united ecumenical spirit. For him, faith meant a devoted humanitarianism toward everyone. He was a devoted comrade–in–arms and gave wonderful support to my work. After giving me the shocking information about Auschwitz and similar camps, he made me promise not to tell anybody what I had heard from him. He considered it necessary for me, leader of the Protestant Good Shepherd Committee, to know what was coming next, but he thought, and I agreed, that we shouldn't make it public because that would cause panic among the Jews and endanger the vague possibilities of organized support. Later we were not so secretive. When I received the Auschwitz report from Géza I told him what I had heard, and when I had been informed by Cavallier it had been only the 22nd of March, that is, the fourth day of the German occupation. There had yet not been any yellow stars or ghettos and the Sztójay government had just come into power. We had then still had the hope that things would be different. Two days later, on the Friday of the first week of the occupation, Dean Lajos Kemény summoned me and, making reference to German sources, he told me exactly the same kinds of things I had heard from Cavallier. In those years, being a young man, I was a good sleeper, but in those particular days, my nights became filled with sleeplessness. In the small hours of one morning, I put down my worries and thoughts on paper, and sent them in letters to all the bishops of our Church.

• *What did you write?*

• I wrote that now, as a result of the German occupation, we had come to the point of talking about genocide and that the Sztójay government would be the executioners. In this government, there were not ministers, but Hitler puppets and criminals. We were not to negotiate with them, nor to beg anything from them. What could be of help would be the uniting and joint actions of the Catholic and Protestant churches in order to prevent the coming events. The situation was so unique, that we would have to put aside old dogmas and points of disagreement. I was trying to beg the honorable and exalted bishops not to consider that it was only an assistant minister who was writing these words, but that it really was a well–informed person who had been placed into the task of people rescuing by them themselves. What would be the value of any rescue work, I wrote, if we didn't make all the efforts relevant to mass–rescuing of all those who were endangered as well. I suggested that the church should apply the severest punishment to all those who took part in the fatal events, namely, "the power of the Keys."

• *What does that mean?*

• We Protestants have two main creeds, the sacrament of the cross and Holy Communion. The power of the Keys means that whoever is denied Holy Communion would find the Gates of Heaven closed to him. Such a person would already feel the consequences of this on earth, and after his death, he would not be able to count on salvation.

• *What happened to your letters?*

• I forwarded one to László Ravasz via Gyula Muraközy, one to Imre Révész via the deacon János Hordós, who thank God is still alive, one to Elemér Győry in Miskolc via a deaconess, and one to Bishop Dr. Andor Enyedi in Győr, via a lay–sister.

• *Did they reply?*

• Révész sent back the message that I was crazy and told János Hordós: "I don't recommend that the Reverend Minister send such letters with you, because if you are captured with it, we won't be able to save you." Hordós was ready with a quick reply: "The Reverend Minister didn't hide the fact that there was life–threatening danger to this task, and this is how I accepted it." From Bishop Ravasz I received the admonishment that they had ordered me to do the Good Shepherd work in harmony with the church's directives, and it was not my right to take over the governing of the church. Only three weeks later, when already three hundred thousand Jews had been deported from the countryside, did the faint hope present itself that my suggestions had not been entirely in vain. But I'll tell you about this later.

• *Let's then go back to the point when Géza Soós slipped the German-language version of the Auschwitz Report into your bag. What happened after that?*

• I went back to my office at 5 Lázár Street where I had a small room separated by a glass wall for confidential discussions. At times, other people, mostly translators, worked here, so that we couldn't disturb them. I asked Mária Székely to come into this room, gave her the German text of the report and asked her to read it, sum up its contents, and tell me whether she would undertake the translation of it. Only hours later, terribly moved but in control of herself, was she able to tell me what she had read. As I was listening to her, I had the feeling that she was on the verge of being sick, so I was afraid that she might not have the will-power to translate it. But Marcsi, being of strong spirit, accepted the task. She said that she couldn't do it in the office, but that her flat was suitable. We decided on the secret code that she would use to inform me that she was ready with the translation and out she went.

• *How long did it take her?*

• Seven or eight days later, she brought the Hungarian version typed in six copies. I immediately read one of them and it was then actually that I learned of the entire content of the report. It consisted of 35 to 40 densely-typed pages with some simple, sketchy drawings in-between, of, if I remember well, the camp, the crematoriums, and the system of guarding. It explained in detail the workings of the genocidal machine which had been designed with a merciless logic and gave figures on the deported and killed people and which countries they had come from. Needless to say, it also had a shocking impact on me. While the translation was being done, Géza contacted me and asked that Mária Székely take the sixth Hungarian copy and the original to him at the Foreign Ministry. I know only now, thirty-seven years later, that he then also requested Marcsi to make an English translation of the German.

• *Therefore, you had the Hungarian version in five copies. To whom were they sent, and who delivered them?*

• The first addressee was Dr. Jusztinián Serédi, Archbishop and Cardinal. József Cavallier undertook the delivery when I requested him. I took the report to him and we discussed what he had to do in private. He had earlier been the chief editor of the Catholic daily, *Új Nemzedék* [New Generation], and was on such good terms with Serédi that, theoretically, he could enter his rooms without knocking. He still thought that it would be better if he didn't give the report to the Primate in person, but he gave the guarantee that he would forward it to him. And so it happened. The second addressee was Bishop Dr. László Ravasz, President of the Universal Convent of the Hungarian Protestant Church, and the deliverer was Albert Bereczky, minister at Pozsonyi Road.

• *Where did you give the report to Bereczky?*

• I took it to his office.

• *Had he heard about Auschwitz before that?*

• I don't know, but he knew a lot, of that I can be sure. He suffered a lot from various kinds of diseases, but in the horrible months of 1944, he had the time, energy, intelligence, and courage to do everything. He was uncompromisingly outspoken in his ministerial duties, and even prepared to take insults when it was necessary. He never ran out of cunning ideas, and was the best in this of all of us. At the beginning of the German occupation, he was the one who hid Zoltán Tildy, leader of the *Kisgazda Párt* [Smallholders' Party], later President of the Republic, from the Gestapo. He hid him in the Pozsonyi Road Church and in the center of the Scottish Mission. He also provided a hideway for Gyula Kállai, for the daughter of Árpád Szakasits, and for many others.

The third copy of the report was to reach Evangelical Bishop Dr. Sándor Raffay. Upon my request, the Evangelical Dean Dr. Lajos Kemény took it to him.

The fourth addressee was Ottó Komoly, an architect, and one of the active people in the Jewish community and the Hungarian Zionists. He became the leader of one of the emergency aid departments of the Budapest Red Cross Association after the German occupation but in December 1944, he was captured by the fascists and executed. At the time the report was delivered to him, I knew only very little about him, and was very cautious with him. I asked Dr. Géza Kárpáty, a true friend, and Chief Justice of the Court to take it to him. I was careful to choose a person who was unknown in both clerical and secular circles. My friend Géza dressed in the clothes of his gardener, and so adopted the appearance of a worker, and in this guise went to

Ottó Komoly. He didn't introduce himself, or maybe he gave a false name, and without explanation he gave him the letter. I learned only later that he himself was in contact with the opposition movement, and reported to Géza Soós that he had received a document from an unknown source. When he learned that the document had reached him via the channels of this movement, he asked for permission to make copies of it. I know from Géza that Komoly had been asked to wait for a while before copying it and distributing it. I think it is a reasonable assumption to make that this was how the copies of the report came into circulation. There was even the humorous incident that a man who felt solidarity with me and my work, came to me with a copy from goodness knows which of the original copies, with the aim of giving me confidential information.

Géza said that he would tell me in time what to do with the fifth copy. This time arrived when Sándor Török, who had already been a well-known writer and journalist at the beginning of the forties, was released from detention.

• *This sounds mysterious. Explain it to me.*

• I should begin by saying that on the first day after the German occupation, following the orders of the Eichmann Commando leaders, a Jewish Council was set up in Budapest. Not long afterward, the Catholics and Protestants turned to the government with the request, or rather the demand, that it should allow the setting up of a separate organization, or at least a section in the Jewish Council, for the Christians of Jewish origin. Török, who had been detained with other members of the intelligentsia after the German occupation, was released in mid-May and was appointed as the representative of Christian Jews in the Executive Committee of the Association of Hungarian Jews [*Magyarországi Zsidók Szövetsége*], which was called into life through a government decree at that time. He reported to Cavallier and to me, asking for our help. I learned from Géza that the attention of the opposition movement had been drawn onto him and they made it possible for Török to be granted entry into the Várpalota (Palace Fort), the inner circle of the widow of the Vice-Regent, István Horthy, Countess Ilona Edelsheim Gyulai. She turned out to be the fifth recipient of the Auschwitz Report, and Török was the messenger.

• *Why did she receive it?*

• She was convinced that the Germans had caused the fatal aircraft accident in which her husband, the Vice–Regent, had died. For this, or maybe for other reasons, she became a suitable person for Domokos Szent–Iványi to involve in the opposition movement. Török was chosen to be the person to inform the Countess and, through her, others concerning the situation of the persecuted in Hungary. He would also be the one to take news out from the Várpalota to the persecuted.

• *This sounds logical enough, but it also appears to be somewhat of a comical and adventurous conspiracy.*

• Yes, you could say this when you look at it from a contemporary viewpoint. But the fact is that for us ordinary people, and even for the not so ordinary, to get into the Regent's Palace in those days with some or other political task wasn't easy. The opposition movement had made it possible for Török to do so, which was typical of the kinds of things happening in the spring and summer of 1944. In those months, when general war, persecution, and mass deportations were occurring, seemingly unbelievable conspiracies and cooperation were created between kindhearted or simply farsighted people who would otherwise never have met. They happened as a result of fear, attempts to find a way out, crises of conscience, the will to help, illusions, and naiveté. The same can be said about the conspiracy between Sándor Török and Horthy's widow, because no matter which way we look at it today it certainly was a conspiracy.

• *Did you receive any feedback on the receivers of the Auschwitz* Report and how they responded to it?

• I received no reaction from Serédi, the Primate. About Ottó Komoly's reaction I know only that he asked for permission to make copies. Bishop Raffay only asked the deliverer, Dean Lajos Kemény, about its origin. With his usual bluntness, Kemény replied that it didn't matter from where it had come, but only that every word was true. Horthy's widow, as Török told me, didn't ask about the origin of the document, and didn't seem to doubt its authenticity. I had the most information about Ravasz's reactions, and there is even a written document about it. Albert Bereczky took the report to the Bishop sometime between the 12th and 14th of May, a time when, as throughout the summer, he was lying, seriously ill, in Leányfalu. A couple of days later, on May 15 to be exact, the first deportation trains left from Kárpátalja (Carpatho–Ruthenia) to Auschwitz. This news couldn't have taken Ravasz by surprise because Baron Zsigmond Perényi, the President of the Upper House, had already visited the

Bishop at the end of April and had told him that the Jews were being rounded up in Kárpátalja and the whole of the northeastern part of Hungary, and that they were not being taken to work in Germany, but rather that they were going to suffer the same fate as the Polish and Slovak Jews had. I see the hand of God in this. Bereczky had been able to take the authentic documents to the Bishop while these events were taking place and in the end, this is what prompted Ravasz to send an appeal to Prime Minister Sztójay in the name of the Protestant Universal Convent on May 17th. In the last paragraph of this he wrote, "We have to call Your Excellency's attention to those sad events which lay at the end of the deportations faced by the Jews from other countries . . ."

This was the first time in a letter to the head of government that the Hungarian church leader had referred to the deportations as a Final Solution, the *Endlösung,* as the Germans termed it. It simply means, of course, genocide. It is likely that the Convent's appeal had been composed by Ravasz, who was very good at following the rules of convention and yet still making another party aware of the truth of a situation in such a way that there could be no ambivalence. Bereczky had shown me the draft of this appeal before it was sent, and had been very happy that in its wording, it was possible to trace the effect of the Auschwitz Report. He had pointed out that the government couldn't mislead the churches any longer by saying that the deportees were being taken to work in Germany, and I was happy that the opposition movement had achieved their desired goal by coming into possession, translating, and delivering the Auschwitz Report, in cooperation with the Good Shepherd Committee. When, on May 15, 1944, the first freightcars left the country filled with deportees, every church leader already had a copy of the Report on their desks, an authentic report which made clear what the end of the line was.

• *From your words, I can draw the conclusion that you were optimistic and that you expected a lot from the fact that the church leaders had received the Auschwitz Report.*

• On my own behalf, I can state that I was optimistic. I was hoping that one or the other of our bishops would remember my letter written after a sleepless April night, and that before it was too late, the church leadership would pluck up the courage to take some decisive steps. My hopes were supported by the quick reaction of the Convent, and its letter written on May 17, which made the government aware that we knew what the whole thing was about, in spite of its lies. I also considered it a good sign, thinking it meant a turning-point in Ravasz's behavior, that from that time on he often invited Albert Bereczky, his brother in Christ and the deliverer of the Auschwitz Report, to come to him, when previously he had not paid much attention to him at all. He made Bereczky privy to all the important decisions concerning the Jews.

From the spring of 1944 onwards, the Bishop lay in bed in Leányfalu with a severe case of hepatitis and he only allowed Bereczky, or "Uncle Berci" as we young ministers called him amongst ourselves, close to him. Since 1942, he had been the one around whom the small group making up the clerical evangelical leftwing had gathered. These included László Márton Pákozdi, today an internationally recognized professor of theology, and a lot of eager ministers and deacons. Those that I know of are Dr. Ferenc Benkó, Sándor Borsos, Károly Dobos, József Farkas, Péter Hajdu, János Hordós, Gyula Nagy, and Andor Sebestyén. There were others from the countryside whom I didn't know. Bereczky didn't make a secret of his disgust concerning what was happening to the Jews, and he was worried about the shame and humiliation into which the Hungarian leaders carrying out the Nazi-induced genocide were leading the nation and our Church in particular. He pleaded for the saving of our final vestiges of honesty. It had already been written about Uncle Berci that he was a quiet, pious man who wasn't attracted to politics, but in those crucial times, he obeyed his conviction and beliefs even if it meant risking his life. After delivering the Auschwitz Report, he was less hopeful than me and as far as the Catholic Church leaders were concerned, József Cavallier was outright skeptical about what action they would take.

Unfortunately, he was right. Of course we didn't spend those days meditating and pondering upon what we should do. After the German occupation, JPB was weighed down by worries and duties. Day by day, the authorities spread around their new anti-Jewish decrees in ever-increasing number. At the beginning of April, Budapest suffered its first extensive bombing, as a result of which the city authorities shortly afterward confiscated the flats of a thousand Jewish families, with the excuse of providing shelter to the bombed-out Christians. They gave them 24 hours to evacuate their homes and showed no interest in where they were supposed to move to. They were allowed to take only the most necessary personal belongings, while all the other contents of the flats, including bedclothes, clothes, pots and pans, had to be left behind. This step affected some of the Protestants of Jewish origin as well, and we helped them to move together with other families. We gave money to those who needed it and comforted those in distress.

• *Did you have any information about Jews in the countryside?*

• From mid–April, people who had managed to escape ghettoization and placement into internment camps for deportation, had been coming to us for help. They needed accommodation, clothing, and, again, money. From them we obtained the first valid information about what was happening in the country, but we had other sources of information too. Albert Bereczky sent brave young ministers around the country and they all returned with tragic, shocking reports from everywhere. We were aware that the ghettos and internment camps in the country meant a preparation for later deportation, and the most tragic of all was that we felt incapable of doing anything about it. I can still recall two pleasant memories from this dark period. One of them is that we managed, by means of denominational unity, to organize a forced labor unit to collect clothes.

• *What was this?*

• At the introduction of forced labor, the Jewish community had established the Veterans' Committee (*Hadviseltek Bizottsága*) consisting of First World War Jewish officers who had received medals. Later, upon the initiative of József Cavallier, a Veteran Comrades Group of Christian Jews (*Keresztény–Zsidó Hadviseltek Bajtársi Csoportja*) was set up in the MSZKE. JPB also joined in their work and under the guise of collecting clothes, we managed to select out several especially outstanding Hungarian intellectuals in the fields of science, literature, arts, and public life and take them to Pest, where we provided them with more protected and humane surroundings. The unit's task, that of collecting clothes, was simply a ruse, and even the clique of Szálasi was unable to drive them to the West, so that most of those who found shelter in this unit survived. Unfortunately, our protecting hands could not reach out to Miklós Radnóti, Antal Szerb, György Sárközi, and many other outstanding people in Hungarian cultural life. On the other hand it has to be said that they deliberately avoided these rescue actions. Antal Szerb even gave his free–movement pass to his parents.

The other good thing in this period of danger was that, when we suffered the greatest shortage of money and when we needed it most,

JPB unexpectedly received a sum of money so large that I could not have dreamed of it. This donation solved our money problems for a long time.

• *Where did the money come from and who donated it?*

• I received an invitation from the representative of the Swiss Trade Mission, Mr. Fritz Born. This was already after we had delivered the Auschwitz Reports. He had his office on Fillér Street in Buda, and I took Mária Székely with me. Born began by saying that he was well-informed about my person and about the work of the JPB.

• *How did he know about you?*

• The head of the Foreign Department of the Protestant Church, Dr. Elek Boér, a retired judge, had most probably sent information about our work to the Swiss clergy, and through them it possibly got through to the secular circles. I had already heard about this in 1943 from Sándor Koncz, a minister of mine, when he returned from a sabbatical in Switzerland. He also brought us a thousand *Pengő* worth of Swiss Francs from donations received through Swiss denominations. I assume that this was how Mr. Born had gained information about the Good Shepherd Committee. He also asked for information on certain people from me. I remember, for instance, that I gave a warm recommendation to Mr. Born concerning Gábor Sztehló, an Evangelical minister and friend of mine who had become a colleague in the JPB with a responsible portfolio. I informed Mr. Born about the potential of our work and at the end of our conversation, he said that he would give us a certain sum of money, which I should at once take with me, but counselled me not to inform anybody of the source of this money, which meant that we couldn't enter it openly into our books. After all this, he took out 80,000 *Pengő*, which I had to somehow carry out with me.

It was a huge sum, when we consider that 250–350 *Pengő* was regarded as a good average monthly salary. You can imagine that Mária Székely and I were dumbfounded by surprise and, of course, by joy too. This money represented an exceptionally great help then to us.

• *Did you find out anything about the origin of the money?*

• No, we didn't even ask. It probably came from clerical donations, but then equally probably from Red Cross donations because not long afterward, Fritz Born left his office and became the leader of the Budapest delegation of the International Committee of the Red Cross. When he was in this position, we got into even greater contact with him. I had a big bag in which I took the money to Lázár Street, and I kept it in the rickety cupboard in my room. As long as the money lasted, I asked God in my evening prayers to protect me and to save our money too.

• *You had to legalize this money somehow, didn't you?*

• A good old Protestant tradition came to my assistance when it came to somehow entering the money into our books. In our faith the most respected donors are those who do not make a show of their names, but rather offer the money anonymously, or who simply enter the initials N. N. (without name). Using this tradition, I from time to time gave certain sums of money donated by N. N. to our treasurer, Emil Hajós. I felt sorry that I couldn't even take the risk of enlightening him, although he was a very thorough, trustworthy colleague, he and his wife together. Earlier, Hajós had been the personal secretary of State Secretary Elemér Hantos, Hungary's Permanent Representative to the League of Nations during the Horthy period. His wife is still alive, living in America, and even at the age of eighty, she does her evangelical work with the enthusiasm of a young person.

I would now like to talk about June 15, 1944, a day I shall never forget in all my life.

• *What happened on that day?*

• That was the day on which the decree of the city authorities was promulgated to the effect that Jews, including Catholics and Protestants of Jewish origin, had to relocate within eight days into buildings which were to be assigned to them and which were to be marked with the Yellow Star on the gate. This decree affected a quarter of a million people who lived scattered all over the city in almost 10,000 buildings. Only 2,600 buildings were assigned them. We had to do in a few days what now, in a civilized era, would not be possible even within five years under a generous municipal authority. Even today I cannot imagine how we were able to pull it off, although I was a participant.

Contained in the decree was the clause that whoever did not move within the given time into one of the Yellow Star buildings, would be interned. We had to deal with not only a shortage of flats, but also with human selfishness and the difficulties of living together. I was out in the streets with my colleagues, trying to find space for those who didn't have relatives or friends who would take them in.

Sometimes we had to be aggressive in the interest of a wife, child, or grandparent. Most of the men, of course, were doing forced labor. On the next to the last day, there were still twenty families without shelter. We set off on an expedition stretching way out into the night and by the next morning, we had found a place for everybody. In these days of human trial, June 15 will stay in my memory forever. On that day, early in the morning, I traveled to Győr with József Cavallier. We were on an errand to Baron Bishop Vilmos Apor in the name of László Ravasz.

• *What was the purpose of this errand?*

• Historical writing and memoirs seem to have forgotten about one of the events of June 1944. We, the older generation of Protestants cannot, however, forget it. I'm talking about the initiative of Bishop Ravasz for the traditional churches—Catholic, Protestant, and Evangelical—to write a joint pastoral letter to protest against the persecution of Jews and, if this didn't have any effect, for them to emphasize their demands via other means of public protest. Cavallier's and my journey to Bishop Apor was a significant part of this initiative. I should begin by saying that in all of that which was started up against the Jews after the German occupation, László Ravasz had taken the stance of passivity and noninterference. Even at the first of his two visits to Horthy, he had given hint of this behavior.

• *What did his behavior imply?*

• Although I deeply despised Bishop Ravasz's anti–Semitism (something I have talked about earlier), his initial passivity did not imply his approval of the anti–Jewish decrees. On the contrary, he considered it appropriate to express his and the clergy's opposition by means of passivity and silence. Events were too serious for such silence and impotence and I think Ravasz realized this only with dismay when he received the Auschwitz Report and when, from the second half of May, the news of the deportations reached him through the reports of ministers and bishops in the country and from those ministers sent to the country on fact–finding visits. In his *Pro memoria* notes, which I think he wrote at the end of 1944 or the beginning of 1945, Bishop Ravasz stated that he could feel that they were in an unfavorable situation due to the lack of joint action by the Christian churches, and that he wanted to change this. The very real cooperation between the Good Shepherd Committee and the Holy Cross Society, as he wrote, showed the justification for the need for joint action.

He tried to get into contact with József Cavallier, who visited him at the beginning of May in Leányfalu. The Bishop made it clear to Cavallier that he was prepared to work together with the Catholic Church to protect the interests of the Christians of Jewish origin, at that time only the Catholics and Protestants, and that he was ready to set aside all issues of prestige, and undertake even the initial steps of joint work.

Of course, Cavallier reported this discussion to Cardinal Serédi. Not long after that, following one of the sittings of the Upper House, Cardinal Serédi initiated discussions there in the Parliament with the representatives of the Protestant and Evangelical churches. Those present informed each other about what their churches had or were doing against the increasingly merciless persecution. Because of his illness, Ravasz was not there, so Jenő Balogh represented the Protestant church. It seemed that, as a result of the Ravasz–Cavallier discussion, it would be Cardinal Serédi who would take the leading role in the cooperation between the churches. But time was passing by, the deportations were continuing and the Cardinal still did not do anything to further this joint action. Ravasz called Cavallier again, this time unfortunately only in the middle of June, and asked him to take his letter and the draft of a protest text to Cardinal Serédi.

• *Why did he ask Cavallier to do this?*

• He needed a well–known Catholic personality who could transmit the confidential written text and the accompanying spoken messages directly to the Cardinal. Cavallier was such a person, and he also agreed to Bishop Ravasz's suggestion. But before Cavallier could go to Esztergom to the Cardinal, Ravasz asked him, via Albert Bereczky, to go with me to Győr to see Bishop Vilmos Apor.

• *Why did you go there?*

• We were sent in order to take the letter destined for the Cardinal to the Bishop first, and we also took the draft of the protesting pastoral letter. Our task was to ask for the Bishop's opinion and advice, and to gain his support for the joint action of the churches. Bishop Apor was the patron of the Holy Cross Society of the Catholic Church, and we knew of him as one who was a wholehearted supporter of the view that members of the churches should speak out bravely and clearly against racism and in favor of saving the Jews, rather than the negotiating, behind the scenes stance. I had a special task as well, namely to orally explain the detailed action plans to Bishop Apor in the name of Bishop Ravasz, because it was not advisable to write them down. These action plans referred to ensuring, or I could even say forcing, the immediate halting of the deportations. Before our journey, Bereczky, Cavallier, and myself met. This was the occasion on which Albert Bereczky made us aware of the plan we were to inform Bishop Apor of. When I heard the plan, it became the second time that I could hope for the fulfillment of that which I had written after my sleepless night and sent to the Protestant bishops.

• *What was the plan of action that you had to acquaint him with?*

• I'll give you the main points. The leaders of the traditional churches either in person or through high-level representatives were to appear before the Prime Minister and give the government, according to the Biblical commandment contained in Matthew 18:15–20, "the warning in front of witnesses which would precede public damnation." This warning should contain the point that the churches expect from the government an obligatory promise with a deadline, to immediately put an end to the deportations. If they did not do this, the churches would turn to their flock with a public pastoral condemnation of genocide from the church pulpits. And if even this did not bring any result, the denominations would close their churches in protest, stop the giving of Holy Sacrament to all those who participated in the deportations and their family members, and would not ring the church bells until deportations came to an end.

• *So you and Cavallier took to Apor in Győr the letter destined for Serédi and written by Ravasz, the draft of the united protests of the churches, and the above-mentioned plan, but only orally.*

• Yes. We set off early on the morning of June 15 in a car driven by a doctor unknown to me. Cavallier asked me not to inquire about the doctor's name. Győr had already suffered a large air raid, the results of which were clearly visible. We could feel the depressing atmosphere of the town. Having been informed of our visit, Bishop Apor was ready to receive us. His somber and tense mood showed through his welcoming kindness, and his mood changed only slowly. From him we learned, as he spoke of it with great feeling, that the last groups of Jews from Győr and the surrounding areas were being crowded into the deportation wagons during the very hours of our visit. They had been kept under terrible conditions in one of the town barracks and had been tortured. On his own, the Bishop had asked and even demanded an entrance pass to these barracks from all sources, from the Prime Minister down to the local authorities, so that he could at least give holy comfort to his Catholic brethren of Jewish origin before they went on to their deaths. Not only was he not granted permission to enter, but Interior Minister Jaross and the county sheriff had even threatened him.

• *What was his reaction to what you told him?*

• He listened to us very carefully, read the written texts, and expressed his complete approval for the united action of the churches as it had been put forward.

• *Did he even show approval for the probable closing of the churches, the denial of Holy Sacrament and the stopping of the bell-ringing?*

• Yes. He approved of all of these, and was ready to undertake the actions. He told us that the wicked representatives of hatred could be kept in check only through the public condemnation in front of believers, the complete use of the church's prestige, and the Godly punishment of the sinners. He was not content to merely show his approval in front of us. After lunch, at which we were his guests, he ordered one of his congregants to accompany us and this man showed us around in the Bishop's Palace. In the meantime, he was writing a letter to Cardinal Serédi in which he was requesting him to join in the Protestant initiative. He entrusted the letter to Cavallier, who went to Esztergom the next day to take it to the Cardinal together with the other correspondence which he was already planning to deliver. It is characteristic of the trust Bishop Apor had in us that he didn't seal this letter, and it meant that Albert Bereczky could read it and inform Bishop Ravasz about its contents. He also entrusted Cavallier with an oral message to the Cardinal.

• *What was this about?*

• Bishop Apor was very hopeful that Ravasz's plan would obtain the support and understanding of Cardinal Serédi. So, when thinking of the actual practicalities of the plan, he sent the good advice to the Cardinal that, in the event it would be necessary to send out pastoral letters, the churches should not post them all at once and in huge quantities, but rather get trusty and loyal members of the churches to spread them around, and the church headquarters should send off the letters in small quantities, in different colored envelopes, and from various post offices to the parishes, so that the authorities could not confiscate them.

• *Did you read Bishop Apor's letter to Cardinal Serédi?*

• Yes. On the way back I read it.

• *Do you remember its contents?*

• Not word by word. I haven't seen the letter since then, and I haven't seen it in print. It was a hand-written letter dated June 15, 1944 in very precise, somewhat old-fashioned style on the Bishop's personal paper with the Bishop's coat-of-arms on the top left-hand corner.

• *From your information, I tried to find this letter in the Cardinal's Archives at Esztergom. At first, I was unsuccessful, but later Károly Hetényi Varga, whom I had also interviewed, sent me the authentic version of this letter read out on tape. I later found the original in the Cardinal's Archives, but there was no registration code on it. I'll read out excerpts from it and maybe you'll recognize the text. ". . . I again turn to Your Eminence with the request that you kindly make use of the last resort in your dealings with the government. Today we are at the point that the Protestant Churches have already overtaken us in gathering the courage to take decisive steps. . . . I beg Your Eminence to join in the fervor expressed in the Memorandum of Christians of other faith, or at least, please give an ultimatum to the government at the same time in a similar tone, which, if it is not positively answered, would lead the entire Bishopry to take definite steps. . . ."*

• With conviction I can state that this was indeed the letter which Cavallier and I brought from Bishop Apor in Győr to Cardinal Serédi, and I'm very glad to hear the most important parts of it again.

• *You also well remembered its appearance. The letter has not been published, which is why you have not been able to see it in print. Well, you returned to Budapest from Győr. What happened then?*

• We immediately went to see Bereczky, who was impatiently waiting for us. We informed him of the complete success of our mission and he read the Apor letter. Not many have seen Uncle Berci as happy as we did then. "You see," he said, almost electrified, "one of the fruits of our work for the Jews could be the coming into life of the ecumenical spirit between the churches in the name of love and for the whole of humanity entrusted to us." We then arranged that on the next day, June 16, Bereczky would go to Leányfalu to report to Ravasz. Cavallier would go to Serédi in Esztergom, and I would go to his home later in the evening to see what he had accomplished. Filled with hope, we went our separate ways.

On the next morning on Lázár Street, all the complications and distress of moving people into star-marked buildings came upon me. Time literally flew. Only briefly during the day I wondered what would be the decision of Cardinal Serédi. I had so much faith that he would approve of it, and even if I had doubtful moments, I discarded them. Early in the evening I went to see Cavallier in his flat. When I rang the bell his wife opened the door, made me sit down and only then told me that, on the way back from Esztergom, her husband had had a heart attack. Fortunately the same doctor drove him there and back in his car with whom we had been the day before to Győr and he could help with an injection. Nevertheless, her husband was in a bad condition. I wanted to leave, but she told me to wait until she had informed her husband that I was there. She returned and allowed me to enter her husband's room. Cavallier was lying in bed, and he signalled for me to sit beside him. He spoke in a quiet, calm manner, which I'll try to interpret in the best possible way: "My dear József, I'm not sure whether I'll survive this shock, and so it is very important that you know and tell others about what happened. You know about my career. You know that I have been allowed to enter into our bishops' apartments without prior appointments. Until now I have had the same arrangement with Cardinal Jusztinián Serédi. Today, however, he didn't allow me in. The chief administrator took Ravasz's and Apor's letters into him, so that I couldn't even tell him about the united plan of action, nor give him Apor's oral message. They made me wait for a long time, and then the chief administrator gave me a printed text in an open envelope, saying, 'His Honorable Excellency requests the professor to give this printed text to Mr. Ravasz.' This is exactly how he put it, my dear József, 'To Mr. Ravasz.' All that I was to say was that this was the reply from the Cardinal." Cavallier was in tears, and I sat spellbound, only able to ask about the contents of the Cardinal's envelope. The contents were the Cardinal's newsletter which he had sent to his bishops on May 17.

• *I am acquainted with this newsletter in which Serédi informs the bishopric about all the things he had said, written and asked from*

Prime Minister Sztójay in connection with mitigating the situation of Catholics of Jewish origin between the end of March and May 10.

• Yes, I know. But on June 16, 1944, when Cavallier went to see Serédi, the 10th of May was a long way behind. They hadn't even started the deportations by May 10, but by June 16, hundreds of thousands had been shipped off to Auschwitz. Serédi knew this. He knew their fate as well. He had received the Auschwitz Report at the same time as Ravasz. I would like to emphasize here that I am much too ecumenically minded to desire to paint the leaders of any other churches black—rather, I'm happy when I can say something good about the leaders of other churches. Proof of this is that very important Catholic authorities enthusiastically gave praise to the Requiem which I wrote in memory of Pope John XXIII. So now, when I tell you, on the basis of Professor Cavallier's experiences, the way Jusztinián Serédi reacted to the thought of united action by the traditional churches, which could have meant the final opportunity to stop this tragedy facing the Jews, I'm not speaking as a Protestant Churchman, nor even as a Calvinist debater, but rather, I think, as an authentic witness of that age and story. Within this framework I state that the united action of the churches failed because the leader of the largest church wrecked the possibilities. Separate pastoral letters were published by the denominations, but they were not read out during sermons. This is, however, another story. As an evangelical Christian minister, I would only add, in connection with this failure that there is no forum on earth which can absolve the leaders of the churches of the negligence committed then or now. The negligence of that time is a warning for the present and the future for whoever are the leaders of the churches. The negligence of June 1944 is terrible because the united church action could have saved the lives of 130,000 to 150,000 Jews from the countryside, who had not yet been deported.

• *It could possibly have saved them.*

• Members of the police and the military police had been educated in a religious spirit to obey the orders of the church, and the whole society was saturated by this spirit. If all those who were directly involved in the deportations, and there must have been unwilling executioners among them, if all these had been aware that neither they nor their family members would obtain the Holy Sacraments or absolution, that in the event of their death, they would be denied the extreme unction, if they were Catholic, or the Lord's Supper, if they were Protestant, if their children could not be baptized, and even that the churches might be closed and no bells rung, all of this could have led to such a conflict of conscience, a confusion among all strata of the executioners, the public officers, and the railway workers, it could have given strength to the cries of those opposed to the occupiers and their servants and might have given an enormous impetus to the national opposition movement. I'm sure that many of those directly involved in the deportations would have refused to take part in sending their fellows to death, because when the churches speak in this way, it means that what they are doing is an act of Cain, and they don't want to be like Cain. They would have realized the horrendousness of the parts they were playing.

• *Some of them surely would have realized, but it is not sure that the whole of the church community would have given unanimous approval. Nevertheless, it would have been a great and noble deed in the struggle between barbarity and humanity, and a wonderful expression of their opposition if the churches had followed consistently the moral and ethical ideas and the kind of humanity originating from their beliefs. But let's return to the sick-bed of Cavallier and his report.*

• Cavallier and I had no comforting words to find for each other. I said goodbye to him and went to Albert Bereczky, taking the Cardinal's 'reply,' and informed him about what had happened. We sat in silence, I don't know for how long, and then Bereczky said, "Tell me, Józsi, might this not be the sign of the coming genocide?" This was not the first time we had heard such things from him, and in the tragic months of 1944, the vision of genocide often haunted him. The deportations from the country areas continued, and all the news we received indicated that the whole dastardly thing was carried on without the least opposition. We heard that the 24,000 Jews gathered in Kolozsvár had been driven out from the city and squeezed into freight cars by as few as 40 gendarmes. As it is written in the Bible, "Like sheep being taken to the slaughter," so they went. In the second half of June, there were rumors that it was soon to be the turn of the Budapest Jews. At that time I thought it was crazy not to do something about it, and that we should find a way in which at least the Budapest Jews could do something toward saving themselves. I shared my thoughts with József Cavallier and his assistant in the MSZKE, András Sebestyén. We decided to try and set up a committee, through which we could find a solution. And so it happened. To myself, I later called this committee the "walking committee" (*sétáltató bizottság*).

• *This has rather peaceful connotations.*

• Ah, but on the other hand, the plans being woven in this committee were not peaceful. But first the facts. At the end of June and the start of July we met twice on two Sundays in the Múzeum Street offices of the MSZKE. Those present were: András Sebestyén, representative of the MSZKE, who was chairman of the discussions; Dr. István Földes, representative of the Jewish community; Ottó Komoly, a representative of the leaders of the Zionist movement; Géza Soós, President of the SDG; and Dr. György Kemény, who had earlier been an employee of the *Pester Lloyd.* We knew of him that he was in contact with the still-alive leaders of the illegal Social Democratic movement. Gyula Muraközy, President of the JPB and my official boss, was there too, and, on one occasion, so was Dr. Lajos Kemény, Evangelical Dean of Budapest. I was very pleased that, for the first meeting, András Sebestyén had already brought a worked out plan of action, which he shared with us.

• *What was contained in this plan?*

• Briefly, the following. That we should organize small, mobile, easily accessible groups of two or three, consisting of trustworthy, young Protestants, Catholics, and Jews alike. Their task would be that when the Budapest deportations began, they should go to the star-marked buildings according to a previously arranged schedule, and tell the Jews living there to go together to the nearest public square or park and to sit or lie down there, holding on to each other, without obeying the orders, so that only one by one, and by force, could they be taken away.

• *So, it would have forced the deportation authorities into a show of public, scandal producing, mass violence.*

• That's right. The civil disobedience movements of today use this method with success. But of course Sebestyén, who worked this plan out, didn't know anything about the prospective followers of his ideas. At stake was life or death, and if it had to be death, as was the basic idea, the victims should not make it possible for the murderers to kill in secret, undisturbed. Even to the first meeting, Sebestyén brought a complete, detailed plan with maps and addresses, showing the places to which the different inhabitants should go. And it was because of this aspect of walking out from the buildings, that I called the committee the "walking committee." We accepted the plan, considering it very good. Sebestyén, Soós, Komoly, and Dr. Földes undertook the task of discussing the plan with suitable, trustworthy young people. We asked Kemény to find out whether, when the Budapest deportations took place, the walking and gathering took place, we could count on the Social Democratic trade union workers to support us by means of strikes, demonstrations, or any other means. We also agreed that Cavallier would at the right time inform the Papal Nuncius and, through him, the neutral embassies, so that they would take notice of these events when they happened.

A week later, at the second meeting, the representatives of the denominational youth were present too. I can't give you names since it was inadvisable to write them down, but Sebestyén, who was the coordinator of the whole action, knew who they were. Three came from the Jewish community and I think they were representatives of the Zionist, Orthodox, and Liberal streams of belief, and there were also representatives of one each of the Protestant, Catholic, and Evangelical youth. Kemény informed us at this meeting that the important Social Democratic and trade union leaders whom he had been able to meet had reacted to the plan with understanding and approval, but at the same time with considerable skepticism and coolness as far as direct support was concerned. They didn't believe it would be possible for them to assure us of this assistance. Regretfully, we had to acknowledge these facts.

• *Did you consider the plan feasible?*

• The plan remained only a plan. Thank God the Jews of Budapest avoided deportation then, and later the Szálasi clique was unable to drive anyone to Auschwitz. You ask me for my opinion of the feasibility of the plan? I'm probably not mistaken when I say that many of the younger Jews would have taken up the action. If only 8 to 10 percent of the quarter million Budapest Jews had listened to us, it would have meant that 20,000 to 25,000 people would have been on the streets and in the parks of the city. This would have been a large enough mass to resist, and maybe to force a result. These were my hopes, but I repeat that, thanks be to God, the plan didn't need to be tried out.

August brought a relative calm to the Budapest Jews because of the Romanian withdrawal from the war, the collapse of the Sztójay government, and the coming into being of the Lakatos government. Political pundits saw the forthcoming events in the same way as a cartoon on the front page of the satirical *Pesti Posta* [Pest Mail]: Szálasi is coming as if he were going.

• *I traveled in the same wagon as a group of Pesti Posta employees from Budapest to Dachau in November, when the political prisoners were deported.*

• Unfortunately, not only were the cartoonists mistaken concerning Szálasi, but the instinct of Jewish parents proved to be more accurate. From the beginning of summer, we hadn't been able, at the JPB, to figure out why so many parents were coming to us and to the Holy Cross saying: "We would like to see our children in safety. Please establish some sort of house of protection for them. We are prepared for any sacrifices." This demand spread like wildfire and we had to take it seriously. We also heard about another well–reasoned opinion, that children gathered together in houses would be easy prey for the Germans and the Arrow Cross. We nevertheless started to establish these children's homes, and with this began one of the most difficult, and most successful periods of JPB's work. Because the work was so immeasurably vast, the Evangelical Church, upon my request, unofficiallly delegated Gábor Sztehló to JPB. He had already worked in the area of child rescuing in his own church and was well known for his excellent organizing abilities, his love for children, and for his boldness and inventiveness. The story of the child rescue homes would only be complete by honoring him as having an invaluable part in it.

The pace of the organization of these homes is a good standard by which to judge the outside events. The first home opened with 40 children on October 5. By the end of October, four homes were in operation, with 120 children, and by the end of November we had 400 children and 150 nurses, most of them also under persecution. On December 24, there were 840 children in these homes, with a staff of 245, of whom 140 were mothers with children younger than a year. In the period between October 1, 1944 and February 1, 1945, altogether 2,000 found shelter in our homes, 1,580 children and 420 adults. We had 27 homes working in Buda and three in Pest. The one in Noszvaj, which I have already referred to, made up the thirty–first.

• *In his work "The Politics of Genocide," Randolph L. Braham analyzes the story of rescuing work and writes in abundance about the work of the Good Shepherd Committee and mentions you and Gábor Sztehló personally. He also writes, and here I give a rough translation, that the Good Shepherd Committee's work became increasingly important during the Arrow Cross period when it was able to give shelter to about 1,500 children in these refugee homes. The basis of this work had already been laid down by the JPB two years earlier, when it had established the Protestant Orphanage in Noszvaj to protect Jewish and non-Jewish children in need of care. Braham writes that the financial maintenance of the home was undertaken by Heinrich and Otto Haggenmacher and their families and they also helped with large quantities of food.*

• One of the villas in Buda in which we had set up a children's home was in fact the home of the Haggenmacher family. In Buda we usually were able to obtain large, many-roomed villas, but most of the time, the owners and their children stayed there as well.

• *Why did they offer up their homes?*

• The first, we can be sure, were offered up because of humanistic reasons. The news of this spread, and we helped to spread it, of course, and the later offers had, besides humanistic ideas, probably felt themselves and their families to be in greater security, and also thought they would have more regular food supplies, which was not an insignificant factor. As to whether the Haggenmachers gave money or food, I don't know. They could have donated, since they were famous food and beer producers, and if this was so, they probably gave the donations to the Red Cross. The homes were run by the Good Shepherd Committee, and the ones in Buda were under the direct responsibility of Gábor Sztehló. Besides insignificant voluntary donations, the actual donation of money and food for these homes was done by the Inernational and Swedish Red Cross, with Sztehló himself being the head of the Child-Protection Department of the International Red Cross, and so was in permanent contact with Fritz Born, leader of the Budapest delegation of the Red Cross. From among the JPB employees, I assigned Mária Székely to be Sztehlo's assistant, and she was of great help to him in every aspect of the organization of the homes, and was also an interpreter for him. Mária Székely later became a close associate of Fritz Born and then, from my colleagues, Zsuzsa Bartos became Sztehló's assistant.

• *How did the homes survive the Arrow Cross era and the fighting for the liberation of the city?*

• One of the conditions which I stuck to was that the homes should not ask for protection from the Red Cross.

• *Why not?*

• The financial and food support from the Red Cross was a matter of life and death, and we were grateful for that, but the risk and responsibility for the safety of the homes was the burden of those leaders, that is, the adults who worked there. My other consideration was that the board outside, which might have indicated that it was under protection, could have attracted the attention of the Gestapo or Arrow Cross, and we wouldn't have been able to rely on their honesty and diplomacy. The Good Shepherd homes, formally and in practice, remained refugee homes until the liberation. In fact, there were refugees from Transylvania with their children, and the persecuted children and mothers who made up most of the staff, running away from their murderers, were refugees too.

Events proved me right. Most of our homes survived and remained in good shape during the time of the Arrow Cross madness and the fight for control of the city. Of course we experienced difficult and dramatic situations, for example, in the home on Roskovics Street, directed by Dr. Imre Thaly and his wife. In the middle of December, an Arrow Cross brigade, led by the infamous László Endre himself, staged a raid on the house and took away ten children together with Dr. Thaly to the Arrow Cross headquarters. The doctor managed to take all ten children back with him by being very firm and by making reference to his contacts. On January 3, however, they had to flee from this home because it was in the line of battle and came under fire. Thirty children with their nine nurses had to leave the house during the night and there was only one place they could go—to Reverend Sztehló's home, where altogether 50 children found shelter. Later they were forced down into the cellar and when the chldren were very hungry, they started singing. They all survived. Our home at 33 Lovas Street also came under fire and it meant that 70 children and their nurses saw out the fight for liberation in one of the cellars of the Buda castle. The home at 37 Tamás Street was almost gutted and in a matter of hours we had to find place for 17 little girls in private houses. We did manage to achieve this.

• *Did you have losses as well?*

• When we reestablished connections with Buda, I was able to make a pleasing "balance"—none of the children had died because of war or persecution. All of them at Noszvaj also survived. This surpassed even our greatest expectations. Two babies had died of enteritis and a nurse had been killed by shrapnel. The death of the Christian German nurse left behind in the Haggenmacher villa was shocking. She had been afraid of her armed, murderous compatriots so when she had seen the first Soviet soldier entering the garden gate, she hurried out to greet him. This was when an SS sniper's bullet shot from the neighboring building struck her down.

• *Did the parents of the children survive?*

• Directly after the liberation of the city, 180 children were left unclaimed and so they were taken to our Budafok Road premises, where the Manfréd Weiss and the Mauthner villas provided shelter for them. We even opened a secondary school here. Also at Noszvaj the orphanage continued to operate. At that time our greatest task lay in taking care of the children and needy adults, and this was a fight against famine. We set up a soup kitchen on Vörösmarty Street, for which we obtained help from the authorities, and our colleagues also made forrays into the countryside in search of food. A few weeks later, flour, lard, eggs, and honey—life-saving provisions—arrived in bulk from Nyíregyháza, and this was followed by foreign food supplies too—for example sugar—of which there was a great shortage, and canned fish and meat.

About two years passed before most of our children at our Budafok premises were claimed when relatives returned to Hungary or by others who were willing to take in an orphaned child. After a while even our soup kitchen became superfluous, and its cook, well-known throughout Pest, was able to get back to her original pharmaceutical profession, and she later became one of the chief pharmacists in the Ministry of Health. The Good Shepherd Committee received the services of devoted volunteers, and I would like to list those whom I haven't yet mentioned: Pál Balkány, Balázs Szőke, György Pálos, Mrs. György Szeben, Mrs. Oszkár Brachfeld, Mrs. Adolf Steckl, the Beregi girls of whom one, Dr. Edit Beregi, is today a well-known gerontologist, Mrs. László Hajós and many others.

• *And how did you survive the months preceding the liberation?*

• One week before the Szálasi takeover, József Cavallier warned me that their spy in Arrow Cross had discovered that both he and I had been placed on their black list, which meant they were going to kill us. Cavallier went into hiding, but I stayed where I was. On October

15, the evening of the Szálasi putsch, a lot of my friends offered their homes to me as places of hiding. I moved to the Gellért Hill villa of Judge Géza Kárpáty and Sándor Kárpáty, a pharmacist, which is where the sister of Pál Ignotus and two others had already found refuge. Later I accepted another friendly invitation and moved to the house of Dr. Géza Fehér, an archaeologist and professor, where I was united with my whole family. The professor was living in Bulgaria at the time, so his wife and sister-in-law, whose husband had been a friend of mine who had fallen at the front, transformed the villa into a refugee base, packed with persecuted people. A few of my colleagues knew my address and came to see me from time to time, and even had a telephone connection with Buda, so as far as these circumstances would allow me, I was able to keep the JPB work in my hands. Gyula Nagy, who now lives in Holland, and Sándor Boros, now a minister in Vál, who were my assistants at that time, regularly visited the ghetto, smuggling in food and medicine. Edit Szász, a deaconess made a search for those families willing to give shelter to those forced to be in hiding. Through my military contacts, I was able to obtain valid military passes and to give them to those who needed them. These were the very weeks and months in which those old and yellowing birth certificates and documents proving Christian baptism came in handy. The Good Shepherd Committee obtained 1,500 blank Swedish passes from Raoul Wallenberg and I entrusted them to the Hajós couple for distribution. These were able to save a lot of lives.

• *Did you have contact with Cavallier?*

• No, but I did find out about his almost fatal experience. In the middle of November he came out of hiding and had the courage to go to his office at 10 Múzeum Street. There must have been an informer in the building because the Arrow Cross raided the office and wanted to drag him away. Cavallier reached out for his telephone to call for the help of the Papal Nunciature, when the Arrow Cross soldiers shot at him. It took months to heal the wounds. As a matter of interest, after the liberation of Hungary, the coalition government designated him to be the ambassador at the Vatican as soon as diplomatic relations were to be restored. While he was waiting for this, he worked in the Foreign Ministry.

• *Since we are talking about personal stories, tell me what happened to Géza Soós. Controversial opinions and facts have been published about him. One of these is that, in the autumn of 1944 following General Staff Major Ernő Simonffy-Tóth's visit to Moscow upon the orders of the Hungarian Front, Soós flew to Italy in order to establish contact with the West, upon the orders of the Smallholders' Party leader Zoltán Tildy, and the Communist Miklós Somogyi. When he arrived, his past was checked and his role in the opposition was acknowledged. Within a short time he became one of the suspects in an anti-national conspiracy and he left the country. In the first issue of 'Confessio' in 1983, Ferenc Gergely, historian and one of the organizers and host of the famous conference in Szárszó in 1943, published a memoir of Soós. In this I read that Soós's role in the conspiracy has not yet been satisfactorily explained.*

• From the experiences I gained during our more than ten-year long friendship, I can talk about Géza Soós as a person, his character, and his political views. I knew Géza as having a magnetic personality, someone with an excellent inner compass, and I simply cannot believe that he would have the kind of political misdirection which would get him to involve himself in such a conspiracy against the republic. It is a different matter, of course, when we consider what others wanted or tried to use him for in his absence, in an effort to save themselves, and thus what they said about him at the hearings. There was no Bill of Indictment or sentence concerning him. Expressing myself in Marxist phraseology, Géza was a bourgeois or even radical bourgeois democrat. He identified himself closely with the left wing of the "populist writers." He considered the so-called historical classes of the Horthy Regime, and most of its leadership, as being harmful for the nation. He knew well that only the unity of the workers, peasants, and politically sound intelligentsia, and a party coalition which included the Communists, could defeat this Regime and the consequences of its sinful war. Only this could initiate those democratic changes in which he had believed ever since I had known him.

• *When did you last see him?*

• In the summer of 1946, most probably in August, although I can't remember the exact date. What is for sure is that it was summer. He came to see me early one morning on Géza Street, where I was living with my parents, as well as having my office in a separate room. I was directing the JPB then as presiding minister, and was surprised by his visiting at such an unusual time of the day. He told me that he was coming to say goodbye, and that he was leaving the country because he was afraid that he would be arrested. This was the occasion on which he gave me a copy of that letter which had been sent by the Presidency of the church, to Visser't Hooft in Geneva via him. He also returned to me some of the letters I had written to him. Five or six months later—it was already winter so it must have been the end of 1946 or beginning of 1947—I received a letter from him from Switzerland. In it he wrote that he had made an offer to those concerned that he would return and clear himself of the suspicions that he had taken part in the conspiracy if he received the guarantee that he could do this as a free man. He wrote that he was innocent and that he could prove it. He wrote a similar letter to Bereczky, but because of his involvement in the sharp coalition struggles, Uncle Berci was unable to help him. He had already resigned from his post of state secretary in the summer of 1946 because even he had been a suspect in that conspiracy, or so we heard.

• *Bereczky?*

• Yes, indeed. As a state secretary, he kept his Pozsonyi Road parish, but in practice it wasn't him, but rather Assistant Minister András Hamza, who did the work. Hamza was arrested as a conspirator, but in court he was absolved of any criminal action. His arrest cast a shadow of suspicion over Bereczky, and there probably were people who assumed that he was covering up for Hamza. The historical punchline of the whole affair or, if you like, its political piquancy, is that Hamza went to live in the U. S. where he was a minister until his death. He had been back to Hungary, where he was greeted by both clerical and secular leaders with reverence, and when he died many of the Hungarian newspaper and magazine obituaries acknowledged his activities and his loyalty to his fatherland—nurtured until his time of death and strengthened in the circles of Hungarians living in the States. I am convinced that Géza Soós would have been a welcome guest in today's Hungary at, for example, the fortieth anniversary of the Szárszó Conference, but unfortunately he was unable to come, having died in a car accident at the young age of forty-one. His daughter visited Hungary in the summer of 1983.

• *This is a sad story. Shall we change the subject? László Ravasz wrote about you, the Minister Secretary of Good Shepherd, in Pro Memoria that: "His activities were anonymous, but most blessed and fruitful, so there will be a separate report devoted to them." Was it in fact written?*

• No. Instead, on January 2, 1946 when, according to our traditions, the ministers of the church districts greeted the Bishop with their New Year wishes, his reply included, albeit namelessly, mention of my humble person. He indicated disapproval of any minister who criticized the church in secular journals and thereby ruined its good name. This was addressed to me, and my fellow ministers knew that. I had published articles in several journals and even had had a series of lectures at the Academy of Music published by *Parnasszus* in 1947 under the title of "Christianity and Politics" (*Egyház és Politika*). In these I was not criticizing the church, but rather the kind of leadership Ravasz had provided for it, and was trying to prove that the church was different from the way its leadership had shown it to be in the preceding years in the realm of politics. I have already talked about this. By the way, in the period after liberation, the church leadership, including Ravasz, boasted about the JPB as though it were their own achievement and success, as if the Convent and its Bishop president had given all possible help to it in its work. The raw truth, on the contrary, is that the JPB had received neither office space nor one penny from the church leadership. Just as a typical example, I can share with you that I learned only in 1946 that the Convent's constitution for the Good Shepherd Committee ensured a monthly salary of 600 *Pengő* for the Minister Secretary. In reality, until 1946, I had been receiving my modest income from donations from the various parishes.

I would only like to add one more thing. You had written in your introduction that the International Hebrew Christian Alliance (IHCA) honored my activities through an award, plus £800. I deposited every last bit of this money, which had been changed into local currency by the Hungarian National Bank, into the JPB account. I didn't want for myself any more of an award than that which I had had. One was the simple honor of being able to do this service. The other was that I had been allowed to survive, miraculous though it was, and with the exception of my younger brother Károly, who fell at the Don, my whole family and even my more distant relatives survived the war. Third, I thank God for that extra gift that although large sums of money went through my hands, I emerged from this work as a poor man. . . . On the other hand, an award came to the Good Shepherd Committee from abroad. In 1953 the International Red Cross and the World Association of Jews, in a message to the Geneva headquarters of the World Council of Churches, thanked the Protestant churches in Hitler–occupied Central Europe for their rescuing activities. They listed each one of them and praised them. The message gives special emphasis to the Good Shepherd Committee because it carried out work in spiritual, financial, and networking fields that were an example to all, and its child–rescuing service had been the most successful in the whole of Central Europe. When the news of this 1953 award reached my ears, I had ceased to be the Director of JPB and the JPB itself had ceased to exist.

• *Had its work been considered to have been accomplished?*

• Not officially, but still it had ceased to exist, and I myself, formally as a minister, but on the salary of an assistant minister, worked for three different parishes in Budapest.

• *Why?*

• The history of this is the following. In 1952, some Protestant and Evangelical brethren, who had earlier helped us in our work, were deported from Budapest. I then suggested to the Presidency of the Convent that I should visit them in order to obtain information on their circumstances, thinking that my work in the past was a guarantee that I didn't have any hidden political aims, but only humanistic intentions. My suggestion had already been turned down at the Synod office, and I had to accept this. I thought the whole affair was over, but about a week later, Sándor Fekete, Dean of Budapest, summoned me. I had known him since he was young and in these years he was providing back–up to his district ministers with unlimited authority and zealous enthusiasm. He started by saying that he wanted to speak to me about my political provocation. At first I couldn't even understand what he was talking about, so he made it clear that he was referring to my suggestion handed in to the Convent Presidency. He said: "We have ordained that this matter should be dealt with mercifully in the following manner—resign from the directorship of the Good Shepherd Committee, we won't demote you to the rank of assistant minister, you will get a minister's pass, but your salary will be 1,000 *Forints*, you can't step onto the pulpit, you can give Scripture lessons once or twice a week in a given place, and you can't visit people or families. If you decline these, then we have finished with the religious part of this matter."

You know the atmosphere of those years. I'm not someone who is easily scared, but I could see that it was no joke. I was a married man with three children. I signed my resignation paper and after that, the following dialogue occurred between us: Me—"Who will be my successor?" He—"Nobody. The Good Shepherd Committee will cease to exist." Me—"It would have been easier if the Minister of the Interior, who is responsible for JPB, had dissolved Good Shepherd and the Universal Convent of the Protestant Churches had said they would put an end to that subcommittee." He—"You can't have it your way. You would of course love to compromise the regime. You can be put aside, but Good Shepherd cannot be dissolved."

What happened after this is not really important. This is how the Good Shepherd Committee ceased to exist. My so-called rehabilitation came in 1954 and I was enabled to go to Szigetszentmiklós to be a minister.

• *Your story is unfortunately typical of those early fifties years. We've jumped ahead to 1954, but now let's go back to 1945. As far as you know, did the Protestant Church evaluate and analyze its relationship to Jewry and the consequences flowing from this after the liberation of Hungary, having experienced what it had during those years from 1938 to 1945?*

• There wasn't much of a review of those years, and so there wasn't any official evaluation. Strange and controversial changes and processes became apparent in the new postwar atmosphere. I cannot now undertake to analyze it from all sides. You would need essays in order to do this. But I will try to sketch a few lines of events and happenings the way I saw—and still see—them. One of the changes was that all that had been a question of humanism and had been a task involving people rescuing became viewed after liberation as having been policy.

• *What do you mean by this?*

• I mean that it seemed to be a very self-destructive thing for the Protestant leadership of that time to bring up the question of its role in causing the Jewish tragedy and in stopping it, or at least ameliorating it. I would like to remind you that Dr. András Tasnádi Nagy was, even after the liberation, legally supervisor of the Budapest district of the church and many of the church leaders with power had had active roles in the persecutions during the war years.

This reminds me of an anecdote about a man who has stolen a pair of trousers: he had a very clever lawyer and the court acquitted him, so the whole case was dropped. The lawyer then whispered to the man: "Stand up, man, and give thanks to the court for its good–will!" To which the man responded in a whisper: "I can't stand up, Mr. Lawyer, I'm wearing the stolen trousers." Well, this was the reason why an analysis could not take place. The other issue was the so–called national interest.

• *What do you mean by this, or at least, how does it relate to our topic?*

• I'll explain it to you. Not long after the government and the ministries came back to Budapest from Debrecen, one of the department heads of the Foreign Ministry came to see me. He told me that it was his task to collect data on the Catholic and Protestant people–rescuing services. The separate reports were going to be handed to the Foreign Minister, who would later use them, in the interests of our homeland, in the negotiations preceding the signing of the peace treaty. Upon his request, I put together the data on the Protestant people–rescuing work, trying hard not to either overestimate or to underestimate its importance. They thanked me for my anonymous work without any comment, yet they couldn't have been satisfied with it because they asked Albert Bereczky, who was by that time already the State Secretary of Culture, to complete the report on the basis of my data. I don't know whether this report proved useful for the interests of the Foreign Ministry, and I certainly don't think it was of any use at the signing of the peace treaty. This would surely also have been the fate of a report made by me. It is true, however, that this report was published as early as 1945 with the respected name of the State Secretary as author under the title of *Hungarian Protestantism's Fight Against the Jewish Persecutions (A magyar protestantizmus harca a zsidóüldözés ellen)*.

This was the first published document by a religious author and, as far as the Protestants are concerned, unfortunately the last which dealt with the relationship between the Protestant Church and Jewry. As a pioneering document, it set the tone for how such topics were to be written or discussed. The spirit of this book contradicted Bereczky's earlier theological, denominational, political, and church political behavior and his commitment to the truth. I had the opportunity to give Bereczky my critique of it, and he didn't deny that it was reasonable, but he argued that what he had written was in the interest of the forthcoming peace treaty. On the other hand, the church leadership, even though Bereczky's book overemphasized our deeds and omitted the mention of grave negligence *only* in the interest of Hungary's standing at the peace conference, considered the contents as being on a par with reality and thus started to overestimate what the church had done.

• *What actually are your objections to the book?*

• In the words of Attila József, I can say that it contained facts, but not the truth, and even covers the truth with the facts. What he put down as facts were indeed facts, but they nevertheless covered the truth because of the way they were presented. This truth was explained not by me but by the son-in-law of Bishop László Ravasz, István Bibó in the 1948 October–November issue of *Válasz* [Response] in his wonderful essay *Zsidókérdés Magyarországon 1944 után* [The Jewish Question in Hungary After 1944]. "The churches did not think it reasonable, even between March 19 and October 15, 1944, to put aside all respect for the Hungarian government and its well-known and customary leaders who themselves were showing a lot of respect for the church, but rather to consider those very leaders and their policies, together with their executive bodies, to be on a level with the mad, pagan, and sinful state of Hitler, which provided the guidance for their actions. And this is why, although individual priests, convents, and organizations showed outstanding heroism, the members of the church on the whole displayed as many different variations in behavior as the whole of Hungarian society. This behavior runs on a scale from 'sympathetic help' through 'distanced incomprehension' to 'violent hatred'. "

I emphasize that this had been written by the son-in-law of the Bishop, a man who was privy to the most intimate of details and that he had written it three years after Bereczky's book. At the very first opportunity, unfortunately, Bereczky had given the example of how to cover the truth with facts, using the "national interest" as an excuse. Of course, it had its own consequences and I'll mention only the most typical. The Nyíregyháza Free Council (*Nyíregyházi Szabad Tanács*) was a gathering of both progressive ministers and religious secular men. I had the opportunity to take part in both of its sessions in the summers of 1946 and 1947. It didn't represent just the fringe, and the number and importance of the participants is proof of this. The whole plenary of this Council accepted a declaration concerning relationships toward the Jews. To be faithful to the truth, I have to say that this declaration was put into words by Bereczky with the approval of those present. This was the same Bereczky who had written that book, and now he was giving his statements according to his real viewpoint, by declaring that the church had responsibilities and by emphasizing that the church should express its shame toward the Jews of Hungary by asking for pardon from those who survived. This declaration was referred to in the press. The journalist Endre Hevesi made it public in the article "The Protestant Church Asked for Pardon from the Jews" (*A református egyház bocsánatot kért a zsidóságtól*). The person who had informed Hevesi clearly stated that it was not the universal and official Protestant Church, but only one of its parts, the evangelical and progressive wing, which was asking for pardon.

Just consider: this was happening at the time when so-called "Mindszentyism" became a rapidly spreading infection even in Protestant circles. The plenary meeting of the National Protestant Ministers' Association (*Országos Református Lelkészegyesület*) was convened in Budapest after this press coverage and here the atmosphere was entirely different from that of the Nyíregyháza meeting. The Bishop Chairman, László Ravasz, withdrew the request for pardon amid resounding applause, by saying that the Protestant Church had no reason to ask for pardon from the Hungarian Jews for what had happened. He made use of Bereczky, the author of the book, to contradict Bereczky, the author of the declaration.

These are the kinds of consequences that flow from using the facts to cover the truth. Without using his father-in-law's name, István Bibó refers to the withdrawal of the pardon in the above-mentioned article as follows: "We have made reference to the irritation caused by a declaration which had asked for pardon, in the name of itself and others, from the Jews. We might say that apologizing is not really the most appropriate word, because if we applied it to another person or people, then the danger always lurks above it that it provides opportunities for an overacted self-humiliation on the side of the apologizer, and the moralizing or merciful patronizing on the side of the receiver. A society in which the spirit of taking responsibility is very strong would not have wasted time on phrases or words in this apology, but having adjusted these appropriately, it would have proceeded toward bringing those who were guilty to be held responsible for their actions. This was not what happened in our country. Instead a fairly arrogant refusal was given, and it would be difficult for our society to give up those reasons and aims which it had created on its own behalf in order to shun responsibility. Anyone, therefore, who is going to try to declare anything to be true or important in the name of the Hungarian nation or society concerning this question, will rapidly find himself face to face with the question of who gave you the right to say this? In this situation, the only thing that one can do is to make an assessment and to bear the responsibility that rests upon one's own shoulders."

• *Would you consider Bibó's statements to be relevant even today?*

• Look, I'm trying my best to tell the truth, not in the name of the whole of Hungarian society, but only in my own name. I cannot make declarations. I can only remember and remind. I consider this to be important so that we, the contemporary witnesses, don't take with us to the grave what we have experienced and what we have thought. I don't consider my memoirs to be a private matter, since what I'm talking about—namely the tragedy of the Hungarian Jews and the Christian Jews—is not an isolated incident in the past, but rather as a part of our national history. I consider this in the same way as I would the tragedy of Hungarian soldiers and forced laborers who fell at the Don and the civilians who perished in the country which had become an arena of war. The Protestant Church is both a part of this national historical past and present, as well as being a creator of it. As a minister of my church, I wouldn't be able to live within it if I were to remain silent about what is faulty, problematical, and confessable in it. Maybe there would be some who would ask me, "Who gives you the right to say this?" and I would answer only, "It is my conscience." As far as my church is concerned, I feel that it is high time that it should say and do something important and new in connection with Protestant–Jewish relationships, and in favor of finding common ground. Anti–Semitism has not been defeated in our souls and I consider it a great plus that open discussion doesn't face arrogant refusal in the general society and in our church.

I would, however, like to return to that period after the liberation of Hungary. In truth I ought to mention that although the church refused to make a self–critical assessment of the past, especially in a public forum, it nevertheless had the incentive to look ahead and act. Not even Ravasz was left untouched by the events of that time, namely that the reckless anti-Semite of the past and the present, as Ady referred to him, vigorously took part and even had an organizing role in the spiritual fight against anti-Semitism in the new situation and atmosphere. This is well-reflected in the following excerpt from the May 9, 1946 declaration of the Senate Council of the Hungarian Protestant Church (*A Magyarországi Református Egyház Zsinati Tanácsa*): "Our Church repeatedly condemns and reproves any thought, statement, and action which is in contradiction with the universal laws of humanity in general and the teachings of Our Lord in particular. It expresses its brotherly sympathy toward all those who have been hurt, persecuted, and made destitute by such behavior. It remembers with reverence all those who perished in the persecution. It expresses its belief that it is possible to correct the faults of the past and to lay the foundation of a better future only on the basis of love as made relevant in the Evangelical spirit and it requests all the preachers, teachers, ministers, and supervisors to spread and teach this principal truth of our Protestant Christian belief, with a special emphasis for these times."

• *What did this mean in practice?*

• A large-scale plan had come into being in the minds and hearts of the official church, namely the need to analyze the theological, social, spiritual, and denominational reasons, signs, and problems of anti-Semitism and *to make the deliberate refusal of anti-Semitism the conviction and belief of every Protestant believer.* The presidential council of the Convent adopted a resolution which in fact went further than asking for a pardon. It was made obligatory to, from the 1,200 pulpits of the church, make Israel (not the state) the subject of the sermon on one of the Sundays of Advent every year and to make this sermon focussed mainly upon the tasks and obligations toward Jewish people. The money collected on these particular Sundays was deposited into the JPB bank account and this money covered most of the financial needs of the Good Shepherd's work. An enormous task awaited my colleagues and me. We organized mass meetings in the capital and in almost every provincial town, and we even got to the villages.

I keep one copy of each of our posters in my private museum. For example, one of them reads: "Christianity for Jews—Judaism for

Christians." Prominent clerical and secular leaders volunteered to become our fellow workers, for which we were very grateful. Some of their speeches were published. We offered a series of lectures which were so popular that the audiences could not fit into the churches. At the Vas Street Congregation, the talks had to be broadcast through loudspeakers to the listeners standing on the street. In Makó, my audience was pushed by the crowd right against the pulpit I was standing in. The collected issues of the *Megújhodás [Regeneration]* magazine gives a faithful overview of our services during that time and the press coverage they received.

• *From the contemporary secular and clerical press debates it is apparent that this church service was rejected by the Jewish community.*

• This is unfortunately true and I have to tell you that the rejection and criticism coming from the Jewish leaders gave encouragement to anti–Semitism on the part of the churches, and certainly made our work more difficult.

• *Why do you think they rejected your work?*

• This is not easy to answer. Let's consider it first maybe from the Jewish side. The dispersed rabbis considered nationality and religion as being equal: a Jew is also an Israelite. Anybody, even if previously of the Jewish faith, who belongs to another religion is not Jewish any longer. The Christian mission, although from another angle, considered it the end of Jewishness if somebody took the Sacrament, and thereby became Christian. Both points of view were discarded under Nazi racism. The situation was made even more complicated as a result of the assimilation process, which was considered by the churches to be equal to becoming a Christian. This assimilation process had been interrupted by the Jewish persecution and rather changed it into the other direction. When allowed to function normally, the process was able to transform the Jews of Hungary into Hungarians, who nevertheless could hold on to their religious beliefs. In much the same way, Sándor Petőfi of Serbian origin, Géza Gárdonyi, Gereben Vas, and István Tömörkény of German origin, and Imre Madách of Slovakian origin are also regarded as Hungarian. I could mention the example of Germany, that, even to this day, Heinrich Heine of Jewish origin is the greatest German poet. Contradictory aims and meanings made the definition of Jewish identity difficult and the complex character of the situation is well–reflected in the case of Father Jean–Marie Lustiger, Catholic Archbishop of Paris. Lustiger was the child of Polish Jews. Partisans had managed to hide him and his father in a monastery during the German occupation and after the war, the then Aaron Lustiger became a Catholic, later chose the church as his career, and in 1981, at the age of 54, he was elevated into the prominent and respected role of Archbishop of Paris with the trust of the French bishopry and Pope John Paul II. The Archbishop of Paris still considers himself a Jew, despite his title, because as he would say at an open press conference, by including the New Testament into his beliefs he has not become unfaithful to his Jewishness and to his honorable ancestors. In connection with his statements, questions have been directed to the Chief Rabbi of Paris, who has made the point that anybody who believes in Jesus and serves Him ceases to be a Jew.

On the other hand, the world famous Professor Joseph Klausner of the Hebrew University in Jerusalem has written in his book *Jesus and His Times* that Jesus of Nazareth was the greatest son of the Jewish people. But even if he had come from another people, and not the Jewish, this rigid refusal of solidarity with converted Jews would be unacceptable—that He was Jewish makes it even more unacceptable. Just as a matter of interest, I can add that, when the Archbishop was asked about his opinion on the statement by the Chief Rabbi, he said only: "It is not important what other people consider me to be, but what I consider myself to be."

I have gone into all these details because I have wanted to make it clear that the fight against anti-Semitism in the church had to be fought on two fronts. On the one hand there was the enlightening of church members concerning the satanic, wicked character of anti-Semitism and requesting them to love and respect our Jewish fellows, and on the other there was the need to win over the Jews toward loving and understanding Jesus, who was of their nation. This is the teaching of the evangelism of love, and the putting into practice of Christ's commandment that we love one another. I would like to emphasize that this is not the same thing as fishing for souls or making a collection of converts. I admit that there had been such a trend in the earlier Christian mission. But what I'm talking about, namely the commandment of love, is an obligation to all of those who believe in Christ. On the basis of this, the church can and has to expect from its members to love their Jewish fellows irrespective of whether or not they believe in Jesus, or whether they accept the Savior. Unfortunately the work which started moving into the above direction after the liberation of Hungary was soon interrupted and destroyed by that period which today is politely called the years of the personal cult.

• *What do you consider the church's task in relation to Christian–Jewish relations today?*

• I can respond in one sentence. We have to face the past bravely and honestly and have to continue with this two–pronged battle which has been interrupted and hasn't yet come back to life. That the time is ripe for this can be indicated by the words of two famous Protestant personalities. The writer and teacher Martin Koestler, Evangelical Minister of Hettlingen in Switzerland, had a book published in 1982 titled *Would Jesus Die Through Christianity*? In this he wrote: "Anti–Semitism and persecution of Jews are shadows which have darkened the Church since its very beginnings. There is the one point that the Church cannot deny its Jewish origins, since Jesus was a Jew, and the Old Testament was the Holy Book of the Christians of the first decades. The Jewish sermon and the synagogues became the examples for Christians as to how they should serve God. The basic religious knowledge is the same for Jews and Christians. Then there is the other point that Christianity wanted to appear as a separate religion in opposition to Judaism. . . . Christians started to consider Jews as unpleasant opponents. . . . Gradually, they projected everything that was wicked and against God onto the Jews. . . . The resulting suffering to the Jews is impossible to gauge and unexpressable. We Christians will never be able to escape the shame caused by the fact that we have been persecuting Jews with a passionate hatred for two thousand years. Ignoring the question, or pushing it aside, does not help. We need to experience individual liberation and genuine love. Only a liberated humanism can enable us to develop in this area, and only this would be convincing enough." And finally, a warning by Karl Barth in his Ecumenical Testimonial of 1966: "We cannot forget that we have only one really great ecumenical question, and this is our relationship toward Judaism."

CHRISTIAN SUPPORT FOR JEWS DURING THE HOLOCAUST IN HUNGARY

Uri Asaf

Introduction

While the catastrophe that befell Hungarian Jewry during World War II is now well documented, much of this documentation focuses primarily on the three major protagonists of that tragic era: the perpetrators, the victims, and the onlookers.[1] Relatively little space is devoted to the rescue activities and support provided by Christians on behalf of the persecuted Jews.

The present study aims to fill this void. It provides a listing of Christians who, often at the risk of their lives, came to the support of their Jewish neighbors. Each entry gives a brief identification of the person and his or her contribution.

The collection is by its very nature incomplete. Many names have been omitted because of insufficient information on the specific episode, the survivors' inability to remember the names of their rescuers or helpers, or their reluctance to share their personal accounts to avoid having to relive the trauma of the past. A special effort, however, was made to include all Christians whose positive attitude toward the Jews was documented in published accounts.

---

[1] See Randolph L. Braham's *The Politics of Genocide. The Holocaust in Hungary*: New York: Columbia University Press, 1981, 2 vols. For additional references, see his *The Hungarian Jewish Catastrophe. A Selected and Annotated Bibliography.* New York: Institute for Holocaust Studies, The City University of New York, 1984, 501 pp.

The Christians involved in helping or rescuing Hungarian Jews had varied backgrounds. Most were ordinary citizens who were appalled by the treatment of their Jewish neighbors. Others were associated with a variety of domestic institutions or international organizations. They can be grouped under the following nine categories:

1. *Individuals.* The examples of individual support provided by ordinary members of civil population are by far the most numerous. Hundreds of ordinary Christians brought food for their Jewish friends and neighbors in the ghettos. Many, especially in Budapest, provided shelter for those who dared to hide.
2. *Military Personnel in the Hungarian Labor Service System* [Munkaszolgálat]. The attitude of the guards (*keret*) and the commissioned and noncommissioned officers attached to the many labor service companies deployed in Hungary and along the front lines in the Ukraine and Serbia varied widely. Although many of them acted savagely, bent on participating in the Final Solution, there are also many cases of guards and officers who went out of their way to help the Jewish labor servicemen placed in their charge.
3. *Officials of the Christian Churches.* Most of the leaders of the Christian churches championed primarily the cause of the converts and of the Christian Jews, but several bishops and many of the lower ranking clergymen and women came to the support of the beleaguered Jews in general—especially in the capital. Their help included the provision of false Aryan papers and the hiding of Jews in monasteries and other places. Particularly active in this field were the Good Shepherd Committee (*Jó Pásztor Bizottság*) and the Hungarian Holy Cross Society (*Magyar Szent Kereszt Egylet*)—the two ecclesiastical institutions championing the cause of converted Jews. Also active in the rescue effort was the Papal Nunciature and its staff, especially during the Arrow Cross (*Nyilas*) era.
4. *Clergymen Acting Independently.* Often defying their superiors, a number of clergymen of various Christian denominations provided false baptismal and other identification papers for the persecuted Jews.
5. *Representatives of Neutral Countries.* The representatives of the neutral countries, including Portugal, Spain, Sweden, Switzerland, and Turkey, were involved in the rescuing of Jews through their ability to issue special protective passes. Raoul Wallen-

berg of Sweden and Charles Lutz of Switzerland were particularly active in this manner. Many of the Jews holding protective passes were housed and fed in specially designated buildings in Budapest.

6. *International Organizations.* The delegates of the International Red Cross also played an important role in the rescuing of Jews in Budapest. Special mention should be made of the activities of Friedrich Born and Hans Weyermann, and of Valdemar Langlet of the Swedish Red Cross.
7. *Hungarian Government Officials.* Foremost in this category was Miklós Mester, a high official in the Ministry of Cults and Public Education. Although a member of the Party of National Renewal, the ultra-rightist party headed by Béla Imrédy, Mester played a very important role in easing the lot of many Jews in Budapest, acting in cooperation with Ottó Komoly, the head of the Hungarian Zionist Association.
8. *Elements of the Hungarian Resistance.* Although the Hungarian resistance movement was quite weak, several elements of that movement cooperated with the *Halutzim*, the representatives of various Zionist youth movements, who participated in the rescue effort. This cooperation was mutually advantageous.
9. *Individual Non-Hungarians.* This category includes the many non-Hungarian gentiles, both within and outside of Hungary, who helped or rescued Jews. Foremost among these were the Romanians, Serbs, and Slovaks, many of who were also suffering from the consequences of fascist rule in Hungary. Also included in this category are several foreign missionaries who were assigned to churches in Hungary during the Holocaust.

* * * * *

The Christians who rescued or provided help for Jews during the Holocaust in Hungary are listed alphabetically. The names were obtained primarily from published sources, both periodicals and monographs, which are identified in the Reference section. The list also includes those recognized by Yad Vashem, Jerusalem, as "Righteous Gentiles" by the end of 1987. These are identified by an asterisk (*). Those identified as helpers or rescuers of Jews in personal narratives collected by the author are identified by a plus sign. A set of these personal narratives are available at the Csengeri Institute for Holocaust Studies of the Graduate School and University Center of The City University of New York. The description of each entry is of necessity succinct. The number(s) listed within brackets at the end of each description identifies the bibliographical reference source(s) used.

* * * * *

**Almásy, Tibor:* Professional officer in the Hungarian Army, saved the lives of 200 labor servicemen stationed in Sopron. He removed the yellow stars from the labor servicemen and saved them by dressing them in regular army uniforms. [Yad Vashem, Department of the Righteous; 69: October 2, 1987]

Ambrózy, Gyula: Head of the Regent's Cabinet Office, supported the establishment of the special exemption procedure, administered by Miklós Mester (q. v.). [11; 68: July 6, 1985]

Ambrus, József: Lawyer. In 1943, he undertook the defense of Christian priests charged with "illegal baptism" of Jews. One of his protegés was Zoltán Török, parson of Budapest–Törökör (q. v.). [64: January 11, 1947]

Anger, Per: Secretary of the Swedish Legation in Budapest, provided assistance to various rescue activities during the second half of 1944. [3; 11]

**Angyal, Ferenc (François):* Teacher in the Champagnat School of the Marist Order in Budapest, saved 150 persecuted Jews by hiding them. [48; Yad Vashem, Department of the Righteous]

+Anker, Mária: Hid many Jews in Buda in her apartment, among them the family of György Kemény, his wife and two daughters. Kemény was a journalist of the *Pester Lloyd*, and had been deported by the Germans. [Testimony by Mrs. Yehudit Yaron, Jerusalem, 1987]

Antal, János: Head of the Salesian house in Rákospalota. In that house many persecuted were sheltered and provided with Vatican safe conduct documents. Mr. Antal was arrested but set free after the intervention of the Papal Nuncio. [22]

Antall, József: Head of the social section of the Ministry of Interior, helped the activity of the *Pártfogó Iroda* [Protection Office], (established in 1939), of the Hungarian Jewish Community, aiding Jewish refugees and interned Jews. He also played an active role in the emigration of Jews using the "Danube route" in 1939. Later he was reponsible for 120,000 Polish refugees, 10 percent of whom were Jews. Help given to Polish Jews by the social section was not ignored by the government. [4; 33; 68: December 1987]

Apatin, Iván: Doctor, supplied care and food to Jews living in the Yellow Star Houses. [75: April 15, 1985]

Apor, Gizella (Baroness): Active in the International Red Cross, as a nurse in the Honvéd Tiszti Hospital, she helped Sándor Újváry (q. v.) and Ferenc Kálló (q. v.) in their rescue efforts. [11; 22; 33]

Apor, Vilmos: Bishop of Győr. Ceaselessly protested against deportations. His efforts to save Jews from the Győr ghetto did not succeed. He was also one of the leaders of the Holy Cross Society (*Magyar Szent Kereszt Egyesület*). [11; 30; 48]

Apponyi, György (Count): A member of Parliament, he took part in rescue action with Margit Slachta in Körösmezö in 1941. In 1944 he was himself deported to Mauthausen. [36]

+Arnóczky, Flóra (née Deák): Rescued the father of J. Donát (and others) when he served in the Hungarian labor service system. [Testimony by Dr. József Donát, New York, 1985]

Asboth, Gyula: Air Force officer. Saved the lives of more than 50 Jews by hiding them in his own house. Among the survivors were Lajos Widder, Lipót Ármin, Hugó Salamon, and others. [75: June 1, 1965]

**Auer (Tótfalussi), Erzsébet*: Saved the lives of Ernst Auer (her future husband) and of Jenő Plan by hiding them in her flat, 5 Régiposta St., Budapest. [Yad Vashem, Department of the Righteous]

Babay, Béla: Technician in Kőbánya. He was active in rescue work with Sándor Sima (q. v.). [75: February 1, 1985]

Babics, Antal: Professor of medicine in Budapest. He helped Jewish labor servicemen by "sheltering" them in his hospital department. [14]

Báder, János and Samu: Rescued Jews in Balf, near the Austrian border, in late 1944. [8]

Bády, Ferenc: Roman Catholic priest. He provided hundreds of Jews with Papal safe-conduct letters. He himself was persecuted by the Arrow Cross. [22]

Bajor, Gizi: Actress. She sheltered her Jewish husband, along with his relatives and other persecuted Jewish friends in her house. She was denounced by the Arrow Cross actor, Ferenc Kis. [52]

**Bakonyi, Gábor, Mrs*: She hid three Jewish labor servicemen, including Miklós Földes (Friedman), at Keszthely. [Yad Vashem, Department of the Righteous]

Bál, Ilona (née Turtentaub): Wife of Mór Bál, a Jewish shoemaker at Szatmárnémeti. She was punished because she gave shelter to Jewish labor servicemen in 1943. [16]

Balázs, Lajos: Doctor of theology, parson in Angyalföld. He produced a large number of certificates of baptism, and also sheltered Jews and deserters in his home and in the church. [60: March 20, 1977]

Balkányi, Pál: Was active as a volunteer in the Good Shepherd Committee (*Jó Pásztor Bizottság*. [48]

Balla, Gyula: A tailor from Újpest. More than thirty Jews, among them women and children, found shelter in his house at 60 Erzsébet St. [49]

Balogh, András: Priest of the Reformed Church in Bugyi. He was brought to trial in 1943 for forging and distributing false "Aryan" documents to Jews. [48]

**Balogh, Endre*: Lieutenant of the Jewish Labor Service Company No. 107/32 of Ózd, which was deployed at the Rákosrendezö railway station. He treated his men humanely and tried to save many of them during their march to the West. [Yad Vashem, Department of the Righteous]

Balzsay, András: Salesian priest. He was the guardian and assistant of Mihály Kiss (q. v.) in the orphanage of his Order in Óbuda, and sheltered Jewish children and adults. Many of these refugees were killed during an Arrow Cross raid. [22]

Bán Mrs. (first name was not given in reference): Concièrge in Budapest. She sheltered four Jews in the elevator shaft, among them István Nádasy and his wife, Hilda. Mrs. Bán refused entry to an Arrow Cross man who wanted to conduct a search. [69: October 1987]

**Bánkuti, Ferenc*: Along with his wife, Theresa, and mother, Cecilia (née Schindele), he took Hani Frankel to his mother's house in the village of Mór. [Yad Vashem, Department of the Righteous]

**Báránszky, Tibor*: Priest, worked with the Papal Nuncio, Angelo Rotta, to save the lives of many baptized Jews. He also rescued many Jews from the Hegyeshalom death march. [11; 76: January 17, 1979; Yad Vashem, Department of the Righteous]

Barla, Kálmán: First Lieutenant of Labor Service Company, No. 101/14, stationed at Szentkirályszabadja. He treated the labor servicemen humanely. [16]

Bartalis, János: Transylvanian poet. He rescued Mrs. J. Neumann. [23]

Bartos, Zsuzsa: Helped Reverend Gábor Sztehló in the rescue of Jewish children in Budapest. [48]

**Báthory, Imre*: A Jew by the name of Wiesel was sheltered in his farmhouse in a suburb of Budapest. [63; Yad Vashem, Department of the Righteous]

Bauer, Margarete: Secretary of the Swedish Mission in Budapest. She participated in rescue actions together with A. Nilsson (q. v.) Both were arrested by the Arrow Cross, but as a result of the intervention of Friedrich Born (q. v.), they were released. [3; 11; 34]

Benes, Miklós, Mrs.: ("Aunt Zsófi") worked with Father Lajos Nagybaczoni Nagy in the Scottish Mission, and after November 1944 in its children's home too. She also helped the ghetto with food. [33]

Benkó, József: Owner of a meat processing plant in Muraszombat, he helped Jews with food and accommodations. [54]

Bereczky, Albert: Priest, one of the founders of the Hungarian front [*Magyar Front*] after the German occupation. He played an important role in different rescue attempts concerning the Jews of Budapest. [11; 27; 48]

Bereczky, Katalin: Wife of Zoltán Tildy (q. v.), and daughter of Albert Bereczky. She was active in the Scottish Mission, where she prepared hundreds of documents for Jews. [33]

Beregi, Edit: Member of the Good Shepherd Committee [*Jó Pásztor Bizottság*], provided help to Jewish children. [48]

Berg, Lars: Secretary of the Swedish Legation in Budapest. He assisted in the rescue activities of his Legation. [3; 11]

Bernovits, Vilma: Religion teacher. She worked with Sára Salkaházi (q.v.) in the Girls' Home of the Society of Social Sisters [*Szociális*

Testvérek Társasága] at 3 Bokréta St., Budapest. Both were killed by Arrow Cross gangs. [22; 30; 33; 48]

+Biró Dezsö: Civil Defense [*Légó*] officer, hid 30 to 40 Jews in two apartments in Budapest and employed the persecuted in Civil Defense. [Personal testimony, Jerusalem, 1985]

Biró, István: Lawyer; member of parliament. He helped in the rescue of Jews from the Hegyeshalom death march. [11; 33]

+Bisits, László: Doctor, municipal health officer of Budapest in 1944 and after the liberation. Head of the Budapest Ambulance Service [*Böme*], helped Jewish Böme members and saved deported Jews in Balf with the assistance of Béla Orovecz (q. v.). In his home he employed Terézia Schön as a housemaid, and her husband, Géza Schön, as a driver. [11; 33; 34; testimony by Dr. Endre Szántó, Jerusalem, 1986; testimony of Mrs. László Bisits, Budapest, 1988]

**Bittner, Helmut*: Saved the lives of the members of John Roman–Reich's family by smuggling them out from the ghetto of Újpest. [56; Yad Vashem, Department of the Righteous]

+Boda, Gusztáv: Upholsterer in the workshop of Miklós Kendi in Budapest. He helped Kendi and his family in hiding. [Testimony by A. P. Kendi, Jerusalem, 1987]

Boehm, Ferenc, Dr.: Jewish labor service company commander. He treated the Jewish labor servicemen humanely. He was deported to Sopronkőhida. [33; testimony by David Grünwald, 1985, Jerusalem]

Boér, Viktor: Army officer. During the withdrawal of the Hungarian army on September 18, 1943, in Kiev, he saved the lives of many Jewish labor servicemen from a slaughter intended by the Hungarian military police. He dressed the Jews in uniforms and provided them with arms. On October 15, 1944, Boér defended the Andrássy barracks against the Arrow Cross and was seriously wounded. [77: July 17, 1947]

**Bonetbeltz,, Jean–Baptiste*: A French Marist priest in the Champagnat school in Budapest. He sheltered refugees and was arrested and tortured, as were several other brothers of the Order. [48; Yad Vashem, Department of the Righteous]

**Born, Friedrich*: Head of the International Red Cross in Budapest. A Swiss national, he organized and led a wide ranging rescue activity in the last months of German occupation in Budapest. [11; 48: Yad Vashem, Department of the Righteous]

Borovszki, Ernő: He hid two Jews, Mrs. János Miklós and Szeréna Klein, in his home in Kaposvár, from mid–June 1944. Later he transferred them to the home of his father-in-law, József Albert. [2]

Borsos, Sándor: Priest. He was active in the Good Shepherd Committee (*Jó Pásztor Bizottság*), provided food and medicine to people in the Budapest ghetto, and also helped in escapes. [9; 11; 48]

Borszéki, József: Police lieutenant. He helped Jews with forged papers and at the end of 1944 he helped save the patients of a Jewish underground hospital in Budapest from the Arrow Cross. [62: August 10, 1987]

**Bösze, Miklós and Erzsébet*: Miklós was the superintendent of an apartment house (25 Jósika St., Budapest). The couple sheltered refugees transferred from the home of Lajos Nemes Takách (q. v.). [Testimony by Lea Fodor, Jerusalem, 1984; Yad Vashem, Department of the Righteous]

Both, Raimund: Head of Labor Service Company No. 101/14 of Szentkirályszabadja. He treated his men humanely. [16; 33]

Branquino, Carlos de Liz Texeira: Portuguese diplomat in Budapest. He provided visas for several Jewish families. [11; 33]

Bugyi, István: Head physician in the hospital of Csongrád district, kept Jews in his ward during the summer of 1944, when it was prohibited. [21]

+Burza, László Kálmán: Chemist, helped Eli Tal (Harmat) with his documents. His mother, a hospital assistant, was also active in rescue work. [Testimony by Eli Tal, Jerusalem, 1985]

Carlsson, Göte: Secretary at the Swedish Legation in Budapest, assisted in the rescue activities of his Legation. [3; 11]

Cavallier, József: Leader of the Hungarian Holy Cross Society [*Magyar Szent Keereszt Egyesület*], a central figure in helping Hungarian Jewry after the German occupation. [11; 48]

**Clerc, Bernard*: A French Marist priest in the Champagnat school in Budapest. He was himself a refugee from a Polish POW camp. Because he had sheltered refugees, he was arrested by the Gestapo and jailed. [48; Yad Vashem, Department of the Righteous]

+Csáki, Béla: Manufacturer, 17 Nefelejts St., Budapest. He supplied water for the neighboring Yellow Star House from his workshop and also saved Jewish property. In November 1944 he was interrogated

by the Gestapo at the Hotel Majestic. [Testimony by Dr. László Remete, Budapest, March 29, 1988]

Csányi, István, Mrs.: She cooperated with Raoul Wallenberg in the rescue activities of the Swedish Red Cross along the highway leading to Vienna. [11; 29]

+Csirmaz, István, Dr.: Officer of a Jewish labor service company stationed at Rimaszombat. He was known for his humane treatment of labor servicemen. [Testimony of survivors in Israel: Moshe Sinai, István Sipos, György Kaposi, Zoltán Fried, Abraham Lebovits, Pál Ilovszki; in Hungary: István Schwartz, in 1985]

**Csizmadia, Malvina and Olga*: Saved the lives of 25 labor servicemen of Labor Service Company No. 107/11, stationed at Sátoraljaújhely, by dispersing them at hiding places in the neighborhood. [66; Yad Vashem, Department of the Righteous]

Csógor, Lajos: Doctor in Cluj (Kolozsvár). He rescued Julia Sző. [23]

Csomor, Gusztáv, Dr.: A secretary for Miklós Mester, he was involved in rescue work in Budapest. [11; 27; 68: July 6, 1985]

+Dakó, Sándor and family: Along with his wife, née Rozália Ivánka and their son, Sándor Jr., he hid members of the Balázs family, and provided necessary documents. [Testimony by Ádám Balázs, Budapest, 1985]

**Danielsson, Carl Ivan*: Swedish Minister in Budapest. He was involved in rescue activities and provided housing and food for Jewish children. [11; Yad Vashem, Department of the Righteous]

Darányi, Daisy: She was active in the International Red Cross, working with Friedrich Born (q. v). [11; 29]

+Darvas, Ilona (née Bagó): Hid Éva Ferkó during the Arrow Cross era. [Testimony by Mrs. Sándor Ferkó, Éva's mother, Budapest, 1985]

+Dávid Erzsébet: A matrimony officer in Debrecen, helped with documents and hiding. She was imprisoned in late 1944. [Testimony by Mrs. Ferenc Lenhardt, and Samuel Derzsi, Budapest, 1985]

De Bavier, Jean: Swiss representative of the International Red Cross in Hungary. He supported, among other things, the activities of the Jewish Welfare Bureau (*Pártfogó Iroda*). [33]

+De Pinedo, Hella: Artist of Austrian origin, hid Nisan Hirschmann in her home in Budapest. She also saved several other Jews, among them two children from Szatmárnémeti. [Testimony by Nisan Hirschmann, Jerusalem, 1966]

+Demény, Pál: An engineer, he was one of the leaders of the Hungarian underground movement and hid many Jews. [11; 35; 37; Testimony by D. Gur, E. Teichmann, Israel; Béla Varga, Hungary, 1985]

Demeter, János: Lawyer from Cluj (Kolozsvár), Romania. He rescued Teréz Havas. [23]

Dezséry László: Ensign in the 109/26 labor service company, together with Commander János Török (q. v.) refused to take the company to the West and went with his men to a hiding place (factory shelter) until the liberation. [42]

Dienes, András: Gendarmerie officer in the Ministery of the Interior. He helped the persecuted in many ways. [19]

Dienes, Gedeon: Under the guidance of Raoul Wallenberg, he saved hundreds of people from the death marches by supplying them with protective passes. [11; 29]

Diestl, András: Retired army officer, he took part in the rescue from the Hegyeshalom death marches. He was a civil defense officer of a building located at 15 Csáky St., Budapest. With the help of concièrge István Bana, he sheltered many refugees in the building. [33]

Dobi, István: Postwar member of the Hungarian government. In 1944 he served as a corporal in a labor service company stationed at the mines of Gánt. There he treated the Jews humanely, saved them from physical suffering, and supplied the labor servicemen with clothes. [60: March 21, 1946]

Dobos, Károly: A priest, he was active in helping Albert Bereczky's group in rescue activities. [48]

Döbrentei, Károly: Saved Sándor Tordai by hiding him. [75: April 1, 1985]

**Dobrovics, Mária*: Saved the lives of Mr. Kondor and his daughter Judith by taking them out of the Hegyeshalom death march. She was caught and treated brutally by the Gestapo for her first rescue attempt. [Yad Vashem, Department of the Righteous]

+Domonkos, Lajos: A resident of Rudabánya, he saved Mrs. Béla Reiner and others from the Hegyeshalom death march. He hid them

at a drill station and returned them safely to Budapest. [Testimony by I. Schwartz, Jerusalem, 1985]

Draskovits, Sándor: A sergeant serving with Labor Service Company No. V/2, which was deployed in Carpatho–Ruthenia (Kárpátalja). He refused to execute the orders of Antal Kern to destroy the labor service company under his command, and led his men to a safe place. [16]

**Dreisziger, Kálmán and Karolin*: The Dreiszigers acquired false documents for three Jewish brothers and helped others to escape a labor camp. Kálmán D. was arrested, but saved from death. [74; Yad Vashem, Department of the Righteous]

Dubay, Miklós, Dr.: Admitted Catherine Szenes, the mother of Hannah Szenes, into a shelter hospital administered by a convent in Batthány Sq., Budapest, after she escaped from the Hegyeshalom death march. [78]

Dunay, András: Engineer. He hid and saved Mária, the daughter of Zseni Várnai, a noted poet. [53; 68: June 15, 1985]

Edelmann, Fritz: Smallholder, Mayor of Thondorf near Graz, Austria. He sheltered eight Hungarian Jews in the last days of the war. Among them were : Hersch Marcovici, Dr. Sándor Dancz, and Dr. Endre Pál. [75: August 1, 1963]

Egyed, András: A teacher from the Piarist Order. He organized police protection for the Champagnat School of the Marist Order at 3 Hőgyes St., Budapest, and for other convents active in Jewish rescue in Budapest. He was arrested by the Gestapo. [22; 48]

Elek, Béla: Worked at the Swedish Legation, cooperated with Raoul Wallenberg in the rescue of Jews during the Hegyeshalom death marches. [34]

Éliás, József: Minister (Reformed). Leader of the Good Shepherd Committee (*Jó Pásztor Bizottság*), one of the central figures in the rescue activities of Church related institutions. [9; 11; 33; 48]

Eltér, (first name is not mentioned): A captain, he served as a liaison for Géza Herczegh (q. v.), by bringing to his shelter Jews during the Arrow Cross era in Budapest. [75: June 15, 1984]

Erna, Sister (family name is not mentioned): Nun. She helped Jewish labor servicemen in the OTI hospital in Budapest. [8]

Ervin, Gábor: Converted Jew, Catholic priest, and writer. Until December 1944 he sheltered many Jews in his home. He was murdered together with his mother by the Arrow Cross. [22]

Eszterházy, József: Worked with Sándor Újváry in the Department of Cooperation (*Département de Coopération*) at 3 Tövis St., Budapest. He was also the Department's liaison to the Arrow Cross Foreign Minister, Gábor Kemény. [11; 33]

Etela, Mária: Nun at the Franciscan Mission in Budapest, where Jews were hidden. She and the mother superior of the convent were killed by the Arrow Cross. [30]

Fábry, Pál: One of the commanders of KISKA No. 5, (a pseudo–military unit), he guarded the "Protected House" in Vadász St., Budapest, together with Attila Horváth (q. v.). [11; 17]

**Fájó, Erzsébet*: Saved the lives of the members of the Abonyi family by hiding and forging documents in Budapest. [Yad Vashem, Department of the Righteous]

Farkas, Imre: Worked with Sándor Újváry (q. v.) in the Department of Cooperation (*Département de Coopération*). [33]

+Farkas, István: Captain assigned to Labor Service Company No. I/307. He provided all his men with Papal safe conduct passes and renamed his unit, "Vatican Protected Company," No. I/25. [Testimony by Dr. János Székely, Jerusalem, 1987]

**Farkas, István*: Along with his daughters Zsuzsa and Mária, he offered their flat at 6 Fiumei St., Budapest, as a shelter to Zsuzsa Jakab and several other Jews. [Yad Vashem, Department of the Righteous]

Farkas, János: Vicar at Németlövő (near Szombathely). In the spring of 1945, he saved 70 of 400 exhausted labor servicemen. The others were shot by the Germans. [22]

Farkas, József: Priest, worked with Sándor Borsos (q. v.), helping the persecuted. [48]

Farkas, Zoltán, Dr.: Worked at the Spanish Consulate, Budapest. He persuaded Angel San Briz (q. v.) to supply passports to Jewish families and also cooperated with Sándor Újváry. [11; 33]

Fedák, László: Schoolmaster at Szeklence, in Ungvár region. In 1944 he was a commander of a labor service company. He treated the Jews humanely. [75: May 15, 1985]

Fehér, Géza, Mrs.: The wife of Dr. Géza Fehér, professor of archaeology. She sheltered many persecuted in their home at Gyarmat St., Budapest, among them Rev. József Éliás. [48]

Fehér, Gyula Mátyás: Catholic priest. He provided many Jews with safe conduct letters from the Vatican. He was jailed by the Arrow Cross. [22]

Fehér, István: Army officer. Worked with Sándor Újváry (q. v.) in the Department of Cooperation (*Département de Coopération*). Major Fehér participated in many rescue activities. [33]

Feller Harold: Secretary at the Swiss Consulate in Budapest. He was active in the rescue efforts of the foreign missions in Budapest. He was arrested and beaten by the Arrow Cross, but survived, only to be interned by the Russians in 1945. [3; 11]

**Ferenczfalvi, Kálmán*: Cadet–sergeant, he helped Jews while working at the headquarters of Labor Service Batallion No. 20 at Szentendre to escape and provided them with documents. Three of them survived: Gyula Wohl, Ödön Judkovics, and István Trepper. [71; 75: August 1, November 15, 1987; Yad Vashem, Department of the Righteous]

Ferenczy, Dr. (first name is not mentioned): A surgeon, he helped Jews concentrated in the Óbuda brickyard. [11; 33]

Ferenczy, Erzsébet: She hid Jews in the house of László Szilasi, 17 József Attila St., Budapest. One of the rescued was László Litván. She was married to the sculptor, Béni Ferenczy. [44]

Ferenczy, József: Commander of the Ferenczy group, KISKA VII/2, (a pseudo–military unit). Jewish labor servicemen were active in this group and participated in armed resistance against the Arrow Cross and the Germans. [35]

**Fertitics, Ferenc*: Saved the life of Miriam Grünfeld by smuggling her out of the ghetto of Huszt. [76: May 27, 1981; Yad Vashem, Department of the Righteous]

Fischer, Gyula: Commander of a labor service company stationed in the Pécs area from May 1944 on. Because of his humane treatment of the Jews, he was dismissed by the Arrow Cross. After his dismissal only 100 of the 300 Jewish labor servicemen survived. [64: September 20, 1947]

+Fischer, József: He hid and rescued Erzsébet Schaár in Budapest. [Testimony by György Konrád, Jerusalem, 1986]

**Fischer, Nándor* (Ferdinand): Marist priest in the Champagnat School in Budapest, where he sheltered many refugees. He was arrested and tortured together with other Marist priests. [22; 48; Yad Vashem, Department of the Righteous]

Fleck, József: He and his wife rescued Jews by hiding them in Balf, Győr district. [50]

Földes, László: Active in an Újpest partisan group, he saved the lives of many Jews. [49]

Földiák, István: Participated in many rescue activities of the Department of Cooperation (*Département de Coopération*), together with Sándor Újváry (q. v.). [33]

Földvári, Miklós: Captain of the KISKA 141 unit. In its five companies many Jews were "enlisted," along with 200 Jewish nurses. KISKA 141 supplied food to the ghetto and to the protected houses. On December 20, 1944, the men of KISKA 141 killed two Arrow Cross thugs, preventing them from murdering Jews on the banks of the Danube. [35]

Forgács, Gyula: Priest who helped the persecuted in the Scottish Mission, Budapest. [34]

**Frankó, Dezső and Franziska*: He was a baker in Budapest, where he and his wife saved the lives of Mr. and Mrs. Brandl and their daughter by hiding them. [Yad Vashem, Department of the Righteous]

Fráter, Iván: Counsellor in the Ministry of the Interior. He cooperated with the Jewish Welfare Bureau (*Pártfogó Iroda*), saving the lives of many persecuted. [33]

**Fülöp, Emy*: She hid several Jews, among them Barbara Markovits, in a secret corner behind the library of her apartment in Vörösmarty Square, Budapest. [Yad Vashem, Department of the Righteous]

Galambos, Iréneusz: Teacher at the Benedictine high school in Budapest. He hid many Jewish families in the cellar of the Benedictines' house. [22]

+Galica, Károly, Mrs.: She hid 10 Jews in her house in Napraforgó St., Hüvösvölgy, Budapest. Among them were Mrs. Pál Koerner, her mother and daughter (now Dr. Esther Paran). [Testimony by Mrs. Pál Koerner, Jerusalem, 1987]

+Gajári, family: Hid Jews in their house in Zsigmond St. in Buda. Among them was Margit Tarján. [Testimony of Margit Tarján, Jerusalem, 1987]

Gátföldy, Egon: Colonel, head of Department 43 of the Ministry of Defense. He treated the labor servicemen with benevolence. His deputy officer was Raimund Both (q. v.). [33]

**Gervay, Augusta*: With her daughter Éva (Brencsán), she saved the lives of Olga Wolf and others by providing them with food and forged birth certificates. [Yad Vashem, Department of the Righteous]

Gidófalvy, Lajos: Commander of the KISKA XIII/1 battalion. In this unit many labor servicemen found shelter, and were given documents and some sort of uniform. Gidófalvy also succeeded in preventing the Arrow Cross from destroying the Munkácsy Mihály Street orphanage. He was killed in action in the last days of the siege of Budapest. [35]

Gligorievits, Milan: He was active in the Gestapo in Topolya, where he helped a Zionist group. [7]

Gobbi, Ede: Captain who "protected" Jewish labor servicemen. [11; 19; 75: September 15, 1969]

+Golda, Frigyes: He helped Ádám Balázs with his own documents. [Testimony by Ádám Balázs, Budapest, 1985]

Gózon (first name is not mentioned): Brushmaker in Baja. He saved the lives of four Jewish labor servicemen during their death march from Bor to western Hungary. [15]

Groó, István: University professor. He hid at the Holland–Hungarian Insurance Office (Üllői St., Budapest) 300 Jews and other persecuted. [75: May 15, 1985]

Grósz, B: Along with his stepmother Rózsi, Grósz helped Olga Hirsch escape from the ghetto of Dés and hid her. [47]

Gulden, Gyula: Consul at the Portuguese Consulate after the departure of Branquino (q. v.). He organized rescue operations with Dr. Ferenc Bartha. There were four Jewish houses under the protection of the consulate in Budapest. [11; 34]

Győri, Pál: A ferryman in Vének, Győr district, who gave shelter to many Jews. [50]

Gyulay, Zoltán: Helped Jews to escape the Budapest ghetto and provided them with food. [68: February 1985]

Gyürk, István: Led the financial section of the International Red Cross office at Érmelléki St., Budapest. He was charged by Friedrich

Born (q. v.) with maintenance and food supply for the children's homes. [51]

Haggenmacher, Henrik and Ottó: Wealthy factory owners who helped Jews through the Good Shepherd Committee (*Jó Pásztor Bizottság*), mainly by financial aid to the children's homes. [11; 48; 51; 75: April 1, 1985]

Haining, Jane: Teacher at the Scottish Mission in Budapest. She gave shelter to Jewish pupils. Because of her anti–Fascist behavior, she was deported and killed in Auschwitz. The Mission continued its help until the liberation of the Hungarian capital. [9; 11; 17; 75: December 15, 1984]

Hajdú, Péter: A minister who was active in the Good Shepherd Committee (*Jó Pásztor Bizottság*). [48]

Hamvas Endre: Bishop of Csanád who protested against the deportations from the Szeged ghetto. He rescued 200 converted Jews from deportation. [11; 30; 40]

**Handler, János*: Butcher shop owner in Szív St., Budapest. With his wife Mária (née Wohnke), he hid 16 Jews (among them Dr. János Székely) in the freezing cellar of his shop. He also smuggled food into the ghetto. [Yad Vashem, Department of the Righteous]

+Harályi Fejér, János: Lawyer. He helped Dezső Balázs in his office. [Testimony by Ádám Balázs, Budapest, 1985]

**Hegedüs, József, Zsuzsanna, Zoltán, and Erzsébet*: Sheltered Miriam Ben David as a "nurse" under an Aryan name. [Yad Vashem, Department of the Righteous]

+Hegedűs, László: Helped Ádám Balázs with documents. [Testimony of Ádám Balázs, Budapest, 1985]

**Hegedűs, Alexandre*: Teacher in the Champagnat School of the Marist Order in Budapest, where 150 persecutees were hidden. [48; Yad Vashem, Department of the Righteous]

Helle, László, Dr.: Worked with Sándor Újváry (q. v.) in the Department of Cooperation (*Département de Coopération*). [33]

Herbeck, József: Army officer, and one of the commanders of the "Ruhagyüjtő" (Clothes–Collecting) labor service unit. The majority of this unit survived. [11; 33]

Herbert, (first name was not given): Hid Ede Duschinsky and his wife for a month when the ghettoization in Rákospalota began. [1]

**Hercegh, Géza*: He and his wife sheltered 10 to 15 refugees in the cellar of their workshop in Budapest ("Herczegh Rádio"). Captain Eltér (q. v.) was his liaison. During the Arrow Cross era he brought Jews to Herczegh. [75: June 15, 1984; Yad Vashem, Department of the Righteous]

Hermann, Ferenc and family: Gave help to labor servicemen in Győr district. [50]

Hervay, Tamás: Visited and helped labor service camps. [33]

Hetényi, Béla: Police lieutenant, former journalist. He protected the members of the Romanian Embassy from September 1944, i.e., after Romania abandoned the Axis Alliance. After the Arrow Cross takeover on October 15, 1944, 200 Jews carrying Swiss safe conduct letters joined the Romanians and were sheltered by Hetényi. Their last place was in the cellar of Hotel Pannonia, Budapest. [64: September 21, 1946]

+Hidas, Ágoston: Gave 200 birth certificates to Dezső Balázs, a Jewish lawyer, thus saving the lives of many Jews. [Testimony by Ádám Balázs, Budapest, 1985]

Hóbel, Gy: A communist, saved, together with his wife, the lives of 14 Jewish families, providing them with the necessary documents. [1]

Horny, Ernő: Major–General, National Superintendent of the Public Labor Service System (*A Közérdekü Munkaszolgálat Országos Felügyelöje*) treated the labor servicemen with considerable benevolence. [33]

+Hornyák, Károly, Mrs.: Housekeeper of a German citizen, Paul Schultz, in his apartment in Budapest. She hid the family (wife, son and daughter) of Ervin Steiner. [Testimony by Mrs. Y. Yaron, Jerusalem, 1987]

Horváth, Attila: Ensign, headed a military unit with Pál Fábry (q. v.). They protected several hundred Jews during the Arrow Cross era in Budapest. [11; 28; 37]

Horváth, Boldizsár, Dr.: Surgeon in the St. János Hospital who cooperated with Friedrich Born (q. v.) in rescuing many Jews from the Óbuda brick factory. He was also active in Physicians' Teachers College (*Orvos Tanári Collegium*). [11; 29; 33]

**Horváth, Elek*: Helped the family of Joseph Welwarth of Budapest. Part of the family was hiding in Pécs. [67: June 7, 1965; Yad Vashem, Department of the Righteous]

Horváth, Imre: Captain of a labor service company employed in military factories in Újpest. He arranged for his men to receive Swiss protective documents and treated them humanely. [49]

**Horváth, Irén* (née Csigor): Was a household maid in Budapest. In 1944 she saved the lives of Magda Mauthner and her son Michael. The latter was kept hidden in the provinces. [Yad Vashem, Department of the Righteous]

**Horváth, Károly and Rozália*: A plumber of Rákosszentmihály, who, together with his wife, sheltered 11 Jews (among them Anna Marosi) in the courtyard of their house. [6; Yad Vashem, Department of the Righteous]

**Horváth, Mária*: Chimneysweeper in the village of Nagybajom, who hid the labor serviceman Joseph Galon for a few days. [Yad Vashem, Department of the Righteous]

Horváth, Zoltán: Captain, active in the Department of Cooperation (*Département de Coopération*) of Sándor Újváry (q. v.). [33]

+Horváth (first name is not given): Captain, who enlisted a large number of Jewish men in the Miskolc ghetto for labor service, thus rescuing them from deportation. [Testimonies by I. T. Steinberger, Jerusalem, 1987; Pál Fóti, London, 1985]

**Hubay, Sándor and Katalin*: Hid Péter Klein and his mother in their villa in the Svábhegy, Budapest, identifying them as house servants. [Yad Vashem, Department of the Righteous]

Huszár, Elemér: A converted Jew and priest in Zugliget. He sheltered many Jews and other persecutees until his arrest in July 1944. [22; 26; 48]

Huszti (first name is not given): Professor, together with Lola Kosáry (q. v.) hid Jewish refugees. [68: April 1985]

Hüvös, Iván: Director of Budapest Tramways, his house on Széher St., Buda, was under Swiss protection. He gave shelter to several Jews, including Zseni Várnai, and to other persecuted people. [35; 53]

Ichim, Nikolai: A forest ranger in Ciblesalja, Transylvania. He gave shelter to Samu Dub and his daughter Hanni Mármor and her three children, following their escape from the Synagogue of Lápos. [47]

Iván, Dr. (first name is not known): Surgeon in Budapest, active in the Szabolcs St. camp for refugees. He treated Jewish refugees from

Slovakia and elsewhere. [Testimony by Dr. Endre Szántó, Jerusalem, 1986]

+*Ivánovits, Mihály*: Concièrge at 6 Jászai Mari Sq., Budapest. He hid Jews with Swedish papers as well as other Jews passing by his house. [Testimony by Mrs. László Kenéz, Budapest, 1985]

Izay, Géza: Jesuit priest who helped shelter, feed, and provide with documents many persecutees. He and his collaborators were supported by the Nunciatura of the Vatican. [22; 48]

Jahoda, Károly: Manufacturer in Újpest. He and his wife gave shelter and food to 86 Jews in the Szántó furniture factory, 32 Jókai St. One of these persecutees was Mrs. István Bán. [49]

**Jakab, János*: Hid Ben Tenenbaum and Rivka Schächter in his house in Miskolc. [Yad Vashem, Department of the Righteous]

Jánosi, József: Priest, leader of the Hungarian Holy Cross Society (*Magyar Szent Kereszt Egyesület*) together with József Cavallier (q. v.). He was one of the most active members of religious organizations involved in rescue operations. He also cooperated with the staff of the Swedish Legation. [11; 27; 30; 48]

Juhász, Attila, Dr.: Captain. He helped labor servicemen to survive by his humane treatment while stationed in the Ukraine. In the fall of 1944 he was killed by the Arrow Cross. [11; 18]

Juhász, József, Dr.: Police counsellor who took care of proper burial of Jews and of the Jewish cemetery in Budapest in late 1944. See also: Nyiri, János. [11]

**Juhász, Margit*: Nun. She sheltered Abraham Farkas and his family in her home after their escape from the ghetto of Budapest. She transferred them to Szúnyogsziget for further hiding. [Yad Vashem, Department of the Righteous]

**Kaba, Márton, Dr.*: Captain in the Hungarian army. He hid many Jews, among them Louis Korda, in his house at 4 Kaás Ivor St., Budapest. [Yad Vashem, Department of the Righteous]

Kádár, Iván: Active in the anti-Fascist underground movement. He hid Jews and provided them with documents. [9; 12]

Kálló, Ferenc: Priest who was a prominent figure of the anti-Fascist movement. He sheltered Jews in his home and in the military hospital at Alkotás St., Budapest, with the cooperation of Dr. Ferenc Leitner (q. v.) and others. He was killed by the Arrow Cross. [22; 48; 68: May 6, 1985]

**Kálmán, János*: Liaison officer who worked in the Refugees' Office (*Menekültügyi Iroda*) in the Vigadó house. He sheltered many people, including Jews, in his home at 12 Szt. István Boulevard. [Yad Vashem, Department of the Righteous]

+*Kanizsay, József László, Dr.*: He gave his own documents to László Forgács. Kanizsay's father protected a labor service company billetted at Rózsák Square, Budapest. [Testimony by István Schwartz, Jerusalem, 1985]

+*Kapdebó, Kálmán*: Church musician. He provided baptismal papers to Dezső Balázs. [Testimony by Ádám Balázs, Budapest, 1985]

Kárász, Artur: A bank official and financial director in Friedrich Born's office (q. v.) of the International Red Cross. [11; 48]

**Karig, Sára*: Writer. She was active in the children's section of the Swedish Red Cross in Budapest, and helped in the assignment of Jewish children to protected houses. She also produced and distributed documents for many persecutees. [48; 65: March 1988; Yad Vashem, Department of the Righteous]

Kárpáty, Géza and Sándor: Brothers who hid many persecutees in their house in the Gellérthegy section of Budapest. Among them were the sisters of Pál Ignotus and Reverend Éliás. [48]

Katona, László, Mrs.: She sent blank baptismal forms to Sándor Újváry (q. v.) for distribution among Jews. [11; 33]

+*Katz, Erzsébet*: Hid Jews in her apartment in Ballagi Mór St., Budapest. [Testimony by Mrs. László Kenéz, Budapest, 1985]

+*Keken, András, Dr.*: Lutheran priest at the Deák Square church, Budapest. He prepared 40 Jews for baptism and sheltered many from the Arrow Cross raids. Erzsébet Borovits (née Leopold) and her nine–year–old son were hidden in the church and later transferred to one of Rev. Sztehló's homes. [Testimony by Mrs. András Keken, Budapest, April 20, 1988]

Kelemen, Krizosztom: Head of Pannonhalma Abbey. He protested against the persecutions and hid many persecutees, among them 36 Jews, in his abbey. He prevented the Arrow Cross from searching the abbey. [22; 30; 33; 48]

Kellner, Imre: Fisherman in Baja. He saved the lives of five labor servicemen (J. Engel, V. Rapcsák, E. Rosenthal, I. Székely, and L. Székely), survivors of the Bor–Červenka death march. [15]

+Képehorjay, Ilonka (née Szegedi): The wife of a captain of an anti-aircraft unit. She gave shelter to two labor servicemen until the end of the war. [Testimony of Yaacov Gat (one of the two so rescued), Tel Aviv, 1987]

**Kertész, Dezső*: Former director of the Hungarian Marosevitz Forest Concern (*Marosevitz Fakitermelő Vállalat*). He sent false protective documents to many Jews, including E. Adler and E. Hubert. [Yad Vashem, Department of the Righteous]

Kipper, Berta: A nun associated with the Hungarian Catholic Mission in Paris. She helped Antal Uhl (q. v.) in his efforts to save Hungarian Jews living in France during the 1942 deportations. [11; 33]

+Király, Béla: Captain of a labor service unit. Because of his humane behavior, the father of Mrs. Markish and many of his comrades returned from the Ukraine safely. [Testimony of Judith Markish, Geneva, 1987]

+Király, N. Mária: Medical assistant at the Széher St. Hospital, Budapest, where she saved many Jewish women. [Testimony of N. Mária Király, Stockholm, 1985]

Kis, György: Priest, (converted from Judaism at the age of 4). He was active in the rescue of many Jews with Margit Slachta (q. v.) within the framework of the Association of Social Brethren (*Szociális Testvérek Társasága*). [26; 48]

**Kiss, Barna*: First Lieutenant of Labor Service Field Company No. 101/2, famous for his humane and decent behavior. [6; 11; Yad Vashem, Department of the Righteous]

Kiss, Géza, Dr.: Assisted Sándor Újváry (q. v.) in the Hegyeshalom death march rescue. [11]

Kiss, Mihály: Salesian priest, director of Szent Alajos orphanage in Óbuda, where he sheltered 26 persecuted children. In December 1944, most of them were shot by the Arrow Cross. [22]

**Kiss, Sándor and Eszter*: Sándor Kiss, a waiter at Gundel restaurant, and his wife, sheltered Peter Herczfeld and his mother in their house. [Yad Vashem, Department of the Righteous]

Kluger, Ladislaus: Member of the Swiss Consulate. He helped in the Hegyeshalom death march rescue. [11]

Knight, György: Priest in the Scottish Mission who helped the persecuted Jews from 1938 on. [34]

Kocsis, József: Detective. He was caught in helping a Jewish girl to escape the ghetto of Munkács. [33]

+Köhler, Ferenc ("Pater Köhler"): Led brave rescue missions for the sake of the Hegyeshalom death march victims. Mrs. József Schwartz was brought back to Budapest, one among the hundreds he rescued. [17; 30; 48: Testimony of István Schwartz, Jerusalem, 1985]

**Kontsek, Erzsébet*: Sheltered Rachel Katz and others in the cellar of her house at 10 Horánsky St., Budapest. [Yad Vashem, Department of the Righteous]

+Könyves, Kálmán: Provided a job and documents for Péter Balázs. [Testimony by Ádám Balázs, Budapest, 1985]

+Könyves, Kolonics József: Protested against the brutal treatment of Jews during the deportations from Makó. [Testimony by his son: Dr. Könyves Kolonics, Jerusalem, 1985]

**Kopházy, Erzsébet*: Together with her aunt, Katalin Schück (q. v.) she helped and transferred Jews (among them P. Egri) from Budapest to a secret hiding place in the Swabian–populated Budafok. [Yad Vashem, Department of the Righteous]

+Korányi, Zoltán: Officer attached to the Rimaszombat Labor Service Battalion No. 11. He fought against the brutal treatment of Jews in his unit. [Testimony by István Schwartz, Jerusalem, 1985; Ron Giladi, Jerusalem, 1987]

**Koren, Emil and wife*: Cooperated with Reverend Gábor Sztehló in the rescue of children through the International Red Cross. Mr. Koren worked in the Fillér Street office of the International Red Cross, and Mrs. Koren in the Völgy Street children's home. [75: March 15, 1988; Yad Vashem, Department of the Righteous]

Kormos, Margit, Dr.: Active in Hungarian Holy Cross Society (*Magyar Szent Kereszt Egyesület*), she helped sick Jews. [11; 33]

**Körössy, Antal*: Commander of Labor Service Company No. 108/15. He treated his men decently, thus helping them to survive. [11; Yad Vashem, Department of the Righteous]

Kosáry, Lola (née Réz): With her son Domonkos Kosáry, she helped Jews by hiding them. [68: April 1985]

Kosztics, Milán: Involved in rescue within the framework of the Department of Cooperation (*Département de Coopération*) headed by Sándor Újváry (q. v.). He was employed as a liaison between Újváry and Gábor Kemény, the Arrow Cross Minister of Foreign Affairs. [11; 33]

**Kovács, Katalin*: With her children, Mária and József, she hid Jewish labor servicemen at Siklós. [76: September 18, 1987; Yad Vashem, Department of the Righteous]

Kovács, Pál: Lawyer. He was assigned by Friedrich Born to negotiate with officials of the Ministry of the Interior. Kovács succeeded in preventing the transfer of Jewish children from the International Red Cross homes to the ghetto. [51]

Kovács, Sándor: Bishop of Szombathely. He protested against, and actually saved a few Jews from, deportations by cooperating with certain elements within the local administration. [11; 30; 34]

Kovács, (first name is not known): He saved the life of Mrs. László Radnóti at Kenyérmező, Kaszásüllő. [75: April 1, 1985]

Kriskó, Elek: Greek-Orthodox priest at Kállósemjén. During the ghettoization, Mária Rinder (née Goldstein) and her daughter Jutka were hidden by him. [22]

Krizsák, István: Barber in Budapest. He gave his personal documents to the writer Tibor Déry in 1944. [13]

Ladomerszky, Margit: Actress who saved the lives of her husband, László Angyal, and all the members of his family. [75: January 15, 1965]

**Lánc, Artur*: As a doctor in Gmund, Austria, in December 1944, he saved by good medical treatment, the best possible under the circumstances, the lives of hundreds of Hungarian Jews suffering in the camp. [Yad Vashem, Department of the Righteous]

**Láng, Mária* (née Széll): Sheltered Mária Benedek (née Sopronyi) in her home at 2 Bem József St., Budapest, for three months, saving her from the Hegyeshalom death march. [Yad Vashem, Department of the Righteous]

**Láng, József and Olt, Mária* (daughter): Mária Olt hid Miriam László, her husband, and their baby in a shed in József Láng's country vineyard. In September 1944 the Lászlós succeeded in escaping to Romania. [67: July 13, 1979; Yad Vashem, Department of the Righeous]

**Langlet, Valdemar and Nina*: Swedish diplomat and head of the Swedish Red Cross in Budapest. He and his wife set up a children's home and distributed protective passes. [6; 11; Yad Vashem, Department of the Righteous]

+*Lázár*, (first name is not given): Police captain in Vác. He gave out many residence permits to Jewish refugees of Slovakian origin, thus saving their lives. [Testimony by Avigdor Loewenheim, Jerusalem, 1987]

Lee, Ms. (first name is not given): Worked with Jane Haining (q. v.) at the Scottish Mission in Budapest. Ms. Lee was arrested with Jane Haining after the German occupation. [9; 17]

Leitner, Ferenc, Dr.: Surgeon in Buda in the Honvéd Tiszti Hospital. He helped many labor servicemen, including István Sötér and Ferenc Karinthy. This hospital was used as an asylum during the Arrow Cross era for many persecutees. Other doctors active in the rescue were Medgyesi, T. Ajkay, Gy. Szutrély, G. Major, Tombor, I. Zárday, E. Sántha, L. Konrády, and D. Sári. [22; 68: May 6, 1986]

Lengyel, Piroska, Dr.: Chemist. She saved many Jews in cooperation with the Máthés (see Máthé, Elek) in Kiskunhalas. [28]

Loederer, Emil: Army officer, head of the technical staff. He saved the lives of many Jews in Budapest. [33]

**Loewenberg, Coelestin* (née Loen): Lived in Budapest, and saved the lives of many Jews. She helped many in the ghetto with food. Among the survivors are Zs. Schoenberger, his wife and son, O. Rados and wife, and A. Frank and wife. [Yad Vashem, Department of the Righteous]

Lorenz, Peter: Parish superintendent in Rohr–im–Gebirge in Austria. He hid 16 Hungarian Jews (with the help of some local peasants) in March of 1945 until the arrival of Soviet troops. [55]

Lukács, Sarolta: Deputy chairman of the Hungarian Red Cross, closely cooperated with the Swedish Legation and with V. Langlet (q. v.). [11; 27]

Lukács, Tibor, Dr.: Surgeon in the MÁV hospital, Budapest. He treated Sándor Weingartner in his department, despite the Arrow Cross prohibition against admitting Jews into hospitals. [33]

**Lutz, Charles*: Swiss Consul General in Budapest who created an emigration office for Jews, thus providing protection for thousands. [45; 78: see index volume; Yad Vashem, Department of the Righteous]

Magass, Miklós: Army chaplain who distributed forged documents to the persecutees in 1944. He also frequently visited the ghetto of Budapest. [22]

Majer, Sándor: Sergeant attached to Labor Service Company No. 110/34 which was deployed in the Ukraine. Thanks to his humane treatment, many labor servicemen survived. [11; 47]

**Majoros, Erzsébet* (née Pesa): Sheltered Mrs. Reiner and her daughter and others in her house in Rákoskeresztúr. [Yad Vashem, Department of the Righteous]

Márer, Pál, Mrs.: Lost her Jewish husband Pál Márer, in 1943. In late 1944, she smuggled her brother-in-law out from Fertörákos and brought him to a safe shelter. [8]

Marton, Áron: Catholic Bishop of Transylvania. He protested against the persecution of Hungarian Jewry and against the official anti-Semitic view of the Catholic Church. [45]

Máté, Zoltán: Sheltered hundreds of Jews at 6 Teréz Boulevard, Budapest. In this action an SS sergeant, Grantzner, was involved too. The action was financed by the richer refugees. After the Germans' withdrawal, Máté took care of the Jews until Soviet soldiers reached the house. [64: December 28, 1946]

**Máthé, Elek and Klára*: Organized rescue activities in Kiskunhalas. Later in Budapest, they hid Jews in churches and private homes. Klára helped the persecuted via the International Red Cross. [11; 33; Yad Vashem, Department of the Righteous]

Mester, Miklós: Former Secretary of State in the Ministry of Education and Religion. His opposition to the Arrow Cross leaders László Endre and László Baky was manifested in the Cabinet meetings of June 1944. He exempted many prominent Jews from persecution. Several of his subordinates in the Ministry were involved in the exemption program, including András Molnár, Kálmán Tar, Sándor Simon, Géza Bernáth, János Pusztai, Zoltán Bassola, Endre Giday, and Szabolcs Lörinczy. [9; 10; 27; 33; 68: July 6, 1985]

Mezey, von Dénes: Consular officer at the Swedish Legation in Budapest. He assisted in the rescue activities of the Legation. [6]

**Michnay, László*: Adventist priest. He helped the persecuted among them the daughter and husband of the writer Zseni Várnai. [53; Yad Vashem, Department of the Righteous]

Mikó, Zoltán: Captain. From September 1944 on, he was active in the Extrication Committee (*Kiugrási Bizottság*). He created the Görgey Battalion and the so-called Bimbó street resistance group. Hundreds of people were saved and hidden by him. Ten Jews from the Görgey battalion were captured and executed by the Arrow Cross in the Margit Boulevard jail. [5; 35]

**Mikulay, Gusztáv*: A violin instructor, who saved Jews from deportation in Budapest in 1944. Among those saved was the family of Andreas Zador. [Yad Vashem, Department of the Righteous]

+Mojzes, János: Lawyer. He hid in his home and at other places 30 or more Jews. Among the survivors was Éva Gróf. [Testimony by Vera Molnár and Mrs. Miklós Kendi, Jerusalem, 1987]

Moldovan, Mihai: Miner, Seventh-Day Adventist from Dés. He helped the Jews in the Dés ghetto (the Bungur) with food, and was brutally treated by the authorities. [47]

+Molnár, Kálmán: Concièrge and plumber who in 1944–45 sheltered in his workshop at 67 József Boulevard, Budapest, three labor servicemen, among them Pál Körner. [Testimony by Mrs. Körner, Jerusalem, 1987]

+Molnár, Károly: Waiter in Budapest. He saved the lives of Hédi Tarján and her mother, Margit, by transferring and hiding them in Sárisáp (near Dorog) from October 15 until the liberation. [Testimony by Hédi Tarján, Jerusalem, 1987]

Molnár, Szilárd, Dr.: Financial director of the Krámer Factory of Baja. He succeeded in keeping a whole labor service company in the town by fictive employment until the liberation. [15]

+Molnár, Dr. (first name was not given): A dentist who hid Jews in his home at 10 Veress Pálné St., Budapest. [Testimony by Mrs. Miklós Kendi, Jerusalem, 1987]

Muraközy, Gyula: Priest in Budapest, active in the Good Shepherd Committee (*Jó Pásztor Bizottság*). He intervened with Miklós Bonczos, the Secretary of the Interior on behalf of persecuted Jews. [11; 27]

+Muresán, (first name is now known): A Romanian, deported to Dachau because he smuggled Jewish refugees from Hungary to Romania. [Testimony by Samuel Nussbaum, Jerusalem, 1987]

Nagy, Emil: Former Minister of Justice in the Bethlen government. He hid many Jews in his house on Kissvábhegyi St., Budapest. Among them was Sándor Török, the well-known writer. [48]

Nagy, Gyula: Priest who helped many Jews in the ghetto of Budapest with food and medicine and kept contact with the Jewish Council. [9; 11; 48]

Nagybaczoni Nagy, Lajos: Was secretary at the Scottish Mission. After Jane Haining's arrest (q. v.), he helped Jewish children. [33]

Nagybaczoni Nagy, Vilmos: Minister of Defense from September 1942 to June 1943. He fought for the humane treatment of labor servicemen. He achieved the establishment of better conditions for Jews serving within Hungary. [39; 45; Yad Vashem, Department of the Righteous]

Nagymarosy, Rezső, Dr.: Physician, Brigadier General. His humane behavior contributed to the rescue activities of Dr. Leitner in the Honvéd Tiszti Hospital in Buda. [68: May 6, 1986]

Neményi, Lili: Actress who helped Jews in the ghetto of Budapest. Alajos Artner, the director of Hotel Continental, was persuaded by her to hide many persecuted in the hotel. Many Jews were also sheltered in the house of her mother in Buda. [24; 75: January 1, 1967]

+Nemes, Aladár and Tibor: Army officers. They served at Miskolc and helped Paula Neumann (née Bruckstein) to escape to Budapest. Tibor Nemes also treated the labor servicemen under his command humanely. [Testimony by P. Neumann, Jerusalem, 1987]

**Nemes Takách, Lajos and Gizella*: Takách was a retired colonel. The family sheltered in their home in Csaba St., Budapest, several refugees, among them Lea Fodor. However, after a visit by Father András Kun, the Minorite monk who was executed after the war for mass murder, the family transferred the refugees to Miklós Bösze (q. v.). [Yad Vashem, Department of the Righteous]

Német, Gyula: Brought food to Jews in the ghetto of Hyirjes, Nyiregyháza. Arrested, he was brutally treated by Gendarmerie Sergeant Trencsényi. [25]

Németh, (first name is not mentioned): A baker in Baja who gave shelter to József Schönstein, one of the labor servicemen from the Bor death march companies.

Németh, (first name is not mentioned): Engineer, saved Jews at Balf. [8]

Níkoróc (first name is not mentioned): Former policeman. He helped Jews cross the Romanian border. [12; 78: see index volume]

Nilsson, Asta: Worked as a Swedish Red Cross representative in Budapest and collaborated with Dr. Langlet (q. v.) in his rescue operations. [3; 11; 34]

Nopcsa, Elek, Mrs.: French baroness who helped in the rescue of Edit Laszló. She was on friendly terms with the Marist priests. [File of the Marist priests at Yad Vashem, Department of the Righteous]

**Novák, István*: Resident of the village of Nyiri, Borsod–Abaúj district. He sheltered five labor servicemen on his farm. Among them was Dr. R. L. Braham. [Yad Vashem, Department of the Righteous]

+Nyeste, János: Concièrge in Budapest. He helped Miklós Kendi and his family by hiding them. [Testimony by A. Kendi, Jerusalem, 1987]

Nyiri, János: Cemetery gardener. He arranged proper burial of Jews during the Arrow Cross era. [11]

Ocskay, László: Commander of a labor service company. Hundreds of Jews found refuge in his "Ruhagyüjtö" (*clothes–collecting*) company. [11; 33; 75: March 15, 1967]

+Orovecz, Béla, Dr.: Military health officer in a special ambulance squadron of the Budapest Ambulance Service (*Böme*). Most of the Jewish members of the service survived because of his activity. [Testimony by Dr. Endre Szántó, Jerusalem, 1986]

**Ozoray, Imre*: Colonel, mathematics professor at the Military Academy (Ludovika). He sheltered Jewish refugees in his house at 25 Szentmihály St., Rákosfalva. [Yad Vashem, Department of the Righteous]

Pákozdy, László Márton: Theology professor who worked with Albert Bereczky (q. v.) in helping the persecuted. [27; 48]

+Pálinkás, István: A guard attached to a labor service company. He saved Sándor Szabó and his son by escorting them to a shelter in Kútvölgyi St., Budapest. [Testimony by Sándor Szabó, Budapest]

+Palkovits, Elemér, Dr.: Lawyer. He distributed Spanish protective documents. [Testimony by Endre Vilcsek, Budapest, 1985]

Pálos, György: He was active in the Good Shepherd Committee (*Jó Pásztor Bizottság*). [48]

Papp, (first name not identified): A professor, who cooperated with Reverend Gábor Sztehló in the Good Shepherd Committee (*Jó Pásztor Bizottság*). [11]

+Papp, Győző Viktor: Former officer. He helped Károly Kárpáti and his family to move to Budapest, when the ghettoization started in Debrecen. In the rescue, he cooperated with Vera Radics, who later became his wife. [Testimony by Károly Kárpáti, Budapest, 1987]

Parádi, István, Dr.: Gendarmerie officer. He helped thousands of Jews escape from the brickyard (a concentration site prior to deportation) to the ghetto in Budapest. [75: January 22, 1947]

Pataky, Arnold: Prelate and university professor. He placed his house at the disposal of the persecuted. [30]

**Peiper, Julia*: She gave shelter to Viola Dubov, a Slovakian Jew, in her house at Rákoskeresztúr. [Yad Vashem, Department of the Righteous]

Pejákevich, Mária: Countess who took Jews to a hiding place at the Collegium Marianum. [11; 30; 33]

Pénzes, Boldizsár: Professor. Together with a group of anti–Fascist doctors, he worked with Friedrich Born (q. v.) for the health care of the persecuted. [48]

**Perlasca, (Jorge) Giorgio*: An Italian who worked at the Spanish Legation after Angel San–Briz (q. v.) returned to Spain in October 1944. He distributed thousands of protective passports. Among the protected was the mother of György Mészáros. [Yad Vashem, Department of the Righteous; 28; Testimony of György Mészáros, Budapest, 1987]

Pesta, László, Dr.: Municipal health officer who helped many Jews in the worst days of the Újpest community. [49]

**Petényi, Géza, Dr.*: Pediatrics professor in the children's clinic at Tüzoltó St., Budapest. He filled his private rooms in the hospital with Jews who he listed as "patients," saving them from deportation. [Yad Vashem, Department of the Righteous]

Péter, János: A member of the MADOSZ Party from Kolozsvár (Cluj), he saved Dr. Jenő Neumann. [23]

Péter, Mihály: A Ruthenian worker who helped a dozen Jews from the labor companies stationed at Körösmezö escape to the Russian side in May 1941. [16]

Pétery, János, Dr.: He worked with Gábor Sztehló (q. v.) in the Good Shepherd Committee (*Jó Pásztor Bizottság*). [11]

**Petrovics, László, Dr.*: He sheltered many Jews in his private clinic at 42 Soroksári St., Budapest. [Yad Vashem, Department of the Righteous]

**Pfleger, Albert*: Teacher in the Champagnat School of the Marist Order in Budapest who helped hide 150 persecuted. He provided, among other things, the parents of Edit László with "Aryan" documents. [48; Yad Vashem, Department of the Righteous]

**Pingitzer, László*: Teacher in the Champagnat School of the Marist Order in Budapest, who helped hide 150 persecuted Jews. [48; Yad Vashem, Department of the Righteous]

Pintér, (first name is not known): Sister of the Jézus Szive Napleányok Convent in Budapest. There a Dr. V. O. was sheltered by sister Pintér during the Arrow Cross era. [22]

+Pintér, Mrs. (first name was not given): Wife of a railway worker at Miskolc. She saved the life of Aranka Kaufmann (née Guttmann) by hiding her until the liberation of Miskolc. [Testimony by Prof. I. T. Steinberger, Jerusalem, 1987]

Pongrácz, Ferenc: Count. He was the personal secretary of Carlos Branquino and Gyula Gulden (q. v.), but served as the *de facto* representative of Portugal. He was also active in the Protection Section of the Consulate saving a number of Jews. [33]

Pór (Bauer), József: Priest who was active in the anti–Volksbund movement in Hungary. As a result of this, and his help to the Jews in the ghetto of Bonyhád, he was arrested by the Gestapo and jailed. In the summer of 1944, he sheltered Mrs. Béla Vér in his home. [22; 48]

**Porócai, Veronika*: She hid Jews in her home at 14 Király St., Budapest [Yad Vashem, Department of the Righteous]

Preisinger, Pál Mrs.: Concìerge at 21 Baross St., Budapest. More than 30 refugees were sheltered in this house with her knowledge. [68: April 10, 1970] (See also Szönyi, István.)

Prém, Margit: A schoolmaster in the Scottish Mission, she was deported to Auschwitz. [33]

Prioress, (her first name is not given): She was active in rescue in the convent of the Franciscan Missionary Sisters. During the battle for Budapest she was killed together with sister Mária Etela (q. v.). [30]

**Prucsér, Louis*: Marist priest of the Champagnat School, Budapest. The priests of this school sheltered many refugees. [48; Yad Vashem, Department of the Righteous]

Pungucz, Antal: Armenian–Roman Catholic vicar in Budapest. In 1944, with the help of Dániel Kádár, he distributed hundreds of documents certifying that the bearers had converted to Christianity. [22]

+Radics, Vera: She hid in her house in Völgy St., Hüvösvölgy, Károly Kárpáti, a champion of the Olympic Games of 1936, his wife, Lily, and daughter Krisztina. Later she sheltered the Kárpáti family in Amerikai St., Zugló She also hid Iván Ráber and György Varga. [Testimony of Károly Kárpáti, Budapest, 1987] (See also Papp, Győző.)

Rassay, Károly: Lawyer and member of Parliament. He fought against the deportation of the "alien" Jews through Körösmező in 1941. He cooperated in this endeavor with Margit Slachta (q. v.). In 1944 he was interned in Mauthausen. [36]

Reile, Jakab: "Páter Reile" was one of the most famous priests who helped Jews in Budapest in 1944. He distributed forged baptismal letters, and organized a shelter for more than a hundred Jews in the House of the Society of Jesus. [17; 30; 33; 48]

Reiss, (first name is not mentioned): Jesuit priest. He worked with Páter Jakab Reile in the rescue campaign. [30; 33]

Rendik, (first name is not mentioned): Lieutenant attached to Section K of the Sepsiszentgyörgy Police Department. He helped Izsó Silberstein and his family to leave the local ghetto. [33]

**Reviczky, Imre*: Lieutenant–Colonel, Commander of Labor Service Battalion, No. X headquartered at Nagybánya. He rescued thousands of Jews by calling them for labor service, thus saving them from deportation. [6; 11; 43; Yad Vashem, Department of the Righteous]

+Riccioli, Mario: Director of the Italian high school in Budapest. His Jewish students were exempted from wearing the yellow star. He also saved Iván Füredi from the Gestapo. [Testimony by Consul Ariel Aran, Jerusalem, 1987]

Richter, Béla, Dr.: Public prosecutor and civil defense officer in one of the Portuguese–protected houses at 5 Újpest Rakpart. He made it possible for Jews to enter the air raid shelters. [33]

Rőder, Jenő: Brigadeer General. Appointed by Minister of Defense Vilmos Nagybaczoni Nagy, he improved the treatment of Jews in the labor service companies stationed within Hungary. [39]

**Rohringer, Károly and Sára*: Helped and saved 30 refugees in Budapest. [Yad Vashem, Department of the Righteous]

Román, Gábor: Manufacturer in Kolozsvár (Cluj). He helped several Jews in the local ghetto escape to Budapest with the aid of the Zionists. [23]

Rotta, Angelo: Papal Nuncio in Hungary. He protested against the persecutions. In late 1944, the Nunciature issued protection letters for Jews with his consent. [11; 30]

Rufs, Ernst: Swiss diplomat. He was involved in the rescuing of Jews concentrated for deportation at the Óbuda brickyard. [11; 33]

**Ruzicskay, György*: An artist who hid 20 Jews in his studio at 19 Kmetty St., Budapest. [75: May 15, 1985; Yad Vashem, Department of the Righteous]

+Salem, (pseudonym): Waiter in Budapest. He hid dozens of Jews in the house of the Haggenmachers in Hármashatárhegy. Among the saved was Professor Andor Glauber. [Testimony of Dr. Endre Szántó, Jerusalem, 1986]

**Salkaházi (also Schalkház), Sára*: She was the head of a Girls' Home at 3 Bokréta St., Budapest, where 20 to 30 Jewish women were hidden. She was executed, together with Vilma Bernovits (q. v.), by Arrow Cross gangs late in 1944 [6; 22; 48; Yad Vashem, Department of the Righteous]

+Sallai, Gergely István: Reformed priest in the Üllöi Street Church. Later, at Pestújhely, he transferred Eszter Remete (née Berkovits) to the house of Mrs. Szlatényi in Örszentmiklós, where she was hidden as a domestic during the Arrow Cross era. [Testimony by Dr. László Remete, Budapest, 1988]

San–Briz, Angel: Spanish Consul in Budapest in 1944. He helped the persecuted with protective papers. [11; 33; testimony of László Szamosi, Haifa, 1984]

Sándor, Dénes: Teacher of religion. He took an active part in sheltering Jewish refugees in religious institutions in Budapest in 1944. [22; 48]

Sárdi, István: He hid three Jewish labor servicemen from the Bor death march in October 1944 in Baja. [15]

Sárdi, János: Together with his family, he hid two Jewish women in Osztopán, Somogy County, in the weeks following the ghettoization. [2]

Sári, Dezső, Dr.: Lieutenant Colonel, physician in the Honvéd Military Hospital, Budapest. He participated in the rescue activities of Dr. Ferenc Leitner (q. v.) at the hospital. [22; 68: May 6, 1986]

+Sárosi, Ferenc: Owner of the Bokréta pastry factory. He provided work and hiding places for Jews. One of the survivors was Béla Fischer Fóti, Budapest. [Testimony by László Szamosi, Haifa, 1984; 16]

+Sassi, Lajos: Commander of Labor Service Company No. 108/21 which spent 17 months in the Ukraine around the Briansk forests. Thanks to Sassi's humane treatment, the company returned to Kassa without any losses. [Testimony of Tibor Simson Klein, Natanya, Israel, 1987]

**Schueck, Katalin*: Together with her niece, Erzsébet Kopházy (q. v.), she helped and sheltered several Jews. Their secret shelter was in a house in Budafok. [Yad Vashem, Department of the Righteous]

Sebestyén, András: Deputy director of the Hungarian Holy Cross Society (*Magyar Szent Kereszt Egyesület*). In late 1944 he worked out a rescue plan for the inhabitants of the ghetto of Pest. His plan was based on the possible dispersion of the Jewish population in the event of deportation. [48]

Selykó, Mária (née Országos): Resident of Nagylucska, near Szolyva. She was jailed because of her help to Mendel Jakubovics in his escape. [16]

Seprényi, Gyula: First Lieutenant (reservist), Commander of Labor Service Company No. 109/26. He treated his men very decently and humanely. [42]

Seress, László, Dr.: First Lieutenant, Commander of Labor Service Company No. 110/60. Because of his humane treatment, the members of the company survived. [11; 49]

Shvoy, Lajos: Bishop of Székesfehérvár. He protested against the persecution of Jews and the brutality of gendarmes. He was jailed by the Arrow Cross toward the end of 1944. [11; 22; 30]

Sima, Sándor: Technician at Kőbánya. Working together with Béla Babay (q. v.), he saved many Jewish girls from the KISOK stadium. One of the survivors was Mrs. József Nagy, the author of the reference. [75: February 1, 1985]

Simon, László: Secretary in the Ministry of Education who provided many Jews with documents identifying them as pastors of the Reformed Church. [33]

Simor, (first name is not given): Captain. Together with Lieutenant Miklós Szirt and Ensign Izsák, he took over Jewish labor service deserters from the Arrow Cross for digging trenches around Budapest in late 1944. They thus saved the lives of many Jews. [31]

**Sipos Eleonora*: A resident of Budapest in 1944, she smuggled the Steinmetz family from Debrecen to the capital. She also took a boy (son of Jose Eisenberg) to shelter with the Mészáros family in Szabadka (Subotica). [58; Yad Vashem, Department of the Righteous]

Sister Superior (unidentified): Convent of Unio Eucharistica Sisters: She hid many refugees at the Convent located at Apponyi Sq., Budapest. She was imprisoned by the Arrow Cross late in 1944. [30]

**Slachta, Margit*: Politician. She was the first woman member of the Hungarian Parliament. The founder of the Social Brothers' Association (*Szociális Testvérek Társasága*), she protested against anti–Jewish policies in Hungary, led several rescue missions in 1941, when "alien" Jews were deported through Kőrösmező, and was especially active during the Arrow Cross era. She was also involved in a 1943 mission to Rome on behalf of Slovakian Jewry. [6; 22; 36; 48; Yad Vashem, Department of the Righteous]

Somogyi, Imre and Miklós: Imre was a sculptor, his brother Miklós a carpenter. Their good connections allowed them to shelter many Jews, Communists, and deserters in 1944. The brothers were also active in the armed resistance movement during the Arrow Cross era. [35]

+Somogyi, Károly: He helped Jews by providing them with forged Aryan papers and gave shelter to many others in Budapest. [Testimony of István Schwarz, Jerusalem, 1985]

Soós, Géza, Dr.: A high official of the Ministry of Foreign Affairs and President of Soli Deo Gloria. He was also active in the Good Shepherd Committee (*Jó Pásztor Bizottság*). As head of the Hungarian Independence Movement (*Magyar Függetlenségi Mozgalom*), he played an important role in the dissemination of the Auschwitz Protocols. [11; 48]

Spányi, Edit: Clerk at the Ganz factory, Budapest. She saved many Jews by providing them with forged papers. [33]

Stationmaster in Balatonboglár, (unidentified): Hid three Jews of Polish origin. [2]

**Sternéder, Margit*: Aunt and foster mother of Tibor Báránszky (q. v.), the priest who was involved in rescue. She helped Hedvig Szekeres by adopting her baby and later gave protective passes to many others. [Yad Vashem, Department of the Righteous]

Stiasznyi, Éva (Mrs. Bartos): Converted Jew since childhood. She led a children's home in Bogár St., Buda where she hid Jewish children. She also helped Reverend Gábor Sztehló (q. v.) in the organization of his rescue network. [51; testimony of Emil Koren, Budapest, 1988]

Stollár, Béla: Sports journalist. He led an underground group in cooperation with KISKA XIII/1. The group also included Jewish labor servicemen and deserters from the army. Stollár and many of his men were killed in armed combat with the Arrow Cross. [35]

**Straus, Margit and József*: Residents of Munkács. They saved the life of Amos Rubin. [67: July 6, 1964; Yad Vashem, Department of the Righteous]

Surányi, Dezső: Together with Antal Bata, István Már, and Antal Zsugár, his group of technicians maintained the vital telephone connections of the Budapest ghetto. [75: February 20, 1947]

Sürü, János: Chemical engineer. In his house in a suburb of Budapest, he gave shelter to engineer Hugó Székely and his family and to several others until the liberation. [15]

+Svetics, Miklós: Former officer in the Hungarian army, resident of Balatonakarattya. He saved the lives of his future wife, Ibolya, and her family. [Testimony of Chief Rabbi Dr. Alfréd Schöner, Budapest, 1988]

**Szabó, Árpád, Dr.*: An army officer and physician. He saved the lives of Alex Lichtig and his wife by smuggling them by train from Poland to Hungary. [Yad Vashem, Department of the Righteous]

**Szabó, Imre*: An officer in the Hungarian Royal Military Hospital No. 11 and No. 1 in Budapest. He saved the lives of many Jews by keeping them in the hospital with false documents. [6; 57; Yad Vashem, Department of the Righteous]

**Szabó, László*: Baker at the village of Fehércsurgó, who saved the life of Abraham Klein, after he had jumped out of a deportation train and asked for shelter. [6; Yad Vashem, Department of the Righteous]

**Szabó, Julianna* (née Rátkai): She sheltered Sándor Szabó (not related) and his son István in her house in Kútvölgyi St., Budapest. [Yad Vashem, Department of the Righteous]

Szalai, Pál: Arrow Cross Party leader and liaison to the police. He did his utmost during the Soviet siege of the capital to prevent the destruction of the ghetto of Pest (December 1944–January 1945). The postwar People's Tribunal exonerated him with praise. [11; 33]

Szalai, Tibor: Director of the Geological Institute at Budapest. He prepared hundreds of forged certificates of baptism, and provided hiding places. Among the saved was a Mr. Weinstein from Palestine. [33]

**Szalkai, István*: A worker in the MOM factory, Budapest, he sheltered Jews in his home. His Jewish wife found refuge in a village. Among the survivors were Mrs. Ernő Kende and Klára Majoros. [Yad Vashem, Department of the Righteous]

Szapáry, László: Count: He helped rescue Jews within the framework of the Fillér St. office of the International Red Cross. [28]

Szapáry, Erzsébet: Baroness of Polish origin. She was a patroness of Jewish refugees from Poland in 1940. [12; 41; 78: volume 1968]

Száraz, Mihály: Medical officer in Labor Service Company No. 101/2 stationed in the Ukraine. He hospitalized and supplied medicine to Jewish labor servicemen. His humane behavior was fully supported by the commander of the company Barna Kiss (q. v.). [64: January 11, 1947]

Szarka, László: Employed by the Ganz factory and also concièrge at his apartment house where he hid thirty Jews. [68: September 24, 1984]

Szász, (first name not given): Hungarian consul in German–occupied Italy. He helped the rescue activity of Father Marie–Bénoit. Mr. Szász issued hundreds of identity papers for the Jewish protegés of Father Bénoit. [17]

Szász, Edit: Deaconess, active in the Good Shepherd Committee (*Jó Pásztor Bizottság*). She provided hiding places for the persecuted. [48]

Székely, Mária (Mrs. Küllői): She was the secretary of József Éliás (q. v.). She translated and helped in the distribution of the "Auschwitz Protocols." Within the Good Shepherd Committee (*Jó Pásztor Bizottság*), she worked with Gábor Sztehló (q. v.). She also cooperated with Friedrich Born (q. v.). [48]

Székely, Mátyás: Engineer at the Ganz factory. He produced forged documents and hid many Jews in rented apartments. The following cooperated with Mr. Székely in rescue: Böhm, Hervay, Spányi, Szöts, Várhegyi, and Béla Zentai (q. v.). [33]

+*Székely, Piroska* (née Kubányi): X-ray laboratory assistant. She saved the lives of Mrs. Almai and her family, and of others in Budapest. [Testimony by Dr. Endre Szántó, Jerusalem, 1986]

Szekfü, Gyula: Scholar. He revised his views in 1943 and participated in the helping and rescuing of Jews. He worked with József Cavallier (q. v.), and also influenced the Catholic Church in revising its policy toward the Jewish question. [11; 33]

**Szeleczky, Mária*: She saved the life of András Sipos. [Yad Vashem, Department of the Righteous]

**Szelei, Margit*: She found a safe hiding place for Aliz and Vera Dembik. Both survived the Arrow Cross terror. [76: March 23, 1984; Yad Vashem, Department of the Righteous]

Szemes, István: Policeman who smuggled registration forms to save lives. [33]

+*Szemes, Lajos*: Policiman. He saved the life of Dr. László Benedek. [Testimony of István Schwartz, Jerusalem, 1985]

Szemző, Florián: A camp administrator at Kistarscsa. He showed understanding for the plight of the Jews. [11]

Szendrödi, Dr. (first name not given): In charge of food supplies and sanitation in the ghetto of Ungvár. He was removed from this position because of his humane attitude toward the Jews. [11]

+*Szendröi, Ilona*: Medical assistant who saved the lives of many Jews from the Hegyeshalom death march. Among the survivors were the members of the Freund family from Budapest. [Testimony by Dr. Endre Szántó, Jerusalem, 1986]

Szennik, László, Dr.: Worked in the voluntary ambulance service (Böme) in Budapest in 1944. In this capacity, he saved many lives during the Arrow Cross era. [11; 33]

Szentandrásy, András: Police officer in the Óbuda brickyard camp. He turned a blind eye to the activities of Sándor Újváry (q. v.), who thus succeeded in saving thousands of Jews from deportation. [11; 33]

**Szentes, Géza*: He and his wife cooperated with Raoul Wallenberg (q. v.) in rescuing Jews. [73; Yad Vashem, Department of the Righteous]

**Szentes, Mária*: A nurse in the home of the Rajk family from 1932, she sheltered Mária Rajk in her home during the Arrow Cross era. [Yad Vashem, Department of the Righteous]

Szerdahelyi, Elek, Dr.: First Lieutenant attached to Labor Service Company No. 101/14, headquartered at Szentkirályszabadja. He provided good sanitary conditions and humane treatment to the labor servicemen. [11; 16]

+Szikora, István: Officer in the paramilitary Levente movement, who provided lifesaving documents to Ádám Balázs and Péter Balázs of Budapest. [Testimony of Ádám Balázs, Budapest, 1985]

Szilágyi, Tibor: Reserve officer attached to Labor Service Company No. 701/306 stationed at Pestszentlörinc. He improved the conditions of his men. When the company was ordered in late 1944 to retreat toward the West, Szilágyi in fact brought 200 servicemen back to Budapest. Szilágyi also saved many from the ghetto of Pest and the Yellow Star houses by using safe conduct letters. [60: January 9, 1947; 75: December 25, 1946]

Szöke, Balázs: A volunteer in the rescue activities of the Good Shepherd Committee (*Jó Pásztor Bizottság*). [48]

**Szönyi, István*: Artist. Together with his wife Melinda, and sister, Margit, he sheltered eleven Jews in their house at 21 Baross St., Budapest. They provided the Jews with false documents prepared by Jolán Szönyi (q. v.). [68: April 10, 1970; Yad Vashem, Department of the Righteous]

Szönyi, Jolán (Mrs. Komáromy): Daughter of the artist, István Szönyi. A chemist, she prepared forged documents for the persecuted and also hid many Jews. [68: November 1986]

Szöts, Ádám: He helped Jews by forging documents and by hiding them. Among the survivors was Anna Friedmann. [33]

**Sztehló, Gábor*: Evangelical Minister. He was active in the Good Shepherd Committee (*Jó Pásztor Bizottság*). With the Swiss IRC delegate, Friedrich Born (q. v.), he organized the rescue of more than 1,000 Jewish children in Budapest during the last months of the German occupation. [1: 48; 51; Yad Vashem, Department of the Righteous]

Szücs, (first name is not mentioned): He built a hiding place for Jews in a shelter on Hungária Körút, Budapest. [12]

**Talán, Ákos*: He hid two sisters, Katalin and Mária Szilágyi, as maids in his villa in Klotildliget, now Pilisliget. [Yad Vashem, Department of the Righteous]

Tamási, László: Army officer. While attached to the Clothes Collecting Labor Service Company, he saved many Jews by "arresting" and transferring them to labor service companies protected by the neutral states or the International Red Cross. [33]

Târnovean, Simion: A Romanian peasant who helped Joseph Paneth, the Rabbi of Ilonda, Szolnok–Doboka County and his family in their escape from the ghetto of Dés. [47]

Teleki, Ernő: Worked with Friedrich Born (q. v.) in the Hospital Bureau of the International Red Cross. [11]

Tergina, Irén: Nun with the Hungarian Catholic Mission in Paris. She assisted Antal Uhl (q. v.) in the rescue of Jews of Hungarian origin living in Paris. [11]

Thaly, Imre, Dr.: Surgeon who led a children's home of the Good Shepherd Committee (*Jó Pásztor Bizottság*) at Roskovics St., Budapest. He saved the lives of 30 Jewish children there. [48; 51]

Thomka, Gusztáv: Teacher at Bonyhád, active in the anti–*Volksbund* movement. In the last days of the German occupation, a labor service company commander entrusted his 200 Jews to him. Thomka sheltered the labor servicemen until the liberation. (The name of the commander is not identified.) [22; 48]

Thury, Zsuzsa and Böske: They provided persecuted people with documents, food, and also hid many in their home at Naphegy, Budapest. [48]

Tildy, Zoltán: Reformed Minister and postwar President of the Hungarian Republic. He indirectly saved the lives of many members of Labor Service Company No. 106/6 stationed around Debrecen. In the spring of 1943, the company was suspected of arson. Beregfy, the commander of the army corps, and Dezsö Nagy killed a few Jews, and intended to decimate the company. Tildy's connections and intervention led to the dismissal of the commanders. [70: February 24, 1946]

Tisza, Kálmán: Worked with Friedrich Born (q. v.) in the office of the International Red Cross. [11]

Tölgyessy, Edit: She was Friedrich Born (q. v.) associate in the International Red Cross. [11]

Tolnay, Géza: Worked with Sándor Újváry (q. v.) in the rescue activities of the International Red Cross. [11; 33]

Tolnay, Klári and Ákos Rátonyi: Actors who hid Mr. Décsi, a movie theater owner of Budapest, in their apartment. [75: 1985]

Tomek, Vince: Piarist priest who provided Slovakian Jewish refugees with false passports. These documents were obtained from the Slovakian Consul in Budapest, Dr. Spisiak. They also helped Jews in the ghetto of Pest. [22]

Tordai, György: Teacher in Kolozsvár (Cluj), who saved Jenő Frieder. [23]

+*Török, János and István Sárvári*: Detective inspectors who helped the Balázs family. [Testimony by Ádám Balázs, Budapest, 1985]

Török, János: Commander of Labor Service Company No. 109/26. He saved his men by refusing to take the company to the Reich in late 1944, and by finding a shelter for them in Budapest. [42]

Török, Zoltán, Dr.: Parish priest of Budapest–Törökőr. He baptized Polish and Slovakian Jewish refugees in order to save their lives. As a result, he was dismissed from his position in 1943. [48; 64: January 11, 1947]

Török, (first name is not given): Police counsellor in Ungvár, later removed from his task because of his humane attitude at the time of ghettoization. He distributed travel permits to Jews. [11; 33]

Tosch, Nándor: First Lieutenant attached to Labor Service Company No. 101/14. He reduced the burden of his Jewish labor servicemen and treated them humanely. [16]

Tóth, Alajos: Chaplain at Kistarcsa in 1942–43. He baptized many Jews against the warning of his vicar. He was dismissed from his position, and punished for the distribution of forged documents. [22]

Tóth, Endre: Officer, deputy of László Ocskay (q. v.) in the "Clothes Collecting" Jewish labor service unit. [75: December 4, 1945]

Tóth, János: Liaison between the Foreign Office and the Papal Nuncio. [11]

**Tschöll, Leo*: An Austrian, he hid Jews in his apartment in Budapest. Among the survivors were Zehava Arieli and Shabtai Német. [6; 72; Yad Vashem, Department of the Righteous]

Turner, Mária: Secretary of Major István Fehér (q. v.). She provided help to labor servicemen. [33]

Tüz, Viktor: Officer in a labor service company stationed at Köszeg. He prohibited the guards from brutalizing the Jewish labor servicemen, an action which resulted in his demotion. [20]

Uhl, Antal, Dr.: Vicar at Baranyaszentgyörgy. He baptized and provided Christian documents to hundreds of Hungarian Jews living in Paris during the deportations from France. He was assisted by the Hungarian consul, Károly Binder. The headquarters for father Uhl's rescue activity in Paris was the Hungarian Catholic Mission (*Magyar Katolikus Misszió*). [22; 33; 48]

**Újváry, Sándor György*: One of the most successful figures in the rescue operations in 1944. As an official of the International Red Cross, he was particularly active along the Budapest–Hegyeshalom death march route, helping and saving Jews from the hands of the Arrow Cross. He also established the Department of Cooperation (*Département de Coopération*), a rescue–related organization. [11; 30; 33; Yad Vashem, Department of the Righteous]

Újvárossy, Dezső: Colonel attached to Army Corps No. III, headquartered at Szombathely. He recruited Jewish men from the ghettos by sending out confidential recruitment orders. These recruits were thus saved from deportation. [11; 16]

Vajkay, Éva and Rózsi: Employees of the Papal Nunciature. They issued safe–conduct passes to everyone who applied for them, without checking the validity of their baptismal papers. Thanks to their connections to foreign embassies and consulates, they proved highly effective in their rescue operations. [11; 51]

**Valik, Jan and Elsbeta*: A Slovakian couple who sheltered Shoshanna Scharf and her sister in their house in Szered. [Yad Vashem, Department of the Righteous]

Varga, Tamás: Cadet sergeant. He helped Jewish labor servicemen escape in Balf. [8]

Varsányi, Mátyás: Lutheran priest. Active in Buda, he helped converted Jews by supplying them with food and clothes. As a result of his activity, he was arrested by the Gestapo and jailed. Later released, he was killed next to his house. [61: January 15, 1947]

**Vasdényey, István*: Police inspector, commander of the Kistarcsa internment camp. He tried to prevent the deportations from his camp in July 1944. [6; 11; Yad Vashem, Department of the Righteous]

Veér, Imre: Provided hiding places for Jews. Later he was arrested by the Gestapo. [33]. (See also Walter, Ede.)

+Verebély, Tibor: Doctor. He was active in the Óbuda brickyard, and saved many Jews in the Orfi hospital's surgery section. [11; 33; testimony by Dr. Endre Szántó, Jerusalem, 1986]

Verolino, Gennaro: Deputy of the Papal Nuncio. He participated in the establishment of the Vatican-protected houses in Budapest. [59: March 22, 1985]

Virág, Ferenc: Bishop of Pécs. He succeeded in obtaining permission for some of the sick Jews to escape deportation. [30; 33]

Vita, Sándor: Former member of the Transylvanian Party (*Erdélyi Párt*). He helped by administrative means 60 to 70 Jewish families of Kolozsvár (Cluj) escape the deportations. [23]

Wagner, Gyula: Commander of a labor service company stationed at Köbánya after September 1944. He refused to take his company to Mosonmagyaróvár, which would have meant possible destruction, and assigned his 230 men to fictitious jobs around Köbánya. [15]

Waldbauer, Imre: Music professor who hid many Jewish musicians in his Budapest apartment and his villa at Lake Balaton. [11; 33]

**Wallenberg, Raoul:* Third secretary in the Swedish Legation who was given a special mission for a large-scale rescue. His well-known activity in late 1944 and early 1945 concerned the whole Jewish population of Budapest. [6; 11; 17; 32; Yad Vashem, Department of the Righteous]

Walter, Ede: Jews were hidden in his apartment in Sobiesky St., Budapest, and in his brother's apartment. [33] (See also Veér, Imre.)

Weyermann, Hans: Swiss representative of the International Red Cross in Budapest from late 1944. He succeeded in keeping Jewish children from being placed into the ghetto. [11; 29]

Wosinszky, Ernő: Director of a bath house in Balf, where he hid many labor servicemen with the help of his family. [8; 50; 75: May 8, 1948]

+Zaherec, (first name is not given): Concièrge at 34 Páva St., Budapest. He hid the son of the landlord and also helped Irén Reich (née Hoffer), an "illegal" tenant. [Testimony by Irén Reich, Jerusalem, 1987]

Zentai, Béla: Engineer who provided hundreds of Jews with different documents. [33] (See also Székely, Mátyás.)

Zsabka, Kálmán: Commander of Labor Service Company No. XIV/2. An extreme nationalist, who quit the "patriotic" Turul Society in 1941. He not only helped Jews, but also led an armed attack against the Arrow Cross house on Thököly Street. He was subsequently arrested and tortured by the Gestapo. [35]

Zsiros, József: Former theology teacher at Sárospatak who helped Jews in the local ghetto. He also saved Jewish property. [75: May 2, 1946]

**Zsoldos, Andor*: Captain of a labor service company. He saved the lives of the labor servicemen. [6; 76: June 1, 1965; Yad Vashem, Department of the Righteous]

Zürcher, Péter, Dr.: Swiss diplomat in Budapest who cooperated with Consul Charles Lutz (q. v.) in rescue work during the Arrow Cross era. [11; 33]

References

Books

1. Aharoni, R., *A rákospalotai zsidó hitközség története* [The History of the Jewish Community of Rákospalota). Tel Aviv: Lahav Printers, 1978.
2. Andrássy, A., "Zsidóüldözés Somogyban" [Jewish Persecution in Somogy]. *Somogy Megye Múltjából* [From the Past of Somogy County], 1984.
3. Anger, P., *With Raoul Wallenberg in Budapest.* New York: Holocaust Library, 1981.
4. Antall, József, *Lengyel menekültek Magyarországon a háború alatt* [Polish Refugees in Hungary during the War]. Budapest: Atheneum, 1947.
5. Asztalos, István, *Író a hadak útján* [Writer on the Path of Battles]. Budapest: Magvető, 1983.
6. Bauminger, A. L., *Roll of Honor.* Jerusalem: Yad Vashem, 1970.
7. Ben-Shalom, R., *Neevaknu LeMaan HaHajjim* [We Struggled for Life]. Israel: Moreshet, 1978.
8. Bence, Gy., *Szabadító börtön* [Liberating Prison]. Budapest: Farkas Testvérek, 1945.
9. Bereczky, A., *A magyar protestantizmus a zsidóüldözések ellen*

[Hungarian Protestantism Against the Persecution of the Jews]. Budapest: Traktátus Református Kiadó Vállalat, 1945.

10. Bokor, Péter, *Végjáték a Duna mentén* [End Game Along the Danube]. Budapest: RTV–Minerva–Kossuth, 1982.
11. Braham, R. L., *The Politics of Genocide. The Holocaust in Hungary.* New York: Columbia University Press, 1981, 2 vols.
12. Cohen, A., *Hamachtereth Hahalutzit BeHungaria* [Halutz Resistance in Hungary]. Israel: Kibbutz HaMeuchad, 1984.
13. Déry, T., *Két emlék* [Two Souvenirs]. Budapest: Szépirodalmi Könyvkiadó, 1955.
14. Devecseri, G., *Hasfelmetszés előnyei* [The Advantages of Disemboweling]. Budapest: Magvető, 1974.
15. *Évkönyv* [Yearbook]. Scheiber Sándor, (ed.). Budapest: MIOK, 1970–1984.
16. *"Fegyvertelen álltak az aknamezökön . . ." Dokumentumok a munkaszolgálat történetéhez Magyarországon* [They Stood Unarmed on the Mine Fields . . . Documents Relating to the History of Labor Service in Hungary]. E. Karsai, (ed.). Budapest: A Magyar Izraeliták Országos Képviselete, 1962, 2 vols.
17. Friedman, P., *Their Brother's Keepers.* New York: Holocaust Library, 1978.
18. Gál György, S., *Atlantisz harangjai* [The Bells of the Atlantis]. Budapest: Móra, 1982.
19. Gobbi, H., *Közben* [In Between]. Budapest: Szépirodalmi Kiadó, 1982.
20. Harsányi, L., *A kőszegi zsidók* [The Jews of Kőszeg]. Budapest: Magyar Izraeliták Országos Képviselete, 1974.
21. Harsányi, L., *A szentesi izraelita hitközség története* [The History of the Jewish Community of Szentes]. Budapest: Magyar Izraeliták Országos Képviselete, 1970.
22. Hetényi, Varga K., "Akiket üldöztek az igazságért" [Those Who Were Persecuted Because of the Truth]. *Ecclesia*, Budapest, 1985.
23. *História Évkönyv. Az 1944 év históriája* [History Yearbook. The History of 1944]. Glatz, F., (ed.) Budapest, 1984.
24. Kerényi, Mária, *Neményi Lili.* Budapest: Zeneműi Kiadó, 1986.
25. Király, A., *A nyíregyházi gettó története* [The History of the Ghetto of Nyíregyháza]. Nyíregyháza: The Author, 1946.
26. Kis, György, *Megjelölve Krisztus keresztjével és Dávid csillagával* [Marked by Christ's Cross and David's Star]. Budapest: The

Author, 1987.

27. Komoly, O., "Komoly Ottó naplója" [The Diary of Ottó Komoly] in *Ráday Gyüjtemény* [Ráday Collection], Budapest, 1984, vol. 3.
28. Lévai, J., *Fehér könyv. Külföldi akciók zsidók megmentésére* [White Book. Foreign Actions for the Rescuing of Jews]. Budapest: Officina, 1946.
29. ———. *Fekete könyv a magyar zsidóság szenvedéseiről* [Black Book on the Martyrdom of Hungarian Jewry]. Budapest: Officina, 1946.
30. ———. *Hungarian Jewry and the Papacy.* London: Sands & Co., 1968.
31. ———. *A pesti gettó csodálatos megmenekülésének hiteles története* [The Authentic History of the Miraculous Survival of the Ghetto of Budapest]. Budapest: Officina, 1946.
32. ———. *Raoul Wallenberg.* Budapest: Magyar Téka, 1948.
33. ———. *Szürke könyv magyar zsidók megmentéséről* [Grey Book on the Rescuing of Hungarian Jews]. Budapest: Officina, 1946.
34. ———. *Zsidósors Magyarországon* [Jewish Fate in Hungary]. Budapest: Magyar Téka, 1948.
35. *A magyar antifasiszta ellenállás és partizánmozgalom, Kislexikon* [The Hungarian Anti–Fascist Resistance and Partisan Movement]. Liptai Ervin, (ed.) Budapest: Kossuth, 1987.
36. Majsai, T., "A körösmezei zsidódeportálás 1941–ben. Iratok a Körös- mezei zsidódeportálás történetéhez" [The Jewish Deportations from Körösmező in 1941. Documents Relating to the History of Jewish Deportations from Körösmező]. *Ráday Gyüjtemény Évkönyve* [Yearbook of the Raday Collection], 1986, pp. 59–86; pp. 195–237.
37. Mezei, A., "*Beszélgetések Gur Dáviddal*" [A Discussion with David Gur]. *Műhely* [Shop], Budapest, Apr. 1981.
38. Munkácsi, E., *Hogyan történt? Adatok és okmányok a magyar zsidóság tragédiájához* [How Did It Happen? Data and Documents Relating to the Tragedy of Hungarian Jewry]. Budapest: Renaissance, 1947.
39. Nagybaczoni Nagy, V., *Végzetes esztendők* [Fatal Years]. Budapest: Gondolat, 1986.
40. Pál, J., "Hamvas Endre a szegedi zsidóság deportálása ellen" [Endre Hamvas Against the Deportation of the Jews of Szeged]. *Szegedi Könyvtári Műhely* [Szeged Library Shop], Szeged, June

1986, pp. 1–48.
41. *Pedut. Rescue in the Holocaust.* Katzburg Nathaniel, (ed.) Ramat Gan: Bar–Ilan University Press, 1984.
42. Pór, D. and Zsadányi, O., *Te vagy a tanú* [You Are the Witness]. Budapest: Kossuth Kiadó, 1947.
43. Reviczky, A., *Vesztes háborúk–Megnyert csaták* [Lost Wars—Battles Won]. Budapest: Magvető, 1985.
44. Réz, P., *Ferenczy Béni arcképe* [The Portrait of Béni Ferenczy]. Budapest: Európa, 1984.
45. Rotkirchen, L., "The Holocaust Era." *Pinkas Hakehilot, Hungaria.* Jerusalem: Yad Vashem, 1975. pp. 104–118.
46. Sallai, E., *Mozgó vesztőhely* [Rolling, Perishing Place]. Budapest: Magvetö, 1979.
47. Singer, Z., *Volt egyszer egy Dés* [There Was Once Upon a Time a Dés]. Tel Aviv: The Author, 1970.
48. Szenes, S., *Befejezetlen múlt* [Unfinished Past]. Budapest: The Author, 1984.
49. Szilágyi–Windt, L., *Az újpesti zsidóság története* [The History of the Jews of Újpest]. Tel Aviv: Lahav Printers, 1975.
50. Szita, Sz., *Holocaust az Alpok előtt* [Holocaust before the Alps]. Győr: Az MSZMP Győr–Sopron megyei Bizottsága, 1983.
51. Sztehló, Gábor, *Isten kezében* [In God's Hand]. Budapest: A Magyarországi Evangelikus Egyház Sajtóosztálya, 1986.
52. Turcsányi, Gyula, (ed.) *Kivel mi történt?* [What Happened with Whom?] Budapest, 1945.
53. Várnai, Zs., *Nem volt hiába* [It Was Not in Vain]. Budapest: Szépirodalmi Kiadó, 1962.
54. *A vasi zsidók* [The Jews of Vas]. A. A. Loewinger, (ed.) Tel Aviv: Izsák, 1974.
55. Weinzierl, E., *Judaism and Christianity Under the Impact of National Socialism.* O. D. Kulka, (ed.) Jerusalem: Historical Society of Israel, 1987.

Periodicals

56. *The Atlanta Constitution*, May 8, 1974.
57. *Brehmer Nachrichten*, Bremen, (German daily) Nov. 21, 1968.
58. *Daily News*, Daily in New Zealand, Jan. 30, 1979.
59. *Élet és Irodalom*, Budapest, (Hungarian weekly).
60. *Haladás* [Progress], Budapest.
61. *Hírlap* [Newspaper], Budapest.

62. *Jerusalem Post*, Jerusalem.
63. *Jewish Life*, Mar. 8–14, 1985.
64. *Képes Figyelő* [Illustrated Observer], Budapest.
65. *Kritika* [Criticism], Budapest.
66. *La–Isha*, Israel, Feb. 1, 1971.
67. *Maariv*, Tel Aviv, [Israel daily].
68. *Magyar Nemzet* [Hungarian Nation], Budapest (daily).
69. *Menóra*, Toronto (Hungarian weekly).
70. *Népbírósági Közlöny* [Gazette of the People's Tribunal] (Hungarian weekly).
71. *Ország–Világ* [Country–World], Budapest, Dec. 27, 1987.
72. *Die Presse*, Vienna, Jan. 21, 1970.
73. *Le Progrès*, Lyon, 10, 7, 1985.
74. *Toronto Star*, Sept. 11, 1984.
75. *Új Élet* [New Life], Budapest (Hungarian weekly).
76. *Új Kelet* [New East], Tel Aviv (Hungarian daily).
77. *Világ* [World], Budapest.
78. *Yad Vashem Studies*. Jerusalem: Yad Vashem, 1957–1987, vols. 1–16.

THE DEPORTATION OF JEWS FROM CSIKSZEREDA AND MARGIT SLACHTA'S INTERVENTION ON THEIR BEHALF

Tamás Majsai

1.

On November 7, 1940, 24 Jewish families were deported from Csíkszereda by the local military authorities without any official justification. The families were told to leave their homes immediately. The next day, all the families were taken to the no man's land between the Romanian and Hungarian borders. These unfortunate people had to live without shelter for six days, after which they were taken back to Csíkszereda. On the evening of November 16, 13 families, with 42 people, were sent from there to Kőrösmező,[1] a frontier village, to await illegal transportation to Russian territory. According to the official report,[2] 19 people went missing during these actions. The families of most of the missing people were left in Hungary with no knowledge of the fate of their lost relatives.

In June 1942, the local police authorities again attempted to deport at first nineteen, then another twenty-two, Jewish families from Csíkszereda. The consequences of this tragedy were somewhat different from the earlier deportations but the motives behind them were similar. Almost invariably, deportation orders were issued to those families where the breadwinner was already doing forced labor.[3] The justification for these actions was the decree 8.130/1939 ME,[4] which states that "the presence of those who are to be deported, and their families, in the town of Csíkszereda and in the frontier zone in general, threatens defense interests and is harmful in terms of state security."[5]

The documents collected here give the reader a detailed picture of these two events. The contemporary letters and notes concerning the events of 1940 and 1942 can be dealt with together. The victims were Jews from the same town. In addition, Margit Slachta, the head of the Society of the Social Sisterhood,[6] strove in both cases to alleviate the miserable conditions faced by the deportees. Finally, there is an intrinsic connection between the two events: continuity can be seen in the treatment of the Jews in that aggressive action against Jews was a real threat even before the German occupation of 1944.

2.

It is well known that the restriction of the Jews' civil rights had reached its height by 1941. The harshest was the "Race Protection Law" of 1941. It is also true, however, that Hungary was almost the only haven where both Hungarian Jews and those who had sought refuge there could live out their increasingly miserable existences without their actual lives being threatened, even though they had to face a high level of discrimination and a strongly anti-Semitic environment.

It could be argued that this feeling of relative security can be seen as a Hungarian characteristic. However, the most likely explanation is to be found in the network of international political economic relationships and the specifically Hungarian system of domestic politics and the social situation. But this is not the place to explore this subject, for which there is already a large body of work.[7]

It is important to make it clear that, although this Third Jewish Law apparently clarified the position of Jews in Hungary, the attitude taken toward the Jews varied from area to area. For example in the summer of 1941, when the military leaders and extremist politicians were in a position to "solve the Jewish question efficiently," about 20,000 Jews—most of whom were from northeast Hungary and Kárpátalja and were considered Hungarian—were deported through Körösmező[8] to the Galician front, where most of them were killed.[9] According to some sources, plans were made to deport as many as 100,000 Jews living in Hungary.[10] This deportation, apart from its lack of technical expertise, in many ways prefigured the slaughter of Hungarian Jews in 1944.[11] There is evidence of physical violence in the re-annexed territories. At the time of the re-annexation of Felvidék in 1938, 340 people of Jewish origin from Kassa were forced into trucks and transported to the border of Slovakia for the same reasons as those from Csíkszereda.[12] We also know of several other similar police actions in Kárpátalja, as well as instances of maltreatment and deportation in Transylvania. This kind of activity was also commonplace in Csíkszereda.[13] There were repeated deportations after the one at Körösmező though these involved smaller numbers of people.[14] It is well-known that the number of Jews killed in the massacre at Ujvidék (Novi Sad) was out of proportion to the number of Jews in the city.[15]

Although these manifestations of a social and political unconscious were scattered and might perhaps seem insignificant when compared to the millions of Jewish victims in the twentieth century, they were clear indicators of a potential eruption of violence which might come at any time. A significant element in this persecution of the Jews was the suffering at Csíkszereda.

The deportations at Csíkszereda and other similar actions were of course unjustified. Examples of the "accusations" are: ignoring vital national interests, political unreliability, collaboration with the enemy, spying, encouraging dissent against the "great national struggle." These "accusations" may reflect a situation in which the interests of the Jews who lived in territories which were seen as being hostile could not possibly coincide with the interests of those who supported Germany. These groundless charges served only as attempts to legitimize various anti-Semitic actions. Take, for example, excerpts from the monthly police reports on the political situation in Csíkszereda in 1941.[16] One states that

> The Jews saw the outbreak of war between Germany and Soviet Russia as being their last chance. Their mood of hope almost instantly collapsed with the victorious progress of the German and allied troops. This conspicuous behavior by the Jews provoked general antipathy toward the Jews among the inhabitants and they are happy to see that the authorities are firmly implementing the control of Jews and, most recently, their mass deportation from the city.[17]

Another report states that

> The morale of the Jews is low. The deportation order made against 37 families has been put into effect and fully implemented by the military administration. The people of the town were happy to hear that all the efforts of the Jews were in vain and that the police had strictly enforced their orders.[18]

3.

The documents make clear that Margit Slachta, having learned about this new deportation through the Transylvanian branches of the Society of the Social Sisterhood,[19] took up the cause of the victims, either on her own initiative or in response to letters seeking support. Through the medium of the Society, she tried to gain the support of those in positions of power in hope of annulling the orders. She intervened on behalf of the deportees at government offices and contacted prominent figures in secular, Christian, and Jewish circles. At the center of the Society in Budapest, several copies of the summary of the fate of the families deported from Csíkszereda to Kőrösmező were made to send to those from whom she hoped to gain support.

It is not easy to determine the effectiveness of her efforts. The documents do not contain full details of the events. For example, it is not known if others were involved in similar activity. It seems, however, indisputable that her endeavors had a significant effect in limiting the extent of the official actions.

4.

Margit Slachta was born in 1884 in Kassa, where she obtained a certificate as an elementary school teacher. She continued her teacher training in Kalocsa, Győr and Budapest. In 1906, she took part in a workers education course in Berlin. In 1908, having resigned her teaching post, she joined the Social Mission Society, led by Edit Farkas, and devoted her life to social work. In 1919, she organized the Christian Women's Society (also known as the Catholic Women's Party). In 1920, she became the first woman member of Parliament and held her seat until 1922. Her political position was conservative and legitimist, and her parliamentary speeches concentrated on children, women, and the family. In 1923, she left the Mission Society to found the Society of the Social Sisterhood. Drawing on her own personality, she depicted the ideal Sister as having strength of character, awareness, unselfishness, modesty, openness, respect for the law and her superiors, and resourcefulness. She spent part of the twenties in the U. S., returning to Hungary in 1927. In 1937, she founded the Catholic Women's Social Training School. After the war, she was once again a member of Parliament, from 1945 to 1948. In 1949, she fled the country and lived the rest of her life abroad where she continued her work with the Society. She died in Buffalo in 1974.[20]

Her life, and especially her political activity, is to this day a topic of lively debate. She is the subject of widely differing opinions, but it is indisputable that she was among those who clearly and forcefully raised her voice against the prevailing anti-Semitic mood and legislation of the Horthy regime in Hungary. Margit Slachta, although only a minor member of the clergy, confronted the flood of paganism which threatened to inundate society with ideological and theological clarity and particularly with the strength of natural justice in Catholic theology and realizing the proclaimed love of her fellow man. This was at a time when most leading, theologically trained members of the Church were supporters of the prevailing anti-Semitism.

Margit Slachta unambiguously opposed the anti-Jewish measures and was a determined opponent of Nazism. In her lectures in teacher training, in her articles in *A Testvér* [The Brother], the Society's periodical, in *A Lélek Szava* [The Soul's Voice], and in her famous *Világnézeti Credo* [World View Credo], she emphasized fundamental Christian values as a force against racist (religiosity) and condemned "the fanatical supporters of racism."

Her first known action on behalf of Jews was her struggle for the deportees from Csíkszereda. Shortly afterward, in 1941, she intervened on behalf of the victims of the Kőrösmező deportations and with this she became the virtual leader of the handful of people who actively opposed the deportations. She even attempted the apparently impossible on their behalf. For example, she visited the deportation centers and transfer points with three other people and wrote a summary of her experiences during this visit, listing dozens of abuses. She sent this to those whom she thought might help.[21] She also informed Mrs. Horthy of the horrors of the deportations in person.

The second stage of her activity was during the 1942–43 deportations in Slovakia. She provided the refugees with false passports. While inundating the episcopal council with appeals and attempts to persuade them to contact the Slovakian episcopal council with a view to joint action to put pressure on the Hungarian government and the Catholic Church in Slovakia to condemn the deportation. In the spring of 1943, she had an audience with Pope Pius XII, who she hoped would intervene to prevent further deportations. Her visit may well have influenced the Pope's instructions to the Slovakian episcopal council to intervene against the deportations and may have helped to delay the planned executions of the surviving Jews in Slovakia in 1943.[22] Other noteworthy aspects of her work were her attempts to remedy the abuses against those performing forced labor,[23] her active collabaoration with various Jewish welfare organizations,[24] and her membership in a committee of the Catholic Holy Cross Society designed to help converts who were affected by the anti-Jewish legislation. It is not therefore surprising that in 1944 she opened the doors of the Society's convents to every refugee and so saved 2,000 lives.

The Yad Vashem Institute in Jerusalem, in honor of her selfless and humanitarian actions, gave her the right to plant a memorial tree on the Avenue of the Righteous as a token of gratitude because "the memory of the just is blessed."[25]

In order to show her personality and spirituality, there follow some characteristic excerpts from her "New Year Letter" in 1943 which caused outrage at the time:

> Would you like to provide your loved ones with God's help twice over? Find room in your heart for the fate of others, especially those whom you have difficulty in accepting. One of your foes, one who caused you harm, someone who hurt you. Let him into your heart so that when you pray for your loved ones, send a genuine supplication to Almighty God on his behalf. Let a labor serviceman into your heart, who is excluded from fellowship by the spirit of this age. *Dare to rid* your heart of ignorance, unlovingness, and hatred in this deadly serious age, *dare to accept* deep in your heart another mother and her son as your fellow human beings, *dare to bear* her pain and help her to carry her cross. *Dare to proclaim* that the only Christian and statesmanlike way is that of the Minister of Defense,[26] when he stated, without hestitation, that the military work of forced labor was *a service to the homeland and not punishment*, and that, like a soldier, their physical health and honor is protected by law. *Dare to confess* that you feel the same. *Dare to take action.* Dare to ask, wish, urge any relatives you have who are commanders in forced labor camps to be the kind of superior to the forced laborers that they would wish to have for their sons at the front or in prisoner-of-war camps. Emphasize to him the Everlasting Word of Christ: *With what measure ye mete, it shall be measured to you again.* This the Lord will do. He will punish or spare, have mercy or turn away according to your cruelty or compassion.[27]

Margit Slachta, with her exceptionally brave and honest letter, aroused the anger of, among others, László Endre, magistrate, who on February 7, 1943, publicly condemned her in the name of the whole community, at a meeting in Pest County:

> At a time when the entire community of the county enthusiastically and with all its might, supports the national movement led by her Highness the Governor's wife in support of the war families, the community learnt with the deepest horror of an action which runs counter to this movement and endangers it. This action was initiated by Margit Slachta . . . with the slogan "Dare to let the Jewish labor serviceman into your heart." At a time when the community of the county is well aware that the Jews are mainly responsible for inciting the war against them [*sic*]. It is they who set peaceful nations against each other, who finance the armaments factories in the plutocracies, in whose interest it is that more and more blood and tears are shed, against whose damage the Hungarian government strives to protect the body and soul of our nation through positive laws. At this time, to support them or even to pay heed to them instead of our Hungarian brothers–in–arms who are shedding their blood runs totally counter to the universal interests of the nation. The community of the county . . . brands and condemns this . . . unpatriotic initiative which is unworthy of the land of Ilona Zrinyi and Zsuzsanna Lorántffy.[28]

Slachta, however, did not write a retraction. Instead she responded to the magistrate this way:

> No one should take my words to mean that I want you to feel this love for the labor servicemen only as an emotion and not that you should put into practice the truths of our beliefs. . . . I proclaim the following: I stand, without compromise, on the foundation of Christian values; that is, I profess that Love obliges us to accept natural laws for our fellow–men without exception, which God gave and which cannot be taken away.[29]

Notes

[1] Village in the Rahó district of Máramaros County. Now Yasinya, USSR.

[2] See doc. 8.

[3] See doc. 11.

[4] See doc. 16, note 3.

[5] See doc. 16, note 2.

[6] The Society (SSS) was founded in 1923. Its aims were to provide the Church and society with trained professionals to carry out spiritual and social work.

[7] See e.g., Gyula Juhász, *Magyarország külpolitikája, 1919–1945* [Hungary's Foreign Policy, 1919–1945]. Budapest, 1988. (2nd ed.) and *Magyarország története* [History of Hungary]. Budapest, 1978.

[8] It seems that Körösmező played a central part in the deportations prior to 1944. For example, in 1942, a group of Slovakian Jews who had fled to Hungary to avoid deportation were taken across the border there so that they could be handed over to the Germans and, in effect, to their deaths. (See letter from Margit Slachta to Gyula Glattfelder, Bishop of Csanád, dated April 29, 1942.) Excerpts from this letter can be found in Mária Schmidt, "Közöny, szeretetlenség, gyülölet? Katolikusok a zsidóságért" [Indifference, Lack of Love, Hatred? Catholics for Jewry]. *Historia*, Budapest, vol. 10, no. 2–3, 1988, p. 65.

[9] For a detailed analysis of the events, see Tamás Majsai, "A körösmezei zsidódeportálás 1941–ben" [The Jewish Deportations in Körösmező in 1941] in *Ráday Gyüjtemény Évkönyve* [Yearbook of the Ráday Collection], Budapest, vol. 4–5, 1986, pp. 59–86, 195–237.

[10] See Majsai *ibid.*, p. 59, as well as the papers of József Pásztor in *Magyar Zsidó Levéltár* [Hungarian Jewish Archives]. Budapest.

[11] Relevant here is the subtitle of Randolph L. Braham's article treating the same event: "Prelude to the Holocaust in Hungary" in *Yad Vashem Studies*, Jerusalem, vol. 9, 1973, pp. 133–156.

[12] Anonymous letter. November 22, 1938. *Magyar Zsidó Levéltár* [The Papers of József Pásztor].

[13] See doc. 11, and the police political reports.

[14] See Majsai, *op. cit.*

[15] See doc. 15, note 7.

[16] See doc. 19.

[17] Police political report from June. No. 3/9–194.biz. szám 1941. VII. 9. in *Párttörténeti Intézet Archivuma*–(PIA) [Party Histor-

ical Institute of the Hungarian Socialist Workers' Party]. Budapest, 651.f2/1941–7–6.000.

18 Police political report from July 1941. VIII.10. in *PIA*.

19 See doc. 1, note 7.

20 See Magda Palkó, "Slachta Margit" in *Politikuspályák* [Political Fields]. Budapest, 1984, pp. 146–154. Natália Palágyi, *Zádjeli Slachta Margit a Szociális Testvérek Társaságának alapitója, 1884–1974* [Margit Zádjeli Slachta, the Founder of the Society of the Social Sisterhood, 1884–1974]. The same, in an extended form: *A sziv* [The Heart]. 1976/2–8. An objective and historically accurate biography of Margit Slachta has yet to be written.

21 The report can be found in Majsai, *op. cit.*, pp. 219–227.

22 See Károly Hetényi Varga, *Akiket üldöztek az igazságért* [Those Who Were Persecuted for Truth]. Budapest, 1985, 428ff, 477ff, and Schmidt, *op. cit.*

23 See doc. 11, note 2.

24 See Majsai, *op. cit.*

25 *Proverbs* 10:7.

26 Vilmos Nagybaczoni Nagy was Minister of Defense from 1942 to 1943 (see his *Végzetes esztendők*, 2nd ed. Budapest, 1986, p. 159). He summarized the measures taken to improve conditions for the labor servicemen as follows: "I ended the treatment of the labor servicemen as prisoners. I ordered that the labor servicemen should receive adequate supplies so that the required work quotas should not be extracted from walking shadows. I ordered that those who are ill or unable to work should be immediately demobilized. I prohibited maltreatment and corporal punishment. I ordered a thorough investigation and severe punishment for those who brutally maltreated members of the labor service companies by hitting, beating, or blackmailing them." *Ibid.*, p. 100.

27 *A Lélek Szava* [The Soul's Voice]. Budapest, vol. 10, no. 1. Jan. 1943.

28 Ilona Zrinyi and Zsuzsanna Lorántffy were prominent heroines of Hungarian history. The report of the magistrate of Pest–Pilis–Kiskun County for the period between November 16, 1942 and January 15, 1943. Budapest: 2–3 Stádium Sajtóvállalat Rt.

29 *A Lélek Szava.* vol. 10, no. 5, Mar. 1, 1943. For details see Majsai, *op. cit.*

1. The Documents

Note: In the documents the abbreviations have mostly been written out in full. Where it seemed necessary, information in square brackets has been added to aid comprehension and to clarify the text. The documents form part of the papers of Margit Slachta, and they are now in the possession of Ilona Mona, to whom the author would like to express his gratitude for giving access to the papers and also for the valuable and generous help she gave in the compilation of the footnotes.

1.

December 9, 1940, Budapest

Margit Slachta's letter to the parish priest at Körösmező. She asks the priest to help the deportees at Körösmező.

December 9, 1940

Reverend Father,[1]

Please allow me to take some of your time to consider the following matter.

We received desperate news[2] from Csíkszereda[3] that the military authorities have deported thirty Jewish families without any prior investigation. The families suffered for weeks[4] at the Romanian border and were transported to Körösmező about 14 days ago and have apparently been interned in the military camp of the Hármashatárhegy-vadász.[5]

According to our information, most of these people were born in Csíkszereda or elsewhere in Transylvania or have lived there for decades.

By and large, the public administration has been taken over by the civil authorities[6] and the internees have also been handed over to them by the military. The appeal made to us claims that, according to orders from the Ministry, they should have been allowed to return to Csíkszereda. This, however, has not yet happened.

I apologize to the Reverend Father for inconveniencing him with the problems of these unfortunate people but apart from all their miseries, they are terrified at the prospect of being transferred across the Russian frontier.

I am totally disinterested in this matter. I am led by nothing other than the Brotherly Love which was given to us as an obligation by our Lord Christ and by patriotism. We are talking about Hungarians. They are apparently innocent. Like others, they suffered a great deal under Romanian administration. It is horrifying to me that someone should be faced with injustice, when innocent, at the hands of the Hungarian authorities, when they are reunited with their motherland, only because they belong to this or that race.

My respectful request to the Reverend Father is as follows:

Kindly, for the Love of our Redeemer, gather information urgently on the actual state of affairs. Be so kind as to go to the military camp and find out on what grounds they have been interned, look at the condition of their accommodation, whether they have enough food, why they are not allowed to return to Csíkszereda and what has to be done and what can be done to help them.

Please be gracious enough not to rely solely on the information provided by the military leadership. Please question those concerned. I think this is the group of people the State social appointee meant when he talked about the cruel situation they had been put into between the frontiers and people were prevented from giving them food, not even to the children.

I need absolutely reliable information, otherwise I am unable to proceed unchallenged by the relevant authorities, who, although they seek order and often act strictly, are by no means sadistic or inhuman.

Please inform me in writing what expenses they would incur, which they or their relatives could not meet, should they receive permission to return to Csíkszereda.

Allow me to request the Reverend Father to reply immediately. We will be happy to refund his expenses.

Thank you in advance for your love of mankind and your efforts.

I remain, Reverend Father, Yours in Christ,

Mother Superior

I am so deeply concerned about the state of affairs in Transylvania because, as you know, our brothers and sisters worked so hard there during the entire 22 year Romanian era.[7]

Typed original, copy unsigned: there are some insignificant notes at the bottom of the second page of the letter; in the possession of Ilona Mona.

[1] Tibor Závodnyik (?).

[2] The text of the news is likely to be the same as the following notes: "A few weeks ago, the military authorities deported thirty Jewish families from Csíkszereda without any prior investigation. They suffered for weeks at the Romanian border then approximately 14 days ago they were transported to Körösmező and they were interned there. Most of the families concerned were born in Csíkszereda or Transylvania and those who were not born there have lived there for decades. These measures are therefore inconceivable. The Ministry has already taken steps in order to allow the internees in Körösmező to return to Csíkszereda. This decision has not yet, however, been implemented" (from the papers of Margit Slachta: in the possession of Ilona Mona).

[3] Csíkszereda is the county town of Csík County, with a population of about 5,000. In the 1900 census, Jews constituted 6 percent of the population.

[4] In fact, for six days. This event was mentioned by Loránt Tilkovszky in his *Revizió és nemzetiségpolitika Magyarországon, 1938–1941* [Revision and National Politics in Hungary, 1938–1941]. Budapest, 1967, pp. 295ff. The source he referred to, which mentions 200 families is, however, inaccurate. The deportation concerned 78 people (see doc. no. 7).

[5] See docs. 7-9.

[6] Under the terms of the 912/1940.BM decree, which is in addition to 7.800/1940 ME, the civil administration was instituted on November 26, 1940 (see docs. 4 and 9).

[7] Since the 1920s, the Social Mission Society and then later the Society of Social Sisterhood also carried out social work, mother care, and charitable work in Romania, especially in Transylvania. Until 1930, their activities were lead by Auguszta Ikrik and later by Marianne Veress.

2.

December 18, 1940, Budapest

Letter from Bernát Berkovits to Sára Schalkház, in which he thanks her for her help.

December 18, 1940, Budapest

Dear Sister Sára,[1]

I would like to thank you for your generous sacrifice on our behalf which reveals your Christian soul.[2] Your intervention has subsequently proved to be unnecessary. The report from the headquarters of the border guard says that on Tuesday the 10th at 9 o'clock, all eight people were observed from the Russian post in the process of being taken out and later being put on sleighs and driven toward Nadvorna.[3] Now, my aunt[4] would like to visit Sister Margit Slachta to ask for her help in finding her children. I do not know how this will turn out since other inquiries did not prove encouraging. We hope, however, that with God's help their destiny will turn out better and that they will come back to us. Thank you again for your kind efforts.

Yours sincerely,

Bernát Berkovits

Signed postcard from B. B. Izabella u. 52/b,fsz, Budapest to Sára Schalkház, Social Sister, Técső Magistrate's Office, Kárpátalja.[5] *In the possession of Ilona Mona.*

1 Sára Schalkház (1889–1944; from 1943, Sára Salkaházi): teacher, journalist, from 1930, Social Sister. As a member of the Society of the Social Sisterhood she dealt mainly with girls. When her planned missionary visit to Brazil fell through because of the outbreak of World War II, she undertook various tasks: from the spring of 1939 she worked for two years in Kárpátalja as part of the "Hungarians for the Hungarians" movement, as an ONCSA (National Fund for the Care of People and Families) worker. She was a "social lecturer" and carer. From 1942, she was the national leader of the Catholic Working Girls movement. In 1944, she gave shelter to thirty refugees at the movement's villa on Lake Balaton. On December 27, 1944, members of the Arrow Cross took her and some refugees from the Working Women's Home at Bokréta u. in Budapest and they were probably killed on the banks of the Danube the same day.

2 See her letter to Social Sister Petra (doc. 3).

3 Nadvorna: a settlement northeast of Kőrösmező on the Bistrica River in Galicia.

4 Berkovits' aunt might be Mrs. Benő Schultz (see docs. 3-5, 7, and 10).

5 Members of the SSS in accordance with the aims of the Society, took part in different kinds of social work. At this time, Sára Schalkház worked in the field as a worker for ONCSA as a social

appointee of the Rahó district. In this post, she was attached to the local municipal authorities.

3.

December 20, 1940, Técső

Letter from Sára Schalkház to Social Sister Petra, in which she informs the sister of the steps she has taken on behalf of the deportees.

December 20, 1940, Técső

Dear Good Sister Petra,[1]

I have just this instant received your letter[2] and I am answering without delay, especially as I can see a basic misunderstanding. Let me start from the very beginning:

After our telephone conversation, the earliest I was able to set off for Körösmező was the next day [the 15th], a Sunday. This was because the timetable happened to change on that day. I arrived late at Körösmező, at around 4 o'clock and went by sleigh to the parsonage where I looked for the parson, but was unable to find him. I then set off to find Bernát Berkovits whom I eventually found after a long search.

I had a long talk with him and his aunt, whose daughter, son-in-law, and grandchild were taken across the border. It is only natural that the situation became more or less clear only after considerable discussion and explanation. The basic misunderstanding is that *I wanted to go to the captain immediately but they said this was impossible because it was Sunday*, so they asked me to try to make an appeal on their behalf to go to the Russian border post at the Tatár Pass and ask the Russians whether they had seen the people in question. They were prepared to go there even with the gendarmerie or with a military escort. We therefore set off immediately to telephone to Rahó. I wanted to telephone the magistrate there, who I know very well,[3] and ask him to arrange this at the military headquarters. Unfortunately, as it was a Sunday, there was no telephone service in Körösmező so the Berkovits's said that there was a train at 7 o'clock to Rahó. I wanted to take that train, and I thought I would meet not only the magistrate, but also the military commander. So we went to the station but the train had been cancelled. There weren't any other trains except the fast train at 1:30 A.M. So I arranged to come back to Técső on that train and try to telephone the magistrate at Rahó the next day and try to get their permission for them and that I might even telephone to Ungvár concerning the same matter. In any case I would telephone Berkovits on Monday afternoon and tell him the result. They had to stay at the station for some time because they were waiting for someone so we sat together talking. The woman told me about how they had been taken across the border, how they came back and also about all that they had been through since they left [Csík]szereda. I was very sorry for the poor woman because I could see how depressed she was. When the woman went away for a minute and I was left alone with Berkovits, we both came to the conclusion that those unfortunate people would still be alive. The best outcome would have been if the Russians had captured and interned [them]. Meanwhile, a detective came up to me and was introduced to me and we talked about this matter and he told them not to worry because they must have been taken to Stanislaw. I asked the detective if [they] had been taken across at a place where they might soon be able to reach a village and he said yes. I again tried to find the parson but was unsuccessful again. The next morning I telephoned the magistrate at Rahó immediately but he told me they were unable to give anyone permission to go to the border—not even with a military escort. This would be, in any case, pointless as the Russians would not talk to anyone. In the afternoon I tried to get in touch with Berkovits by telephone, but I couldn't find him and I left a message. Everyone told me that the only chance was to get information from the Foreign Ministry.

Dear good Sister Petra, I feel I have done everything I could. I couldn't do any more because I was in the middle of so much work here and I was able to do this only by, in a way, escaping from Técső, missing a day's work and staying up all night.

I cannot give you definite information, I only know what I have been told: that [they] have been taken across totally illegally having received an assurance from the local captain that he would wait until Tuesday then, on Sunday night, he took them over unexpectedly and the next day, on Monday, the order to set them free arrived.[4]

I also know from them that there was a 79-year-old man among them, a little boy of seven and two mentally handicapped women who had lived on charity in Csíkszereda.[5] When they were put on a cart, the little boy was sobbing because he was so afraid. They said that even the soldiers were moved, only the captain was unaffected. I have no definite information, only what I heard from them, but I can tell you something else which is nothing to do with this but it is shocking to think that this could happen in Christian Hungary.

This is what happened: while I was waiting for the night train, I had to sit in the station restaurant because there was no heating anywhere else. I had supper there and then I thought I would have a little nap with my head on the table. But it didn't work out like that. A group of people came along: someone in a railway uniform (red epaulettes with two gold stars), two civilian gentlemen and two ladies. One of the gentlemen and one of the ladies soon left, the rest of the group: the uniformed man, one civilian gentleman and the owner of the restaurant started carousing. They were soon soused and they managed to get a gramophone from somewhere and started to dance, etc. They started to shoot their mouths off. They sang, they hollered and screamed. It was terrible. They danced. At another table, three Ukrainian men and three Ukrainian women were sitting with a glass of beer each. They were laughing at the drunk Hungarian gentlemen. One of the men poured wine into their beer and asked Jura for a dance. Jura, however, merely shook her head and, with difficulty said in Hungarian, "I can't, it's Pentecost." (She wanted to say "Advent.")[6] The hollering got louder until in the end they were a drunken choir shouting, "Then Jesus took the bread, broke it and said, 'This is my body' and took the wine and said, 'This is my blood. Do this in remembrance of me.' So let's do it! Drink! . . ." You have to imagine that this took place while they were shouting drunkenly and drinking. I was clenching my fists in rage and crying and quickly said two rosaries. I was indescribably tired and sad, it was around 12 o'clock. I should have found out their names so I could have reported them to the police. I didn't dare reprimand them because I was afraid because they were saying such nasty things. And the station was so far from the village. . . . So that is what happened in Christian Hungary a few meters from the Russian border. . . . And they were Christians. . . . In fact, they even sang all the *circumdederunt me*[7] . . . drunkenly . . . and the Ukrainians were watching the Hungarian gentlemen.

I have just received a postcard from Bernát Berkovits which I will enclose.[8] His full address is on it, he can give you definite information. I do not know if I have to write an official report.

I have an awful lot of work so I'll finish quickly. If I need to write any more to dear Sister Margit, please let me know.

With grateful Love,

Sister Sára

[handwritten signature]

Typed, signed original, in the possession of Ilona Mona.

1 Erzsébet Rónai, member of the SSS at this time working at the "mother–house" in the headquarters of the Society in Thököly Road in Budapest.
2 This letter is not known.
3 Dr. Ernő Gorzó. See doc. 2, note 5 to see how they know each other.
4 The order arrived on Monday the 9th. See docs. 2 and 6-8.
5 See doc. 7.
6 The four weeks before Christmas in Christian liturgy.
7 *Circumdederunt me* [They have surrounded me]: the first words of a Latin funeral hymn.
8 See doc. 2.

4.

January 2, 1941. Csíkszereda

Letter from Mrs. Benő Schultz to Margit Slachta asking her to save her children.

January 2, 1941

Dear Sister Margit,

I have only today found time to thank you for the boundless brotherly love you gave us. I have been ill since I got home and I was hardly able to get to [Csík]somlyó by sleigh to take the letter which I received but unfortunately the Head Sister was not at home so I could not talk to her.[1]

I have not yet received any news of my children. All my hopes lie in Sister Margit being able to take me to them or at least to find out if they are still alive. Because I could not imagine so much love and conscientiousness in anyone else in this kind of matter. I am extremely worn out, physically and mentally, by these terrible events and the uncertainty surrounding the fate of my children makes this worse. I have a constant waking nightmare in which I see that terrible winter storm into which they were dragged and I cannot imagine that such cruelty can exist in human souls.

My dear Sister Margit. Do all you can and let me know the result because I will have no inner calm until I know their fate. Nobody, nobody can understand the pain in a mother's heart as well as you can and a man might not be resolute enough. Furthermore, a man is affected by social and political ambition of which my Sister Margit is completely free. Because a woman's soul is suited to motherhood she can understand more deeply another mother's pain. I beg your help, give my children back to me.

The pain is much worse here at home because my regular guests only disturb me and the relatives of missing families also bring their pain to me. My home is a house of tears. This is made worse by the fact that public opinion here and the town's leaders refuse to accept that we have returned and they do not take into consideration that we have escaped from the jaws of death but we can hear voices saying that they should abide by the decress of the military administration and so they see us as having officially been deported.[2] This is said by responsible leaders. The only thing I do not understand is why? They themselves cannot tell us what our crime is, except that we are Jewish. This is held against only those who fall victim to a horrifying action based on a random selection.

One more thing I have to mention is your book of which I have unfortunately read only a little due to my frequent visitors and also because I find it difficult to concentrate my attention in this state of mind but I hope that I will live through better times and that when reading it for a second time I will enjoy its deep thoughts.

I would like to thank you again for your kind support and all the efforts you have made on our behalf. At the same time I would ask you to keep this matter in mind because you could do nothing which was more Christian. Wishing you lots and lots of success in your work. With love,

Mrs. Benő Schultz
[handwritten signature]
Rákóczi ut 113, Csíkszereda

Typed, signed original; the address at the end of the letter is in a different hand from the signature. In the possession of Ilona Mona.

[1] Letter unknown. Members of the Society ran the local maternity

home. Their leader was Emma Strobl (1906–1968). Her Society name was Sister Gerta.

[2] See Doc. 1, ref. 6.

5.

January 10, 1941

Letter from Margit Slachta to Mrs. Benő Schultz. She informs Mrs. Schultz about the steps taken on behalf of the missing at the office of Commissioner Miklós Kozma.

January 10, 1941, Budapest

Mrs. Benő Schultz, Csíkszereda

Dear Madam,

I only received your kind letter on the 7th although it was dated on the 2nd January, posted on the 4th and it arrived in Pest on the 6th.

I am indescribably sorry about not being able to inform you of any results yet because I can only proceed slowly due to pressure of work.

Unfortunately I was unable to talk to [Kozma], the Commissioner of Kárpátalja on the 27th.[1] I made another attempt to contact him the next day but I received the answer that he had been obliged to return to Ungvár so it was necessary to contact him in writing. This I was only able to do today. It was, however, sent by registered mail with an acknowledgment of receipt made out only for him so I expect to receive the acknowledgment of receipt soon.[2]

Meanwhile, however, we have written several copies of what you, Madam, have sent us[3] and I have sent one to Károly Pakocs, the canon and representative for Szatmár on whose heart the fate of Transylvania weights heavily.[4] He returned yesterday and will take steps in the relevant places. I hope I will soon receive definite news both from him and from Ungvár. I will write immediately.

How can the local authorities continue with this persecution? This I do not understand because you kindly told us that the Ministry of the Interior had ordered the return. Is there no written record of this? I think the first priority is to obtain this written report. Furthermore, G[ábor] Pál,[5] the representative, is not in Pest at the moment. I think he must be at home. He ought to take the case up with the authorities in Csíkszereda.

I fully understand how painful and excruciating it must be to think about your missing loved ones. I beg you from the depths of my heart to recite the prayer which shows that you trust in Providence. Put the fate of your loved ones, again and again, into the hands of Providence. People's trust pays respect to the Good God and He often helps merely to show us that our trust in Him is not in vain and He wants to reward us so that we trust in Him despite the circumstances.

I am sorry that you made such great efforts with my letter and that you had to travel by sleigh when you were ill. Please take care of yourself. I will write as soon as I receive news.

Greetings and I include your important and painful case in my prayers.

Typed original, unsigned copy; the address at the top left is most likely to have appeared only on this copy. In the possession of Ilona Mona.

1 Miklós Kozma (1884–1941) was one of the leading figures in the counterrevolutionary movement from the end of 1918. Among other posts, he was the head of the Propaganda and Defense Department of the National Army in Szeged and one of the leaders of MOVE (*Magyar Országos Véderő Egyesület*; Hungarian National Defense League). He was a prominent political figure in the Horthy régime. He was primarily a supporter of the Gömbös group. From 1920, he was general manager of the Hungarian Telegraphic Correspondence Office, from 1925 to 1935 and again from 1937 to 1939, he was president of the Hungarian Telephone Information and Radio Service Co. In 1934, he became a member for life of the Upper House of Parliament. From 1935 to 1937 he was Minister of the Interior. From 1939 to 1941, he was Commissioner of Kárpátalja.

2 See doc. 6. The date of the receipt is January 10.

3 This summary was apparently written by Mrs. Schultz. See also doc. 1, ref. 3 and doc. 10, ref. 2. Margit Slachta's papers contain several versions of this summary written in several different styles. One of these versions was sent to Miklós Kozma (see doc. 7) and another version to Ferenc Biró (see doc. 15).

4 Károly Pakocs, canon, papal representative, parliamentary representative, writer and poet.

[5] Gábor Pál, lawyer, parliamentary representative for Transylvania.

6.

Letter from Margit Slachta to Miklós Kozma, Commissioner. She asks for an investigation on behalf of the deportees to Körösmező.

XIV Thököly út 69
Budapest Tel: 296611 January 10, 1941

To: Miklós Kozma Esq. Ungvár
Commissioner

Your Excellency,

I am extremely sorry that circumstances did not permit me to relate the following matter to you in words during your brief visit to Budapest nor the one which I wish to enclose.[1] Herein I would like to lay forth the details concerning the causes of and the circumstances surrounding the present matter and explain why it is I who asks Your Excellency to investigate these matters; I who am completely disinterested in the subject.

I received this case as a social worker. I do not know how they found me. They perhaps heard about me through my sisters working down in Csík. I do not want to avoid doing anything which is in my power because, due to my Christian convictions, I want to work against all injustice, and, because I am Hungarian, I would like to prevent any trends which might discredit our homeland in front of anyone, especially the re–annexed territories and in this way might loosen the relationship between the re–annexed territories and the motherland.

I am also, however, lead by anxiety when I ask for judicial protection from the relevant forces on a basis of principle and ask you to prevent tyranny appearing here and there because it can rapidly cause disruption. Today, anarchy affects other people, but tomorrow or the next day it could be the turn of those classes which abuse the weaker ones and their fate will drag us down as well. The weakening of justice generally undermines law and order which has been so good up to now in our country. If we have come to the state where the authorities are not able to fully control the entire system and they have to turn a blind eye to the excesses of local small pashas, then the principles of law, at least in some respects and in some places, should remain intact; as, for instance, in Kárpátalja, which is in the fortunate position of having a Commissioner who is the ex-Minister of the Interior and thus appreciates the importance of retaining judicial principles and who, first and foremost, cannot allow those who are appointed to protect the nation and its people to abuse their positions in his territory.

I asked the Security Department of the Ministry of the Interior on the telephone to take measures before the unfortunate people in question were taken across the Russian border at Körösmező. It was a Saturday, the weekend, so I was unable to talk to the Ministerial Secretary, Head of Department, but only to the receptionist who reacted cynically and did nothing although, when I asked again on Monday, he said that he had telephoned to the border post at Körösmező, though this was merely a formality. The extent to which this was a formality can be seen in the following: Gábor Pál, the representative for Csíkszereda, repeatedly demanded the freeing of those interned in the military camp. The Ministry has taken steps in accordance with this. The orders, even after weeks of demands, arrived there either too late or in vain; the border guards ignored them. After their inhuman action, the Ministry of the Interior apparently said that the case was closed.

I now turn to Your Excellency and ask you to kindly take it into your hands and see it through in the interests of law and order and in the interests of your dignity. Anarchy can only be stopped at the source. I would also like to ask you to kindly officially command a search for those who are missing so that those who are alive can return home and so that those who are dead can be identified and so that anyone who acted inhumanly and arbitrarily should be brought within the bounds of the law.

I would like to apologize for inconveniencing you. I put this case into Your Excellency's hands with faith and at the same time hoping that revealing myself in this affair does not bring my disinterest into doubt and that my actions are based on Christian, Hungarian principles.

With greatest respect to Your Excellency,

Margit Slachta

[handwritten signature]

Typed, signed original. Országos Levéltár [National Archives], Budapest K 429 (Kozma documents) 36.cs.871.t; at the top of the letter there is a stamp of receipt reading: Commissioner of the territory of Kárpátalja, arrived January 13, 1941, ref. 871, original reference no., further reference number, appendix; handwritten on the back of the letter: no. 139/1-941. Immediately. With me. [illegible initials].

[1] See doc. 5.
[2] See doc. 7.

7.

December 1940

Summary report on the persecution of the Jews deported from Csíkszereda: The Csíkszereda–Körösmező case, November-December 1940.

In the afternoon of the 4th of November this year, twenty-four Jewish families from Csíkszereda received notice from Colonel Elemér Éder, the commandant of the city, requiring them to pay sums of 20–100 *pengős* in lieu of public service into the city's finance office by 12 o'clock the same day. As the notice arrived in the afternoon no one paid that day, especially because the city mailman would not allow the papers to be taken out of his hands and read. In the afternoon of the next day, all twenty-four heads of the households were summoned by Albrecht, first lieutenant, the deputy commandant of the city, to his office and, in harsh tones, gave them half an hour in which to pay the stated sums. This they did, but the city finance office was unwilling to give anyone receipts for the received sums.

In the evening of November 7th, the same families received summonses from the police which stated that they should appear before the head of the Special Branch at 8 A.M. on the 8th concerning their citizenship. On the morning of the 8th, the heads of the households were informed by the police that they would be deported in accordance with the orders of the city commandant and that they should be out of the country by 1 P.M. The police refused to look at any of their papers or listen to anyone but sent them back with a gendarmerie escort to pack as much as they could carry on their backs.

The deported families are:

1 Izidor Popper, timber merchant, with his wife and two children who were born in Csíkszereda and although their father is of

Galician origin, the family has lived in Transylvania for forty-five years.

[2] Benö Schultz, timber merchant, reserve first lieutenant with many medals, with his wife. Born on Hungarian soil, also his grandfathers. His documents were in his pocket.

[3] Árpád Hochfelder, timber merchant, with his wife and his seven-year-old son. His citizenship position is the same as that of Benö Schultz, who is his father-in-law.

[4] Adolf Berger, ironworks owner, with his wife, who is seriously ill, and his son. Born in Bukovina, but has lived in Csík for forty years.

[5] Mrs. József Brüller, wife of a timber merchant, with her daughter. Mr. Brüller was out of town that day so his wife and daughter were dragged away while he escaped harm. Mrs. Brüller suffers from diabetes, she is sixty-five.

[6] Salamon Werber, merchant, with his wife and two children. Born in Szatmár, as were his forefathers.

[7] Albert Grünwald, of independent means, seventy-nine years old, with his two mentally handicapped children. He has lived in Csík for sixty years, where he moved from Erzsébetváros. His forefathers were also Hungarian.

[8] Ernö Salamon, agricultural merchant, with his wife and nine-year-old son. Born in Transylvania, his forefathers also lived there.

[9] Manó Mózes, tinker, with his wife and four children (from six to sixteen years). Born in Gyimesbükk, his forefathers might have been of Romanian origin.

[10] Zoltán Indig, merchant, with his wife and eight-year-old daughter. An old Transylvanian Jewish family.

[11] Dr. Nándor Ádler, clerk, with two children and his seventy-eight-year-old mother, from a Transylvanian family.

[12] László Léderer, timber merchant, with his wife and one and a half year old child. Born in Brassó where his forefathers also lived.

[13] Samu Ligeti, sign-writer and painter, with his wife and son, who are Christian. Born in Kolozsvár, where his family has always lived.

[14] Mrs. Dávid Mózes, widow, seventy-five-years-old, with her four children. Of Romanian origin, but all her children were born in Transylvania where she has lived for fifty years.

15 Franciska Grossberg, merchant. Of Polish origin, but has lived in Csík almost all of her life.

16 Izidor Nagler, [leather] merchant. Born in Transylvania, his forefathers are from Galicia, with his two children.

17 Manó Nagler, leather merchant, son of the above, with his wife.

18 Emil Glanz, timber merchant, with his wife and child. Born in Bukovina, has been in Csík since 1916.

19 Adolf Wasser, kosher butcher, with his wife and two children (six and eighteen months). Born in Abauj-Torna County.

20 Sándor Dénes, lawyer, with his wife and fourteen-year-old son. Born in Transylvania, his forefathers also lived there.

21 Jenö Klein, gut-dresser, with his wife and four small children. Klein lived in Romania with a Hungarian passport when it was under Romanian control.

22 Mrs. Léb Wiesel, widow, with her three children. Born in Máramaros, day laborer.

23 Dávid Herskó, photographer, with his wife. Born in Romania.

24 László Fried, clerk. Born in Csíkszereda, his parents have always lived there and still do. His Christian fiancée was with him.

The above twenty-four families were taken out to Gyimesfelsölok on November 18, and were taken across the Romanian border in the valley of the Ugra stream, the wildest part of the Gyimes mountains. This was at a place where it was impossible to go forward because of the dense forest and the military guards would not let anyone back. Some of the younger, more enterprising ones fled, while the old, the sick, the children and those who were unwilling to abandon them stayed there without shelter until November 14, when the group, worn out by cold and starvation, was taken back to the courtyard of the gendarmerie in Csíkszereda and in the evening, they were put into the prison. They "had a rest" there until the evening of the 16th, then they were transported to Körösmező, to the 3rd Division of the Border Guard Battalion. They had to pay their own and their relatives' traveling expenses.

The families taken here are:

1. Izidor Popper
2. Benő Schultz
3. Árpád Hochfelder
4. Adolf Berger
5. Mrs. József Brüller
8. Ernö Salamon
9. Manó Mózes
10. Samu Ligeti
11. Izidor Nagler
12. Manó Nagler

6. Salamon Werber
7. Albert Grünwald
13. Adolf Wasser

On their arrival, the captain in charge had no idea why they had been sent there but when he asked his superiors they informed him that they had to be taken across the Russian border. The families were provided with two rooms in the military camp, where they slept on straw which had been spread out over the cement; men and women together without even the most basic washing facilities and they were exposed to abusive soldiers and NCOs. For instance, Lieutenant Asztalos made the men clean out the toilets and used the informal mode of address to the women[1] and locked them up because they were protesting about being taken over the border separately from their families.

The unfortunate people, ill as a result of sleeping on the cold cement, were expecting to be set free; their hopes fueled by occasional post cards from their relatives. The mail only got to them occasionally at the whim of the officer in charge. On December 5, however, instead of being set free, the process of classifying them started and, regardless of family ties, they were put into small groups and were taken at night across the Russian border at various points.

The situation was the same as it had been at the Romanian border. Those who could, escaped back to the land where they were born and where they belonged. The process of taking them across the border lasted until December 9, when an order arrived by telegraph from the Ministry of Defense setting all of them free. By this time, however, only Izidor Popper and his family were still at the camp and they were released the next day.

As a result of inquiries and a search initiated by their relatives, it was discovered that six families were missing, which means that they had either fallen into the hands of the Russians which would be preferable to the other possibility which is that they were lying somewhere in the depths of a forest, frozen solid by a raging snowstorm.

According to information from the military headquarters, eight people were seen being taken in the direction of Nadvorna by Russian border guards and these are: Árpád Hochfelder, timber merchant, with his wife and son, [Adolf Berger, the ironworks owner with his wife and son],[2] and Mrs. József Brüller and her daughter. This group was taken over the border on the evening of December 8, but they all returned because none of them wanted to leave their families. At 7 o'clock on the 9th, they were again taken across and at 9 o'clock [P.M.]

news arrived by telephone from headquarters that they were free. No one went in search of them. This is how the Russian border guards must have found them and picked up this group who were mostly ill or handicapped. (Mrs. Brüller, whose husband stayed behind, had blood pressure of 280, was diabetic and was lame; Mrs. Berger, who had high blood pressure, became blind in one eye as a result of lack of medical treatment at the military camp; Mr. Hochfelder, who had crushed a leg, was with his seven–year–old child and his wife, had been separated from her parents who had been taken across the day before and who she believed were somewhere in the forest without shelter.)

Other missing people: Manó Mózes, tinker, with his family; Albert Grünwald, seventy–nine, of independent means, with his two mentally handicapped daughters; and Salamon Werber, merchant, with his family.

Even the military headquarters was unaable to give any information as to the whereabouts of these people because the army's mission "ended" when the families were taken across. According to reports, one corpse was found in the forest, but it has not yet been identified. As every missing family has relatives who are desperately seeking help and as the relatives of those who were taken into Russian territory against their will would like to bring them back to safety, we demand that you establish the precise whereabouts of these people in order to provide the relatives with definite information about the fate of those missing. It will also, however, be necessary to re-unite the broken families in order to avoid the kind of unthinkable situation where Mrs. Brüller's husband, for example, is in the country, while his family is, if the military reports are reliable, in Russian territory.

They appeal to the highest level of the relevant authorities to kindly take the necessary steps with all haste, that is:

1. Determine the whereabouts of those in Russia and arrange for their return.
2. Conduct a search for those missing.
3. Identify the dead.

Typed, four page original, K 429–36. 871.t.

[1] Translator's note. As in French, two forms of address exist in Hungarian. The use of the informal would have been humiliating in these circumstances.

[2] This family must have been omitted due to a typing error. They

are found in another version which is in the possession of Ilona Mona.

8.

February 14, 1941, Ungvár

Report by Arisztid Meskó, police superintendent, to Miklós Kozman, Commissioner, concerning the investigation into the deportation of Jews to Körösmező.

Hungarian Royal Border
Ungvár
No.: 139/1 - 1941

Subject: The deportation of 40 Jewish people from from Csíkszereda to Körösmező
Request: verbal
Attached: 6 documents[1]

Ungvár
To the Commissioner

I hereby report that I have conducted an investigation into the case of deportation of forty Jews from Csíkszereda to Körösmező by the border police unit in Körösmező. I have ascertained the following:

On November 21, 1940, twelve Jewish families, comprising forty individuals,[2] arrived in Körösmező from Csíkszereda. They were given a short note and sent on their way by the 104th Army Service Corps HQ with the purpose of taking them to Russian territory.

Captain Sándor of the Border Guard Corps refused to take responsibility for transporting the Jews to Russian territory. He therefore wrote a report to his superiors concerning their transfer. As it was not in his power to send the Jews back to Csíkszereda, their starting point, he lodged them in the barracks of the military camp of the Border Defense Regiment HQ until such time as he received further orders from his superiors. The two rooms with which they were provided were well-ventilated and clean but as he was unable to provide them with beds, he was obliged to have straw brought to the rooms. It was impossible to separate men and women due to the shortage of rooms, but the accommodation was in any case in accordance with the wishes of the families.

It is not the case that they were exposed to abuse from soldiers and NCOs. Nor is it the case that Lieutenant Asztalos used the informal mode of address when speaking to the women nor that he locked up some of the women. It is true that he made the men clean the toilets but he made them clean only those toilets which they themselves used and he could not have ordered soldiers to clean them.

They received, as civilians, the best treatment; they were allowed to walk in the yard of the military camp during the hours of daylight and some of them were even permitted to get kosher food from the village. There may possibly have been occasions when Lieutenant Asztalos used a somewhat firm tone of voice when addressing them but as a good officer and disciplined soldier he always used a firm and military tone when addressing his men and this might be why the Jews perceived his military manner as being rude and curt. It is not the case that the Jews did not receive the mail which was sent to them, nor is it the case that there were delays in giving it to them. The Border Defense Regiment immediately handed them the letters or any other mail which was sent to their address.

Captain Sándor, the commander of the Border Defense Regiment, received an order from his commanding officer on December 2, 1940, which ordered him, in collaboration with the border police unit at Körösmező, to smuggle the forty Jews who had been transported from Csíkszereda to Körösmező across the Russian–Hungarian border in groups or individually. Captain Sandór, in accordance with this order, started taking the Jews across in small groups on the night of December 5, 1940, and this action was carried out within his own sphere of authority without the collaboration of the border police unit.

By December 8, 1940, he had taken thirty–six Jews across with the help of the sentries from the Border Defense Regiment at the Tatár pass, Páncélház and Mohelki, thus only the Popper family (four persons) remained. They should have been taken across on the night of the 8th. However, because eight of the forty Jews who had been taken across returned to Hungarian territory, in the evening hours of December 9, they were again taken across to Russian territory. As a result of this, the transfer of the Popper family would have happened in the evening hours of the 10th but at 7 P.M. on the 9th a telegram arrived at the HQ of the Border Defense Regiment from the Ministry of Defense ordering the immediate release of the detained Jews. As soon as he received the telegram, Captain Sándor telephoned the sentry of the Border Regiment at Páncélház, who was responsible for the transfer of the eight Jews and told them to escort the Jews back to the military camp in the event that they had not yet been transferred to Russian territory. Since they had already been transferred by the superior officer of the sentry of the Border Defense Regiment, they could neither be escorted nor set free.

The Poppers: Izidor Popper, timber merchant in Csíkszereda, Mrs. Izidor Popper, Zoltán Popper and Judit Popper, who were awaiting transfer, were set free in the morning hours of December 10, 1940, and told to return to Csíkszereda, their starting point. They were provided with a letter and they left the territory of Körösmező the same day.

The persons mentioned in the appeal as having been taken to Russian territory are: Adolf Berger, born in Csíkszereda in 1879, Jewish, ironworks owner; Mrs. Adolf Berger, born in Hosszúmező in 1880, Jewish wife of an ironworks owner; Manó Berger, born in Csíkszentmiklós in 1909, Jewish, of independent means; Árpád Hochfelder, born in Nemesör in 1900, Jewish, married, merchant; Mrs. Árpád Hochfelder, born in Gyergyótölgyes in 1909, Jewish, married, wife of a merchant; György Hochfelder, born in Csíkszentsimon in 1933, Jewish, student; Mrs. József Brüller, born in Stó, Galicia in 1882, Jewish, married, housewife; Eszter Brüller, born in Kézdivásárhely in 1906, Jewish, single, housewife; Salamon Werber, born in Szatmárnémeti in 1886, Jewish, married, merchant; Mrs. Salamon Werber, born in Gyimesbükk in 188[?], Jewish, wife of a merchant; Menyhért Werber, born in Brassó in 1920, Jewish, photographer; Rozália Werber, born in Brassó in 1928, Jewish, single, student; Manó Mózes, born in Gyimesbükk in 1896, Jewish, married, day-laborer; Mrs. Manó Mózes, born in Galatz in 1896, Jewish married, wife of a day laborer; Sára Mózes, born in Galatz in 1922, Jewish, single, seamstress; Mátyás Mózes, born in Csíktapolca in 1926, Jewish, single, student; Lajos Mózes, born in Csíktapolca in 1928, Jewish, single, student; Albert Grünwald, born in Csíkszereda in 1861, Jewish, married, merchant; Róza Grünwald, born in Csíkszereda in 1894, Jewish; and Ida Grünwald, born in Csíkszereda in 1914, Jewish, single, housewife. The head of the police unit has conducted a thorough search in order to determine the whereabouts of the abovementioned but with no success.[3]

In the course of the investigation, Captain Asztalos visited the sentries at the Hungarian-Russian border at the Tatár pass, Páncélház and Mohelki and during the interrogations he ascertained that the abovementioned Jews had been taken across to Russian territory at three places. A member of the patrol at the unit in Mohelki, who was among those who conducted the transfer, saw the transferred Jews being intercepted by a Russian patrol, put on three sleighs, and escorted to Nadvorna.

I also hereby report that it is not the case that a corpse was found in the forest near the border. Along the border, there is one track which is used by patrols on their rounds. It is impossible to take any other way, because of the snow which is often one and a half meters deep and if it did happen that any of those who were transferred did return to Hungarian territory, it could only have been by means of this path and had he frozen to death, the patrol would certainly have found him.

In the course of the investigation, the head of the police unit visited the abovementioned places, with a patrol. He thoroughly examined the tracks along the border and the border but found no corpse.

Ungvár, February 14, 1941
Head of police HQ:
Dr. Arisztid Meskó
[handwritten signature]
Hungarian Royal Superintendent

Typed, four page, signed original; OL K 429/36.cs.871.t.

[1] Not known.

[2] Doc. 7 gives the number as thirteen families and forty–two individuals (Tilkovszky gives Meskó's figures on pp. 295ff.) Similar minor differences occur in other places.

[3] According to docs. 7 and 10, in fact, twenty–one people were missing.

9.

Ungvár, February 18, 1941

Letter from Miklós Kozma to Margit Slachta: His reply concerning the case of the Jews deported to Kőrösmező.

Commissioner of Kárpátalja — February 18, 1941

Esteemed Sister Margit Slachta

Budapest

Dear Esteemed Sister,

I received your letter dated the 10th of January and having investigated the case, I have established the following. No unit within my sphere of authority took part in this matter. The Border Defense Corps is not under my authority. In civilian matters, they are responsible to the Ministry of the Interior. In any case, the whole matter is beyond my sphere of authority.

Now, as for the facts: first, it should be established that the entire case was undertaken by the military HQ in a period when civil authorities had absolutely no influence on the military because Transylvania was under military rule.[1]

According to the Hungarian Royal Border Police HQ,[2] who are responsible to me, the complaints against the Border Defense Regiment at Körösmező are not in accordance with the truth because the Border Defense Regiment did not take the individuals concerned across the border without the authorization of their superiors. Later, in accordance with orders from a higher level, the transfer began. This was later halted by a telegram from the Ministry of the Interior, but by that time, most of them had already been taken across and only the Popper family remained. They were then released.[3]

I have conducted a thorough investigation concerning the presence of corpses in the forest along the border. As the snow is nearly always one and a half meters deep in the border region, there was only one path on which travel was possible. This path is used by border patrol units on their rounds. If any of those transferred had come back to Hungarian territory it would have been by means of this path and had he frozen to death, the patrol would certainly have found him. In the course of my investigation, the chief of the border unit, in person, conducted a thorough search along the paths by the border but found no corpse.

In general, the Russians, in fact, intercepted the Jews, they were seen being transported toward the interior of the country.

I would also suggest, as this is a military matter, that you also kindly contact the Minister of Defense.

Please accept my sincere respect,

Kozma
[handwritten signature]

Typed, signed original with handwritten notes (see notes 1 and 3 below); in the possession of Ilona Mona.

1 In pencil alongside this paragraph, written by Margit Slachta [?] are the words: "This is the same old recipe; one body passing the buck to another." Concerning the military administration, see doc. 1, ref. 6.

2 See doc. 8.

3 These last two sentences are underlined in pencil and the notes alongside written in pencil by Margit Slachta [?]: "This is that method. A trick."

10

March 10, 1941, Csíkszereda

Letter from Mrs. Benő Schultz to Margit Slachta. She gives Margit Slachta some of the details of the deportation and some more information and asks her for further assistance.

Rákóczi út 133
Csíkszereda
March 10, 1941

Dear Sister Margit,

I have been intending to write to you for some time but I have been prevented by illness or by circumstances. The other day, I received your kind letter and I will try to give you a detailed answer.[1]

I did not honestly expect any other response to our complaint to the Commissioner of Kárpátalja's office. It is true that we were in the hands of the military authorities and I myself came into contact with the police only after my escape from the forest. Partly because I wanted to ask for permission to search for my children at the border and partly because they asked me to provide them with information about those who escaped from the forest because, without this, they were unable to answer the telegram from the Minister of the Interior.

I gave them the information they needed but when I started to make complaints about the Border Defense Regiment and told them that I had been forcibly separated from my family, the duty officer was reluctant to include it in the report. Nor did he want to include the fact that Lieutenant Asztalos locked me up because I asked him not to separate me from my children nor the fact that he addressed me informally as if I was one of his men. He did not want to include in the report that the men were made to clean the toilets nor First Lieutenant Szlávik's order that Mrs. Popper, who was on the point of being released, and her daughter should scrub all the floor in the barracks.

I still maintain that all this is true and restate them because I experienced them and suffered them along with all the other petty humiliations that I had to suffer at the hands of these gentlemen who are not fit to wear the uniforms of officers. As for the reports, they are no surprise either because they had the audacity to report that all of us had escaped across the border. This can be substantiated by Károly Herskovits, head of the religious community, who saw these reports at the Army Ministry.

Dear Sister Margit, I do not want to go into details of the suffering we had to face again. What I stated in that report which I sent to you[2] was only a small part of it. I do not expect great results from the investigation because I see that Colonel Éder, who sent us there and who harassed us at the Romanian border, is still merrily hunting in the mountains of Csík and enjoying the hospitality of those who helped him in this affair.

The only thing I would like to achieve and for which I again ask your help is to find my children. What they have reported from Csíksomlyó; that everyone has returned home, is incorrect: twenty–one people are still missing and my loved ones are among them. As I heard from Mr. Károly Herskovits who made inquiries at the Russian Consulate where he was told that all the twenty–one people who are still missing are there, but that their internment can come to an end only after an investigation through diplomatic channels. This process may take until May and we cannot foresee its results. So, until then they are locked up, their liberty is denied to them and cannot send any mail. Innocent people, ill women and children, have to endure this trial only because they were chosen as victims at the whim of one individual.

I would like to ask you to help me to somehow arrange it with the Foreign Ministry that this period will be shortened and my loved ones will be able to come home. I have no experience in these matters, I do not even know how to begin. I am waiting and wringing my hands day after day when I see that there is no mail. The relatives of all the twenty–one people are in this state because all twenty–one have parents, brothers and sisters, and husbands here at home.

I cannot write much about the situation here. I am not even interested in it, I am so apathetic that I am only interested in my loved ones.

I am almost ashamed that I am inconveniencing you so much with this matter when you have to spread your effort in so many different directions. I beg you not to bother with investigations or punishment as they will almost certainly prove fruitless. Let us leave punishment to God. Let us concentrate on bringing them back now that we know for sure that they are there. This would at least relieve those families who are separated from their relatives.

I thank you with gratitude for the eternal efforts you are making on our behalf and I would very much like to repay it to some extent.

With heartfelt greetings,

Mrs. Benő Schultz

[handwritten signature]

Typed, signed letter in the possession of Ilona Mona.

[1] The letter which apparently informed Mrs. Benő Schultz about Miklós Kozma's reply (see doc. 9) is unknown, but presumably held out the prospect of an investigation. See below.

[2] See doc. 5, note 3.

11.

June 16, 1942, Csíkszereda

Letter from Mrs. Károly Herskovits to Margit Slachta. She asks for help on behalf of the nineteen Jewish families deported from the town.

June 16, 1942, Csíkszereda

Dear Sister,

In our desperate situation the only way out seems to be to appeal to your noble heart which is well-known throughout the country with this respectful request.

A few days ago the local police HQ issued deportation orders to nineteen Jewish families from the town. We do not know why this took place but it can be assumed that someone aims to make the town free of Jews. We assume this because, since the fortunate re-annexation of Transylvania, Jews have been almost constantly deported from the town. This assumption is likely to be correct because similar actions have not, thank God, taken place in the neighboring towns.[1] Our behavior has never given the authorities any grounds for these strong measures. We are Hungarian citizens; many of us were born in Csíkszereda and others have lived here for decades. None of us have ever faced criminal proceedings; we have never betrayed our homeland in word or deed; we have always fulfilled our obligations as citizens and we have, all our lives, earned our bread through honest work.

As the authorities have not told us why the deportations took place, we kindly ask you, dear Sister, to intervene with the relevant authorities, asking them to re-examine these actions against us because the actions may be based on a false impression and we have to give the deportees a chance to clear up this kind of misunderstanding which can have such serious consequences.

Most of them have been called up to do military service. We, their families, stayed here with the infants, defenseless and without support.[2] If we have to leave now we will become homeless, we will have to sell off our simple possessions and, overnight, we will have to face great deprivation.

Until such time as our husbands return, we beg you to kindly mention our difficult situation to the relevant authorities and try to persuade them to allow us to stay in our old, humble homes where we can, albeit barely, get by until the good God returns our breadwinners to us.

We would like to call your kind attention to the urgency of this case as the police have told us that they will take the sternest measures if we do not leave within a few days regardless of our appeal against these measures.

In the hope of the fulfillment of our respectful request we give you our heartfelt thanks for your kind protection and we offer our sincere respect.

On behalf of the women of Csíkszereda,

Mrs. Károly Herskovits

wife of the head of the religious community

[handwritten signature]

Typed, signed letter in the possession of Ilona Mona.

[1] In fact, similar actions did take place in Transylvania, although not in the neighboring towns. See doc. 12.

[2] According to Decree 2.870/1941.M.E., Jews were not permitted to perform military service after April 16, 1941. Instead they performed "civil work." Here, they were not allowed to hold positions of authority. Being a "civil worker" not only meant legal discrimination, but also often involved physical humiliation and brutal treatment.

12.

June 18, 1942

Letter from Margit Slachta to Countess Móric Esterházy. She asks for support on behalf of the deportees from Csíkszereda.

June 18, 1942

Deeply respected Countess,[1]

I was given so much joy by your kindness and by the fact that you have taken an interest in this poor, forsaken cause. God bless you for this.

I enclose only information concerning Ernő Sümeg. The position of the previously mentioned family is no longer so urgent. I will not go into the details. They are very sad.[2]

However, an express letter has this minute arrived from Csíkszereda.[3] These unfortunate people, in number 140, were, after the re-annexation, deported and taken across the Russian border at Kőrösmező by the military commander in December.[4] Most of them have fled back but, for example, the daughter, the son-in-law, and the grandchild of Mrs. Herskovits are missing[5] because they would not even do so much as to take them across together. This was an unlawful act. This is anarchy of the highest order and it takes place in secret. They did it at Borszék as well and later they brought them back but the people they had taken away had already given up their homes and sold off everything they could.[6] I feel that this is a case of great importance which the Minister of the Interior,[7] a man of influence, could stop. I would be grateful if you could let me know by telephone tomorrow if you will take up this case.[8] The general situation is rapidly deteriorating; it seems that the Hungarian state would like to follow the example of Slovakia.[9]

With deep respect,

In the copy of the letter from Csíkszereda, I omitted the greeting so as not to reduce the chances of success as a result of my name because the Minister of the Interior is angry with me.
Typed, unsigned copy, at the top left corner in pencil: Mrs. M. Esterházy, in the possession of Ilona Mona.

1 Countess Móric Esterházy, member of the Presidential Council of the National Association of Health Protection and the Hungarian branch of the Red Cross. Her husband, Count Móric Esterházy, former Prime Minister, Minister without Portfolio, and parliamentary representative of the Party of Hungarian Life (*Magyar Élet Pártja*).

2 This case is unknown. On the basis of doc. 13 it can be assumed that it was also a case concerning the protection of Jews performing labor service in which Margit Slachta and Baroness Edith Weiss were involved. See doc. 13.

3 This is probably the same as doc. 11.

4 She is referring here to the 1940 case. Her memory seems to be faulty because only forty-two people were in fact taken to Körösmezö and the total number of deportees was seventy-eight. See doc. 7.

5 Margit Slachta seems to have confused the author of doc. 11 with Mrs. Schultz.

6 This case is not recorded elsewhere.

7 The Minister of the Interior at the time was Ferenc Keresztes-Fischer.

8 Mrs. Esterházy's response is not known.

9 Between March and July 1942, 60,000 people (60 percent of the Jewish population) were deported from the Republic of Slovakia. Margit Slachta was involved in attempts to save them. See introduction.

13.

June 18, 1942, Budapest

Letter from Margit Slachta to Baroness Edith Weiss. She informs the Baroness about the steps she has taken on behalf of the Jews in Csíkszereda.

June 18, 1942

Dear Edith,[1]

Mrs. Esterházy devoted two hours of her time to the appeal case. Her position is totally intransigent.

I am writing because of the letter of which I enclose a copy. I have also sent a copy to the Countess and asked her to intervene with the Minister of the Interior, since she herself offered to intervene with him to gain exemptions for certain deportees (the Láng family). At present she does not want to do the K. Koch case. I therefore sent only the case of two labor servicemen to her, plus the Csíkszereda case.

B[álint] H[óman] Min[ister][2] said, among other things, that they have found only one patriotic Jew in the whole of Transylvania, the hotel proprietor in Nagyvárad, who spoke out under the Romanian regime. How nice it would be if we could give him precise information, perhaps even names, about those who were patriotic either up there or in Transylvania. I will write a letter to him soon about today's audience then I could also include that.

It was so nice that you visited this morning,

Best wishes,

Typed, unsigned copy, in the possession of Ilona Mona.

[1] Little is now known about Baroness Edith Weiss, although she must have been an important figure in Jewish life at this time. Her main contribution was in Jewish social work. She was a member of several social and charitable organizations. She played an important role in saving the victims of the 1941 deportation.

[2] Bálint Hóman (1885–1953), historian, university lecturer, member of the Hungarian Academy of Sciences. He was Minister of Religion and Education between 1932–1938 and 1939–1942.

14.

June 22, 1942, Kolozsvár

Letter from Judit Veress, Social Sister of Margit Slachta, giving information about her visit to the vicar in Kolozsvár.

Dear Good Sister Margit,

Thank you very much for your letter. My heart was aching when I read of these actions which shame Christianity. I was myself witness to similar scenes while I was there last year.[1]

The vicar[2] read through everything thoroughly and hesitated for a while but eventually he came to the conclusion that he could do nothing without knowing the situation and said that in any case he was not Bishop Majláth,[3] whose word immediately gains the attention of the authorities. While we were talking it came to my mind that there was Archdeacon Ferenc Biró in Csíkszereda, who is a very good friend to the Society, and also a friend of the local police chief who is a daily communicant and a deeply Catholic man. I think that if you, dear good Sister Margit, were to write to the Deacon, he could achieve a great deal in local affairs through that police chief. The Reverend Archdeacon always mentioned your name with such great respect and love when I was in Csíkszereda and we were talking about the work of the Society. I am terribly worried that this reply may be a little too late; this morning I told everything to dear Sister Petra, at least I think it was her, on the telephone. Yesterday I called [Nagy]várad and gave them the answer because I thought that you, dear good Sister Margit, had also gone to the meeting and I thought that the information would get to you sooner in this way. We are very much looking forward to the results of this meeting. Sister Marianne has sent a telegram to say that she will not stop but will only pass through on the way to [Csík]somlyó. We will meet her at the station. I wish we could meet you, dear good Sister Margit, at the station again soon. I long to see you and to have a little talk with you. The "brightness"[4] in Szegvár has often been obscured by clouds but I still feel that I came to a profound love of the will of the good God, and I ask you, dear good Sister Margit, to sometimes include me in your prayers. I offer to do this every day in my grateful, childlike soul.

I kiss your hands with deep respect and loyalty,

Sister Judit

[handwritten signature] June 22, 1942, Kolozsvár

Typed, signed original in the possession of Ilona Mona.

1 Probably a reference to the deportation orders.

2 Possibly Imre Sándor, Protonotary Canon.

3 Count Gusztáv Majláth (1864–1940), prominent Bishop of Gyulafehérvár (Alba Iulia) from 1897 (first assistant bishop, later bishop). His successor was the famous Áron Márton.

4 The Society had a novitiate in Szegvár. This sentence refers to a personal experience of Judit Veress.

15.

June 22, 1942, Budapest

Letter from Margit Slachta to Archdeacon Ferenc Biró. She asks him to intervene on behalf of the Jews deported from Csíkszereda.

Archdeacon Ferenc Biró
Csíkszereda

Reverend Archdeacon,

Let me turn to you concerning a local matter and ask you to devote some of your precious time to intervene in it.

It is a grave and difficult problem. It concerns nineteen Jewish families in Csíkszereda who are to be taken out of the town because it is a military zone.

Please do not be surprised that I am writing about this case which is so distant from me. I write and do whatever I can, first, because we are talking about people and second, for our homeland.

In November of the year of the re–annexation, the local military commander picked up twenty–four families and their woes are described in the enclosed document.[1] May I ask you to return this document to me at some point. At this time I had already become very interested in this case from a Hungarian point of view. It caused me great pain to hear that hardly had they been returned to us when they faced such experiences. I would not concentrate all my efforts on the realization of Christian values if we had not experienced, both this year and last, shocking and atrocious acts performed by the supporters of "racial fanatics."

Last year there was a vast deportation, Jews were taken across at Körösmező by the thousands on the grounds that their presence was illegal.[2] Most of them died at the other side of the border. In order to see for ourselves, a small group: Countess Erzsébet Szapáry,[3] Governor Pakocs,[4] Count György Apponyi[5] and Szabó,[6] the secretary of the Pest Archiepiscopal Vicar and papal representative, went to Körösmező and saw what was taking place there. Ujvidék was even more horrible.[7] Now local petty pashas are harassing their fellowmen just for the sake of it in the name of "martial law" or even without any pretext. A lot of tragic things are also happening in the labor service camps.

I have recently learned that Jewish families are again being rounded up in Csíkszereda. They claim their innocence—for that matter, the deportees' innocence was proved in 1940 too, during the first similar action. I now turn to you Archdeacon with a request to kindly visit the police chief, who we have heard is a good Catholic, and kindly ask him to deal gently with these unfortunate people, especially with those families whose breadwinner is in a labor service camp.

I write with a bleeding heart that lurking anarchy exists. If this kind of order is received, it in no way means that the authorities up here want the same. The Minister of the Interior categorically condemns these actions. Those who plan this kind of thing, perform these atrocities in the name of "martial law."

The police chief is in a position to achieve a lot:

1. He can establish if there are, in this case, any grounds for the implementation of martial law.
2. He can tell us if the families concerned *gave any grounds* to the authorities for the deportation from the town which plunges them into poverty.
3. He is entitled to delay the action if not cancel it. (The Minister of the Interior will support him. *I tell you this in confidence.* It is useful, however, if he knows the feelings of his ultimate master.)
4. He could look into the conditions to which these unfortunate are sent and if they have no place there, he could surely demand that they should not be sent out until they have a place to go to.

We are living through intensely painful times. Who shall we turn to for merciful compassion if not to the priests of the Church and such loyal sons of the Church as the police chief?

I apologize for inconveniencing you and ask for God's blessing for the Archdeacon. I remain, on June 22, 1942,

Your devoted servant in Christ,

Mother Superior of the Social Sisters

Allow me to enclose for your perusal a copy of our journal.[8] It expresses our point of view. We work for the victory of this point of view and we believe only in this.

Typed, unsigned copy, the top left address may be missing from the original, in the possession of Ilona Mona.

[1] This is possibly the same as doc. 7. See doc. 5, note 3.

2 The Körösmező deportation took place in July–August 1941. Approximately 20,000 Jews were deported to military zones in Galicia, where most of them were executed. See Tamás Majsai, *A körösmezei zsidó deportálás 1941–ben* [The Körösmező Deportation in 1941] in the *Yearbook of the Ráday Collection*, 1986, vol. 4.

3 We have not found any more information about Erzsébet Szapáry.

4 Károly Pakocs canon, papal representative, member of parliament, writer and poet.

5 Count György Apponyi (1898–1970), legitimist politician who was opposed to the Germans. He was elected to parliament several times. In 1944 he was arrested by the Gestapo and taken to Mauthausen concentration camp.

6 Imre Szabó (1901–1976) Catholic priest. In 1938 he was given the title "confidential papal representative." From 1931 he worked for the *Budapesti Helynökség* and was secretary of this organization between 1935 and 1944. (This information was gained from Margit Beke, archivist of the primacy). Szabó was in the group instead of Bishop Endre Hamvas, Archbishop and Archepiscopal Vicar, who was unable to travel with them. (See *Nemzetgyülési Értesitő* [National Assembly Bulletin], Budapest, 1947, 592–612.)

7 Over several days from the end of January 1942 a "clearing action" was carried out by military and gendarmerie units. It was in fact a brutal massacre in the course of which about 5,000 people, including 1,000 Jews, were butchered.

8 Its title was *"A Testvér"* [The Brother].

16.

June 29, 1942, Csíkszereda

Letter from Mrs. Károly Herskovits, wife of the head of the religious community, to Margit Slachta. She thanks her for her support and asks her for further assistance and informs her about the present situation.

June 29, 1942, Csíkszereda

Dear Sister,

There are no words to express our gratitude for the loving concern with which you made our case your own. Seeing and feeling your interest in our fate, an interest which springs from the most noble sentiments, I feel the need to give you a clear picture of our present situation because I am afraid that I may have been too biased because I was too surprised and touched to describe the situation here clearly and comprehensively enough to your representative [whose name] I could not remember due to my embarrassment.[1]

In order to understand the situation, I think you should know the following important points:

The deportations may have been instigated by the military but it is *the civil administration* which carries them out. The deportation orders were issued by the police at the primary level and appeals could be made to the provincial police chief in Budapest and, at the highest level, to the Minister of the Interior. We have learned that our appeals have been sent back to the police here to be supplemented and they will be returned to the Budapest HQ for a decision by the 7th of July.

Meanwhile, further deportation orders have been delivered to twenty–two families, that is, forty–one families in total would be made homeless. Most of them are from the older generation and have lived here for thirty or forty years and are well–respected individuals. Some of the deportation orders had to be received by relatives because the head of the family had been called up.

The text of the deportation is the same in every case[2] and all the deportations are to take place groundlessly, on the basis of Decree 8130/1939.M.E.[3] Given an objective investigation, it could be established that all the accusations in the deportation orders are, without doubt, groundless.

We ask you, dear Sister, to kindly use your influence so that the local police will allow us to stay in our homes pending the decision of the Minister of the Interior and we will have complete faith in the justness of this decision and we will regain our inner calm. We should not become homeless after a lifetime's hard and honest work, especially because they are unwilling to take us in any other part of the country.

The reason why we do not attempt to find a remedy for our problems here and turn directly to your noble self, is that those prominent and influential people who sympathize with us and with whom we have spent most of our lives are afraid to speak out on our behalf because the authorities, as normally happens, would brand them as "Jew–lovers," "Jewish hirelings," etc.

We will implore the Almighty to assist you, dear Sister, in your blessed acts and to grant you a long healthy life in order that you can bring continued comfort to all your persecuted and needy fellow men.

On behalf of myself and of those who share my fate may I thank you from the bottom of my heart for your compassion and I can assure you of complete discretion.

Gratefully yours,

Mrs. Károly Herskovits

[handwritten signature]

Typed copy in the possession of Ilona Mona.

[1] Probably Viktor Muszély, religious teacher in the bishopric of Vác. See doc. 18.

[2] The text of the deportation order: "The Royal Hungarian Police HQ in Csíkszereda. No. 1942. Subject: the deportation from the Hungarian town of Csíkszereda of ____________, and the members of his family, residents of Csíkszereda. *Final notice.* Profession __________, No. ______, __________ Street, with __________, wife of the above, living in the same household with __________, his children. On the basis of Par. 1, Section 1, Subsection b of Decree no. 8130/1939.M.E., I hereby order the deportation of the above-mentioned from the Hungarian town of Csíkszereda and also that they are to be placed forthwith under police supervision. Within fifteen days of the receipt of this order, the deportee is required to give notification of his intended place of residence after the implementation of this order. In the terms of Par. 6, Section 1 of Decree 760/1939.B.M., which deals with the implementation of the above-mentioned decree, I forbear from placing them in custody until a final decision comes into operation. Appeals against my final decision can be registered within fifteen days of receipt. These should be addressed to the Provincial Police HQ, Royal Hungarian Police and should be made to me, either in written or verbal form. *Reason*: I had to take this decision because the presence of the deportee and his family in the Hungarian town of Csíkszereda and in the border zone, in general, threatens defense interests and is harmful in terms of national security. I forebore from placing them in custody as empowered to do by Par. 6, Section 1 of Decree 760/1939.B.M. due to the inconvenient condition of

the cells in Csíkszereda. Copies sent to: __________, resident of Csíkszereda, __________, __________. 1942, Csíkszereda. Head of Police, Police HQ: __________, Hungarian Royal Police Commander." [Typed copy in the possession of Ilona Mona.]

[3] The text of Par. 1. of Decree 8130/1939 M.E.: "The police authorities will (a) place under police supervision or (b) deport from their place of residence or place in police custody, those whose presence in certain localities or certain parts of the country is disturbing in terms of law and order or national security or harmful to the economy."

17.

1942, Csíkszereda

Letter from Mrs. Lipót Török to Margit Slachta. She asks for her help in revoking a deportation order.

Dear Sister,

I, the undersigned, Mrs. Lipót Török, née Erzsébet Kohn, resident of Csíkszereda, being unable to find any other way out of my desperate plight, turn to your nationally well-known noble heart. I ask you:

My husband fifty–two years of age, Hungarian born, of the Jewish faith, was a lawyer in Csíkszereda, who, following the end of the Romanian occupation, as a result of the well–known *numerus clausus*, was prevented from becoming a member of the Chamber of Lawyers in Marosvásárhely.[1] He has been unemployed for two years. I was born in Gyergyóditró, in Csík County. I have two children: One, László, eighteen years of age, is a sixth year pupil at the Jewish vocational school in Budapest, the other is Klára, fifteen years of age. They were both born in Csíkszereda.

We all therefore come from here. My husband has lived continuously in Csíkszereda since 1898. He was a member of the Hungarian Party during the Romanian occupation,[2] a time when this meant not only financial and moral sacrifice but was also dangerous. He was a supporter of every Hungarian cause: schools, churches, cultural movements. He employed Hungarian office staff, his apprentices went on to become prominent local figures; public notaries and examining magistrates.

Three weeks ago the local police HQ issued deportation orders to nineteen Jewish families and also placed them under police supervision. We cannot understand the reason for these deportations since we have always been loyal citizens but, as Jews have been constantly deported from our town since the re–annexation of Transylvania on the most unlikely pretexts, it seems likely that someone wants to totally rid the town of Jews. The best evidence for this is that a further twenty–two Jewish families have received summonses, apparently on the same grounds.

My situation is all the more desperate in that, in addition to the threat of deportation, my fifty–two year old husband and my eighteen year old son received "SAS" (immediate) call–up papers on the 20th of this month. So here I am alone, facing deportation and under police supervision and distraught. My husband, of the same pedigree, is performing military service along with my son, but they cannot help me either. I stand here defenseless, homeless and without support. I will have to sell off my simple things because I have no place to take them to. I cannot get a reasonable price for them and I will suddenly have to face extreme deprivation and will be homeless at a time when my husband and son are serving the homeland.

I beg you to inform the relevant authorities of my predicament and use your influence to allow me to stay in my modest home where, although living from hand to mouth, I and my daughter will try to make ends meet until my husband, my breadwinner and protector, and my son return, God willing, from serving our country.

Allow me to draw your kind attention to the urgency of this matter; the police have informed us that, if we do not leave in a few days, irrespective of our appeal which is before the Provincial Police Chief in Budapest, they will implement the harshest measures; we will be interned. Although we have tried to find places to stay, we have not been taken in anywhere because there is apparently an order[3] which forbids anyone taking in those who have been deported on various pretexts from Csík County or the border zone of Transylvania.

In the hope that you will listen to the pleas of an unfortunate woman and that you will give a helping hand to a poor woman pursued by fate, whose only sin is that she was born a Jew.

Yours sincerely,

Mrs. Lipót Török

[handwritten signature]

Typed, signed original in the possession of Ilona Mona.

[1] The number of Jews who could be registered with various professional bodies was limited to 20 percent by Par. 4 of the 1938:XV. Law (the so-called First Anti-Jewish Law) and further reduced to 6 percent by Par. 9 of the 1939:IV. Law (the so-called Second Anti-Jewish Law).

[2] National Hungarian Party: "The only well-established political organization of the Transylvanian Hungarians as a minority in terms of nationality" with the help of which "first and foremost . . . wishes to maintain the continuity of [Hungarian] national unity" (see *Erdélyi Magyar Évkönyv, 1918–1929* [Transylvanian Hungarian Yearbook 1918–1929], Vol I, István Sulyok and László Fritz (eds.). Kolozsvár: Juventus, 1930, pp. 8–10). The Party was formed from the short-lived Hungarian People's Party on December 28, 1922 in Kolozsvár. The Jewish population played an important role in the Party.

18.

July 2, 1942, Budapest

Letter from Viktor Muszély, teacher of religion to Margit Slachta. He informs her that he has passed on a message which was sent to Csíkszereda.

July 2, 1942, Budapest

Dear Sister Margit,

I managed to take the messages to Csíkszereda.[1] The women affected than you from the bottom of their hearts.

Mrs. Herskovits told me that the news I had brought was worth more to them thank you, Sister Margit, could imagine. Because their case is in the hands of the police and not the military HQ.

Their appeal will be heard at the Provincial Police HQ on July 7. If it seems necessary they will ask you for further help at that time.

I pass on their grateful greetings to you.

As for myself, I thank you very much for your help concerning the Central Hotel.[2] I enjoyed myself very much there and in Csík. The sisters were very hospitable in [Csík]somlyó as well.

With respectful greetings I offer myself to your prayers.

Viktor Muszély
Teacher of religion

6. Erzsébet u., Újpest

Handwritten letter in the possession of Ilona Mona.

[1] The contents of the messages are unknown. They may have been in connection with the case mentioned in doc. 16.

[2] The Hotel Centrál in Kolozsvár was owned by the Catholic Church in Transylvania. The Social Sisterhood ran the hotel.

19.

July 10, 1942, Csíkszereda

Letter from Emma Strobl, Social Sister, to Margit Slachta. She tells her about her conversation with the police chief of Csíkszereda.

July 10, 1942, Csíkszereda

Dear Good Sister Margit,

I received your letter dated June 23rd and the enclosed papers the day before yesterday. Thank you for the occasional kind words along with the official ones.

Today, I managed to go down to the police chief, who I have known for some time and who loves and respects our Society so much that he would like his daughter to join us. He had already heard about this case; the Archdeacon must have already talked to him. We had a long talk. His main argument, which was free of the usual hatred but was based on a string of sad experiences, was that we should believe him when he says that they Jews should be removed from here into the heart of the country for the security of our country. He argued that wherever there is a border incident, spying, or inciting discontent, they always find a Jew behind it.[1] And their natural and instinctive self–defense makes them friends of the English and they are too close to Russia here at the Romanian border. Under no circumstances will they be allowed to stay here. And we should not think that this is the will of only one man; it is not his or any one person's decision, a lot of people are backing it.

I tried to tell him about the excesses because, for instance, we saw one sad case here in which a man was taken to the Ukraine on military service on the very day that his wife had died. He was not even allowed to stay for the funeral because the unit was leaving. And then those girls on whose behalf you, dear Sister Margit, intervened . . . but then he brought out a book about Hungarian Communism . . . and asked if we had so easily forgotten.

He also said that one should not see only one side of the coin—and we see only that one—he would like to talk to you, dear Sister Margit, to show you the other side in person. He convinced me in the sense that these unfortuante people will have to leave and that innocent people will have to suffer for crimes of the wrongdoers. They do not have to go to the Ukraine, where the men are to be taken on military service, but to the interior of the country. They received thirty–nine deportation orders: not the families, but each individual, that is, the adults, received one each.[2]

I have visited the Herskovits: they are slightly comforted and are hopeful. I have heard rumors that apparently some kind of "edict of tolerance" has arrived from the Ministry of the Interior (a Székely man told me this), I do not know if it is true. The police chief did not mention anything about it.

I am very sorry, dear Sister Margit, that I was unable to arrange these things better. I think the Archdeacon must have given you a similar answer.[3] I again emphasize that it was not hatred but a string of sad experiences which he expressed. I know, however, that telling him how we view these matters was not worthless and that further measures may reflect some of this but we cannot even think of achieving what we asked for. In any case, the 7th of July has passed and they are still here.[4]

I sent the full list of names to dear Sister Marianne[5] because she had asked for it. If it seems necessary, she will surely send it to you.

I kiss your hands with deep childlike respect.

Sister Gerta[6]

[handwritten signature]

P.S. The police chief has just telephoned again on the subject of our conversation this morning and said that they are not going to implement any sterner measures (taking into custody, arrests, etc.) and they have given them the right to appeal and until an answer is received from a higher level, no steps will be taken against them here. So you see, my visit was by no means worthless, the good God needs nothing but willingness. Thank you again for appointing me to this task.

Typed, signed original, in the possession of Ilona Mona.

[1] However, the monthly police political report for December 1941 states: "The morale of the Jews is low, their behavior is subdued and distrustful. No Zionist or other activity has been detected." (Police Report from December 1941 3/biz.–1942.sz., 1942.I.9*PIA*.)

[2] This contradicts docs. 11 and 16 as well as the text of the deportation order itself, which orders deportation along with all family members.

[3] See doc. 20.

[4] Cf. doc. 18.

[5] Marianne Veress was the leader of the district Society work in Transylvania from 1930 to 1942.

[6] Emma Strobl (1906–1968), director of the maternity home in Csíksomlyó.

20.

July 17, 1942, Csíkszereda

Letter from Archdeacon Ferenc Biró to Margit Slachta. He has intervened on behalf of the deportees but is unwilling to undertake similar tasks again.

July 17, 1941, Csíkszereda

Dear Sister,

I enclose the case of Mrs. H[erskovits].[1] I took her case to the relevant authority on July 10 (we had a service) and received the answer that you have already received an *order* from the highest authority the [?]. I am sorry, but if there is such power *there*, please do not involve me again because I do not accept *this kind* of Church work.[2]

With love,

Ferenc Biró

Archdeacon–priest

Csíkszereda

Handwritten, unsigned visiting card, in the possession of Ilona Mona.

[1] Probably the same as doc. 16.

[2] See doc. 15.

DESTRUCTION OF SLOVAKIAN JEWS AS REFLECTED IN HUNGARIAN POLICE REPORTS

Maria Schmidt

In 1941, the Royal Hungarian Minister of the Interior ordered the commanders of provincial police headquarters to submit monthly political reports on the events occurring in their areas. Reports had to be sent not only to the Public Security Department of the Ministry of the Interior, but also to the newly established State Security Center (*Állambiztonsági Központ*). These summaries yielded information about the right and left wing political movements, all events worthy of being commented upon, the political and economic crimes, and the ethnic–national movements and the Jews. These reports were prepared on the basis of guidelines provided by the Ministry.[1]

Fifteen detailed reports were submitted about the fate of Slovakian Jews.[2] Heads of police of the towns of the *Felvidék* (Upper Province), namely Rozsnyó,[3] Léva,[4] Kassa.[5] Losonc and Rimaszombat[6] sent first–hand accounts of the fate of the Slovakian Jews. In their objective reports, reflecting official police style, they sought answers primarily to the following questions: What was happening to the Jews in Slovakia? To what extent did these events affect Hungary? What police measures were to be taken on the basis of these events?

The Hungarian police officers and their superiors in the Ministry had detailed information about the situation the Slovakian Jews found themselves in. The reports provided information about three distinct phases in the persecution of Jews in Slovakia.[7] The first described the deprivation of rights, robberies, confinements, and threats, which were all preparations for the "Final Solution."[8] These were followed by descriptions of ghettoization: the herding of people into transit and forced labor camps. The last series of reports contained descriptions of the "Final Solution," forced removals, deportations, and transportations to unknown places.

Detailed reports were written for the Hungarian police organizations about the measures taken against the Slovakian Jews. The way the Jews were herded together and deported was described as follows:

> The authorities in the whole of the territory of Slovakia are strictly carrying out the measures made against the Jews living there. They are continuing with the record-keeping and the gathering up of Jews of both sexes between the ages of sixteen and forty-two. Regardless of sex, those Jews reaching the age of sixteen are taken away from their families to unknown places.[9]

> . . . most Slovakian Jews have been deported[10] and only those were allowed to remain whose skills are regarded as necessary. According to reports, even these are to be deported before the end of this year. Deportations are to be carried out by the Hlinka guards. All their belongings have been taken into State possession without compensation.[11]

> In Slovakia the gathering up of Jews is continuing. According to travelers coming from Slovakia, the Hlinka guards, with the help of the German SS, make surprise attacks on pre-selected Jewish families at night. They put them on trucks and transport them. In certain towns and localities, there are only one or two Jews left. The portable belongings of the Jews are placed on auction among the inhabitants, and their fixed property is taken into State possession.[12]

> The Hlinka guards which are carrying out the work of gathering up the Jews have allowed rich Jews to stay in their homes in a lot of cases. According to rumors, these Jews who are temporarily left in their homes, are constantly being sucked dry by the Hlinka guards, because payment of a certain amount of money ensures that they stay in their homes for the time being.[13]

The Ministry of the Interior and the civil servants working in key positions in other governmental organizations were able to receive information about the genocide going on inside Slovakia, from among others, the police reports quoted above. Similar reports arrived via the channels of the Foreign Ministry, the Hungarian Railway Company (MAV), and the various churches. All these sources unanimously confirmed that the planned and comprehensive elimination of the Jewish inhabitants of Slovakia had started. It was well-known that the measures taken against the Jews were of a total nature. Being sent away, the confiscation of possessions without compensation, and the rounding up and transportation of persons to unknown destinations applied without exception to all Slovak inhabitants who were considered to be Jewish. Those whose deportations had not yet been effected were able to stay in their homes only temporarily.

The press censor in Hungary prevented the publicaiton of detailed news concerning the anti–Jewish crusades going on in neighboring countries. The news published here and there and the threatening speeches made by Slovakian politicians, however, called the attention of even the broader public to the horrible realities. It did not remain a secret to the inhabitants of Hungary, therefore, that Nazi Germany, together with the Slovak puppet state, had started the planned elimination of the Jewish inhabitants.

As a result of the increasingly serious anti–Jewish measures, many Slovakian Jews tried to seek refuge amidst their friends and relatives living in Hungary. All of this was of concern to the police authorities because of the great number of Jews crossing the border. Some sources estimated the number of Jews at 12,500,[14] while others at from 7,000 to 8,000.[15] The bringing in of such a large number of people was supported by an organized system of smuggling and forging of documents, besides the help of the relatives and friends themselves. This is why the police officers of the border areas paid so much attention to the prevention of Jewish infiltration. Police officers of high rank[16] were not exaggerating, therefore, when reporting about well–planned and organized actions, the existence of smuggling, and other organizations producing forged documents, and about the highly supportive and helpful attitude of Hungarian Jews.[17]

The Slovakian Jews' attempts to escape are described in the reports of the police officers of Léva and Losonc:

> In the interest of preventing the infiltration of Jews from Slovakia, I have ordered the regular inspection of the homes of Jews. By the end of last month, the anti–Jewish actions taken by the authorities in Slovakia had already resulted in a significant infiltration of Jews towards Hungary. As a result of the measures I have taken in order to prevent this, I have had twenty–seven refugee Jews caught and have handed them over to Slovakian border authorities. Hungarian Jews have been facilitating this infiltration partly as a result of racial considerations, and partly as a result of their

> commitments to their families. They have been providing shelter for those refugees, have been helping them with food and have been trying to organize their transportation to Budapest. . . . I have already started administrative procedures against those who have been providing refuge and assistance to the incomers and have booked sixteen people. Of these, six Jews have been taken into police custody, five have been placed under police supervision, and one is under clandestine supervision.[18]
>
> As I have already mentioned in a previous report to Your Excellency, the State of Slovakia has been putting into effect anti–Jewish procedures so radical that its effect has been to push the number of Jews seeping into Hungary to undesirable levels. It is in vain that I take people in for questioning: they are simply brought in again, not once or twice, but sometimes even up to five times. The whole situation can only exist as it does not because of the deliberate actions or negligence of the Slovakian border authorities. According to confidential information at hand, these officials, and other nonofficial people, are dealing in such smuggling of Jews in return for money. . . . The local Jews do everything to help their Slovakian relatives to come over and it has been confirmed that a whole organization has been set up to assist the smuggling and forging of documents. It is rumored that recently several documents have been faked in Kassa and distributed for use.[19]

In spite of the above-mentioned measures, and as a result of the high level of support and devotion on the part of friends and relatives emphasized in the reports, the Slovakian Jews found refuge in Hungary in significant numbers. Those Jewish inhabitants of Hungary supporting others found themselves under increased supervision by the authorities, who were regularly checking the flats of Jews living in their districts. Even the smallest of telltale signs would result in their detention for police questioning. Those found to be supporting refugees were interned or placed under police supervision, while the refugees themselves had to face repatriation.

The Hungarian authorities, primarily officials of the Ministry of the Interior, were kept informed of the tragedy facing the Slovakian Jews not only from the reports, but also by some members of parliament who stood up against Jewish persecutions.[20] As a result of their intervention, border authorities became more lenient toward the Slovakian refugees and put a temporary halt to their repatriation. Nevertheless, the border police kept up its vigilance as the following report indicates:

> In March the infiltration of Jews from Slovakia showed another increase. Mainly children have been smuggled over, in the knowledge that Hungarian authorities would not send them back. Large numbers of Slovakian Jewish children have already reported to the KEOKH[21] in Budapest and applied for residence permits. Two Jewish women from Kassa, Rozsi Katz and Mrs. Herman Schwarz, have been arrested for smuggling in Jews and producing false documents.[22]

At the beginning of 1943, Sano Mach, the Slovakian Minister of the Interior, announced the resumption of deportations. The Kassa police reported:

> Sano Mach Slovakian Minister of the Interior, in a speech delivered in Rozsahegy on February 8, 1943, announced a merciless struggle against enemy propaganda and stated publicly for the first time that every Jew, irrespective of whether he was up to then exempt, would be deported out of Slovakia. It is a fact that, as early as the 9th and 10th of February, several Jewish families in Rózsahegy who had had residence permits were arrested and taken to internment camps. The news of this spread like wildfire among Slovakian Jews and by the following day the flight toward Hungary had started anew. This fleeing has been welcomed by Slovakian authorities, for in this way, they can cut down on deportation costs payable to the Germans, while still having free use of the possessions left behind by the Jews.[23]

The illegally operating rescue organization, the so-called "Working Group," consisting of members of the Jewish Council of Bratislavia, provided assistance to the Slovakian Jews, and Polish Jews temporarily seeking refuge in Slovakia, in getting to Hungary. They guided the refugees to gathering places which had been set up close to the border. Their ability to go across the border was closely linked to everyday events. One of the methods, which was quite cunning, was based upon cooperation from the Slovakian authorities, while meaning relatively little danger to the refugees themselves. They reported to the local bureau of the state security authorities (*Ustreda Statnej Bezpecnosti*) that people of suspected Hungarian nationality had appeared in Slovakia and had been committing various financial misdemeanors. On the basis of these reports, the security officers ordered the cases to be investigated and the perpetrators to be expelled, and thus deported to Hungary. The "offenders" were given police escort to Presov, and were then taken south to the Hungarian border, which they legally crossed.[24]

Entire organizations were established to smuggle in Slovakian and Polish refugees. Some provided help in return for money, others were undertaken on a voluntary basis. This was reflected in a report from Ungvár:

> In September, the KEOKH and the K Department of Ungvár found out about a smuggling organization from Galicia, through Vereck, Szolyva and Munkács to Budapest, and during the investigation, 50 people were taken into police custody and some of them were from Munkács. This infiltration of people is under constant surveillance, and so far we have managed to catch 250 fleeing Jews and 30 people assisting them.[25]

The Kassa and Rozsnyó police reported:

> It is an outstanding event, that, in contrast to the smuggling in so far of Slovakian Jews, which has decreased to a minimum, a great number of Polish Jews are coming in via Slovakia. In the last month, I have arrested 31 Polish and two Slovakian Jews.[26]

> There is an expected increase in the seeping in of Polish Jews through Slovakia. This is given encouragement by the Slovakian authorities once they have taken possession of all their valuables. In Eperjes, a one-time Jewish timber merchant by the name of Edelmann is providing the organization for smuggling activities, also supported by JOINT. He provides the refugees with cash, dollars and fake German documents.[27]

> The Slovakian government planned to round up a great number of Jews on March 15 and deport them to occupied territories. For varied reasons, however, this did not happen, and rumors have been spreading that the Slovakian government will nonetheless carry out its plan to round up Jews, and Sano Mach, Minister of the Interior, is traveling in person

> in territories densely populated by Jews and is making arrangements in the cases of those Jews who are to be taken. According to rumors, once the Jewish question has been resolved, the Slovakian government wants to begin the application of the Final Solution to the Gypsy question. It wants to put Gypsies into internment camps, in the same way as Jews.[28]

Not long after the announcement of resumption of deportations, the Vatican interceded at the government level. Through its extended diplomatic network, and on the basis of first-hand reports and requests for help sent to Rome, the Holy See was in possession of reliable information concerning the fate of the deportees. Diplomatic notes sent to Prime Minister Vojtech Tuka pointed out that Jews deported to the territories of the Polish province were not put to work, but were slaughtered in various camps. Slovakian bishops gave support to the protest of the Vatican and in this way the Jews, most of whom had converted to the Christian faith, and therefore exempt from deportations, received a period of grace.

> Deportation of Jews out of Slovakia has been temporarily halted, but rumor has it that, during the summer of this year, all the Jews will be shipped off and the number of baptized and exempted Jews will have decreased even further. Another census of the Jews has been carried out, and from this, new actions can be expected.[29]

> They have recently put an end to the rounding up of Jews and those who remain in the territory of Slovakia are employed at various levels in the work force. The round-up and placement in internment camps of Gypsies, similarly to Jews, has also been halted for the time being, and only some Gypsies who shun work have been taken to forced labor camps.[30]

> In Slovakia, the resettlement orders concerning Jews and Gypsies have been altered to the effect that it doesn't include Gypsies who can play music, so now even the brick-laying Gypsies are learning to play music.[31]

> The Slovakian Minister of the Interior has again limited the traveling of Jews and in future they will not be allowed to travel or leave their permanent place of residence. They are given permission to travel only in exceptional cases. Those

> traveling in violation of this order will be placed in labor camps.[32]
>
> From one of the internment camps close to the Hungarian-Slovakian border, several Jews have escaped and are supposedly hurrying toward Dobsina in order to get onto Hungarian territory. The further round-up of Jews is not occurring and the Jews left behind can temporarily carry on with their civil occupations within certain limits.[33]
>
> The distribution of Jewish land has started in Slovakia. . . . 150 hold (85,50 hectares) of Jewish land has been shared out among the members of the Hlinka Guard. There will again be strict steps concerning the Jewish deportations in Slovakia and they are going to take back all the special exemptions. As a result of this, an infiltration into Hungary from among the Slovakian Jews is expected. The fever to obtain documents has started again among the Slovakian Jews and there is an especially great demand for certificates of Hungarian citizenship and Hungarian passports. It is supposed that the Jews to be included in the count will be placed in a camp in Nyitra, from where they will be transported to the territory of the Polish province.[34]

Those Jews left behind in Slovakian territory after the 1942 deportations met their fate in the fall of 1944. After the crushing of the Slovakian uprising at the end of September, 12,000 to 13,000 Jews were sent to Auschwitz, and some to Sachsenhausen and Theresienstadt.

The deportation of the Slovakian Jews was carried out from the immediate region of the Hungarian border, and most of those taken were Hungarian-speaking. Almost all of them had family or friends living in Hungary. The reports quoted in this study gave a relatively detailed description of the events and tried to be objective. The police officials restrained themselves from providing any comment on the events, and added neither positive nor negative opinions. The measures taken against the Slovakian Jews primarily meant for them a problem of dealing with foreigners, and they saw as their main task the prevention of these foreigners from infiltrating into Hungary, and to punish the Hungarians who helped them.

In 1943–44, i.e., until the German occupation of Hungary, the government's policy indicated more flexibility and patience toward the refugees and their helpers, which caused an increase in the trust Hungarian Jews had for their political leadership.

The reports, as well as the number of Jews that were allowed to come into Hungary—seven to eight thousand—indicate that the Jewish inhabitants of the northern parts of Hungary not only experienced from close quarters what was happening in their neighborhood, but most probably also had the opportunity to get first–hand information from the refugees themselves about what they had had to go through.

The Jewish and non–Jewish inhabitants from the northern part of Hungary became eyewitnesses to the genocide of the Slovakian Jews. Their feelings of anxiety and terror are well–reflected in the following report, this time in connection with the Hungarian Jews:

> There is panic among the Jews that as soon as the Russian army reaches the Carpathians, the Jews who live in the areas adjoining the front will be interned. They can also, however, envisage a worse fate: the retreating Germans will "get rid of" the Jews. The Jews are also afraid of the possibility of air raids (a possibility also recognized by the authorities) because in this event they expect possibly bloody anti–Jewish actions by members of extreme right–wing movements.[35]

> The Jews are afraid of enemy air raids on Hungary because they fear that pogroms would be carried out by the extreme right wing, while in the other case the Germans would not tolerate the presence of Jews close to the front or in the adjoining areas, and they would solve the problem of evacuation in the same fashion as they have done in Poland.[36]

The Hungarian Jews were more closely touched by the tragedy affecting their Slovakian neighbors than the similar fate of the Polish, Austrian, or German Jews, and this time not only because mostly Hungarian–speakers were bieng dragged to death, but also because they were coming to realize that the net was tightening around them. Their fears of "evacuation in the same fashion as they have done in Poland" and that "the retreating Germans will 'get rid of' the Jews" became a tragic reality in the summer of 1944. The genocide of the Hungarian Jews occurred in the same stages, from "preparation" and "concentration" to "the Final Solution," as had already occurred in neighboring countries. The fate intended for the Jews couldn't have been a surprise for the Hungarian government and this is proved beyond doubt by the contents of the above–mentioned reports.

Notes

1 This author received about 450 reports obtained from 80 different places, all written between June 1941 and May 1944. This article deals only with the portion of the reports pertaining to the situation of the Jews. For other aspects of the reports, see Maria Schmidt, "Provincial Police Reports—New Insights into Hungarian Jewish History" in *Yad Vashem Studies*, Jerusalem, Vol. 19, 1989.

2 The number of reports were as follows: 1942, 8; 1943, 6; 1944, 1. The reports are filed in the archives of the Party Historical Institute (*Párttörténeti Intézet*) under the following numbers: 641.f.2/1941–1944, 651.f.2/1941-7-6000. Dr. Edit Petri was my assistant in the selection of the material.

3 Six reports.

4 Three reports.

5 Four reports.

6 One report each.

7 In the territory of Slovakia, which became independent in March 1939, there were, according to the data of the December 1940 census, 2.5 million inhabitants, of which 88,951 (3.6 percent) were Jewish.

8 Early on, in the first month after its foundation, the young Slovakian state passed an anti–Jewish law and later, in September 1941, a so–called Jewish Codex was put into practice. This contained 300 anti–Jewish measures, all seeking to limit the political, social, and economic rights of the Slovakian citizens considered to be Jewish.

9 Rozsnyó, June 1942, 651.f. 2/1942-7-6006.

10 According to information obtained from *SS–Hauptsturmführer* Dieter von Wisliczeny, one of the coordinators of the deportations, 52,000 Slovakian Jews were transported to Auschwitz, Treblinka, Lublin, or Majdanek between March 26 and June 26, 1942. The fate of the remaining 36,000, most of them converted to Christianity, was suspended until the fall of 1944.

11 Rimaszombat, July 1942 651.f.2/1942-7-6006.

12 Rozsnyó, July 1942 651.f.2/1942-7-6006.

13 Rozsnyó, August 1942 651.f.2/1942-7-6006.

14 Ladislav Lipscher, "The Jews of Slovakia 1939-1945" in *The Jews of Czechoslovakia*, p. 201.

[15] Rezsö Kasztner, *Bericht des Jüdischen Rettungskommittee aus Budapest.* [Basel]: Vaad Ezra V'Hatzala Bo' Budapest, [1946], p. 12. The report of this Budapest Zionist Rescue Committee, dated November 22, 1943, estimated the number of Slovakian Jews arriving in Hungary between 1942 and 1943 at seven to eight thousand.

[16] These were either the commanders of police headquarters, or their deputies.

[17] The Jewish inhabitants of Slovakia formed an organic part of Hungarian–speaking Jewry in terms of language and culture.

[18] Léva, May 1942 651/f.2/1942-6006

[19] Losonc, June 1942 651.f.2/1942-7-6006.

[20] See Maria Schmidt, "Közöny, szeretetlenség, gyülölet" [Ignorance, Lack of Love, Hatred]. *Historia*, Budapest, vol. 10, no. 2-3, 1988. See also her "Action of Margit Slachta to Rescue Slovakian Jews."' *Danubian Historical Studies*, vol. 1, no. 1, Spring 1987, and "Margit Slachta's Activities in Preventing the Deportation of Slovakian Jews" in *Remembering for the Future.* Oxford, 1988. (Conference Proceedings, Theme I, pp. 207-11.)

[21] *Külföldieket Ellenörzö Országos Központi Hatoság* [National Bureau for Control of Foreigners].

[22] Kassa, April 6, 1943, 651.f.2/1943-4-1006.

[23] Kassa, February 1943 651.f.2/1943-4-1006.

[24] Report by Dr. Wohlstein-Voldan, former member of the Central Jewish Committee and one of the organizers of the above–mentioned rescue activity, dated December 10, 1967, as quoted by Lipscher, "Jews of Slovakia," p. 222.

[25] Ungvár, September 1943 651/f.2/1943-4-1006.

[26] Kassa, September 1943 651.f.2/1943-4-1006.

[27] Kassa, September 1943 651/f.1/1943-1006.

[28] Rozsnyó April 1943 651.f.2/1943-4-1106.

[29] Kassa, May 1943 651.f.2/1943-4-1006.

[30] Rozsnyó, June 1943 651.f.2/1943-4-1006.

[31] Kassa, August 1943 651.f.2/1943-4-1006.

[32] Rozsnyó, September 1943 651.f.2/1943-4-1006.

[33] Rozsnyó, November 1943 651.f.2/1943-4-1006.

[34] Kassa, January 1944 651.f.2/1943-4-1006.

[35] Kassa, November 1943.

[36] Kassa, January 1944.

THE FORCED LABOR OF HUNGARIAN JEWS AT THE FORTIFICATION OF THE WESTERN BORDER REGIONS OF HUNGARY, 1944–45

Szabolcs Szita

This paper presents the main characteristics of the German labor camps, which employed Hungarian Jewish forced labor to build the fortifications in the region of the two frontier counties of western Hungary. Their history is an important, but only partially known, chapter of the Holocaust in Hungary.

On December 3, 1944, 2,000 Hungarian labor servicemen arrived from the Hungarian capital in closed railway cars to Pozsonyligetfalu (German, Engerau; Slovakian, Petrzalka), annexed to the German Reich in October 1938. The German command of the defense works distributed them into groups of 150, and forced each worker to wear a yellow star on his clothing. The deportees were quartered in old barracks, but mostly in farm buildings, lofts, barns, and cement floors. Even on the first night, many suffered frostbite and a number of people died from exposure to cold.

The Engerau labor camp consisted of two major units, divided into seven sections. One of the major units was a military barracks along the Köpcsény (Kittsee) road, while the second was located in a field between the railway line connecting Vienna and Pozsonyligetfalu and the Matador works. It is impossible to definitely identify the location because of the subsequent construction of buildings.[1] The sections of the camp were called Auliesl, Fürst, Schinawek, Wiesengasse, Leberfinger, Bahnhofstrasse, and Krankenrevier. They were named after local owners and local streets.

The prisoners of the labor camps building the fortifications of the Poszony bastion were mainly engaged in work along the "construction stripes" (*Baustreifen*) that extended outward from the Hungarian–German–Slovakian border toward Köpcsény–Berg–Hainburg. In addition to labor along the fortifications, the prisoners were also sent to work at the lumber yard of Adolph Hersch and the local unit of the Semperit. The Germans quartered the French, Yugoslav, and Ukrainian workers in barracks along the fortification works, and also employed Soviet prisoners of war who were kept separated from the others.

As in the other camps of the defense line, the Hungarian deportees were guarded by SA (*Sturmabteilung*) personnel and by so–called political leaders (*Politischer Leiter*). Initially, the SA patrol was under the command of Edmund Kratky, who was later replaced by *Wachkommandannt* Falkner.[2] The headquarters of the 24–member SA patrol, active around the clock, was set up at Köpcsény. A railway station platoon (*Bahnhofstreif*) was also organized. Its task was to supervise the station, the cars, and their passengers. At times the patrol would fire at suspicious individuals without any provocation and would also take aim at would–be escapees.[3]

The ruthlessly driven Hungarian deportees were mainly employed felling trees and did quarrying, in addition to digging trenches. They had to work seven–day weeks with a bare minimum of food. The daily march from the quarters meant a great strain for the increasingly exhausted people. Prisoners who collapsed would be shot and buried on the spot by SS guards. SS camp commander Starzinski allowed the slaughter as a result of which the number of the camp inmates was constantly decreasing. Furthermore, young Hungarian Arrow Cross thugs who had been transferred to the Reich would engage in driveby shooting at the Hungarian Jews who had to work along the highway.[4] Among the prisoners were the film director Róbert Bán, the actor József Gáti, and the writer Andor Endre Gelléri.

Initially, the population of Pozsonyligetfalu (2,000 to 2,500 of whom were Hungarians) tried to help the workers. As a sign of sympathy some residents threw pieces of bread from their windows to the workers dragging themselves along the road. However, the SA guards shot at the open windows. As a consequence of such terrorism the streets were depopulated and the curtains drawn whenever the groups of servicemen appeared.

On March 29, 1945 the Hungarian deportees of the Niederdonau Defense Line were made ready to march because of the approaching front. Work on the trenches was abandoned and the camp command prepared for the withdrawal and westward transfer of the "muscular power still fit for use." That afternoon, the Austrian SA guards murdered one female and 102 male captives in the dispensary.[5] At 10:30 p.m. between 1,500 and 1,600 Hungarian survivors were marched off on foot. Many of the limping, emaciated, frostbitten victims were unable to keep up with the march and were shot by the guards.

The columns of victims arrived at Bad–Altenburg after the long march through Berg and Hainburg. The captives were camped at a river port on the Danube and were subsequently transported by three river barges towed by the tugboat *Dyonisos.* Unfed for the six days of the journey, the starving, sick, and increasingly apathetic pariahs arrived at the Mauthausen concentration camp on April 6. After Pozsonyligetfalu was returned to Czechoslovakia, five common graves were opened at the northwestern wall of the village cemetery, where the corpses of 460 prisoners were found,[6] of which 86 could be identified on the basis of their blood–soaked papers and Hungarian military documents.

The 700 Hungarian servicemen of the "middle" section of the defense line were crammed into an emptied wine cellar on a farm between Fertöfehéregyháza (Donnerskirchen) and Feketeváros (Purbach) in December 1944.[7] They were employed felling trees and building fortifications. The senseless toil, the daily beatings, the tortures of the morning and evening roll calls lasting for hours combined with freezing temperatures and typhus to cause many deaths. Nikolaus Schorn, in command of the fortifications of the Austrian segment, and Otto Seitz of the SA were particularly brutal.

Schorn usually beat the prisoners with a thick club, and a guard named Laska hit the marching men with a shovel. Victims of brutality lay everywhere in the work areas outside Fertöfehéregyháza. Execution was the answer to any act considered "punishable" by the guards. Schorn, who had earlier been an *Ortsgruppenführer* (district leader) gave a premium of ten cigarettes to the guards for every Hungarian Jew killed, and he even threatened those Jews who were ill or absent from work with gassing .[8] The seriously ill would be "cured" by isolation in a stable without windows or a door; the feverish would he lain in snow without garments. This is how a survivor described the situation:

> Whoever was taken to the "hospital" knew that he had to die, while anybody not reporting at the morning call, not standing sufficiently straight, cowering, or pulling a blanket over himself, was inevitably sent there. People were dying off like flies. . . . Who was not shot was frozen and if he

tried to crawl into the camp he was shot dead.[9]

The camp set up in the wine cellar outside the village was evacuated on March 29, 1945. The Hungarian prisoners were marched off toward Mauthausen. The common graves, when exhumed, contained more than 500 corpses at the outskirts of Feketeváros. The Hungarians found their final place of rest in the martyrs' graveyard of the Jewish cemetery of Rákoskeresztúr in Budapest.

The servicemen of the fortifications, about 1,110 people,[10] were quartered in the drying and storage rooms of the sugar mill of Cinfalva (Siegendorf), 16 km west of Sopron. They were set to work on anti–tank traps, trenches, roadblocks, or on the railway lines between Somfalva and Cinfalva. The later reports of the survivors at Cinfalva speak about "tolerable" treatment and quarters, and at times even about the occasional help of the Austrian population. No data remain about executions and tortures.

Yet large numbers were exposed to rain and snow, as they were working outdoors; they also suffered various injuries. The meager food supply did not cover even a fragment of the laborers' daily needs. The morning "coffee" was only black water. As a "supplement" to the daily soup made of potato skin, the prisoners were forced to consume dried sugar beet, slices of beet that otherwise would have been used for animal fodder, and molasses that they chanced upon. Their lines were thinned by colitis, typhus, and general debilitation.

In March 1945 almost two–thirds of the prisoners of the Cinfalva camp were emaciated, injured, or sick. On March 25 the journalist and poet János Vajda fell victim and was interred in a paper bag. His remains were not located until 1961.[11] When the camp was evacuated on March 27 and 28, the Nazis marched off about 300 to 400 prisoners able to walk—and work—from Cinfalva. They went partly on foot, and after an eight–day train journey they arrived in Mauthausen. The sick, who had remained at Cinfalva, experienced the joy of liberation there on April 1.[12]

In December 1944, Fertörákos, famous for its Roman quarry, was also one of the stations for the so–called "protected" labor service companies. These were protected by the legations of neutral states until November, when between the 27 and 29 they were put into railway cars at the Józsefváros station of Budapest.[13] The Germans allocated barns, dilapidated sheds, occasionally pens and lofts for the camp. In sum, 110 labor servicemen were jammed in. Papier–mâché barracks were erected along impromptu streets while earthen huts were built to serve as "quarters." György Tamássi (Wagner), one of the leading lights of Hungarian scientific literature, died in one of these hovels at Christmastime.[14] In December Antal Szerb, an eminent figure in Hungarian literature, spent ten days in the village with the erstwhile company of labor servicemen no. 701/304. He was martyred. Géza Ranschburg, a world-famous psychologist, ended his life as a prisoner of Fertőrákos. His father, Pál Ranschburg, died of starvation while in hiding in Budapest.

István Dobi, a well known politician of the Smallholders' Party, did his military service for months at Fertőrákos. In his autobiography Dobi described the labor camp as the "harshest and cruelest place of work in Hungary," where the commanders "did all they could to utilize all the horrible methods and means at their disposal to torment and destroy those poor Jews."[15]

Some of the "pastimes" of the SS at Fertörákos included shooting at the barracks or at the laborers. The following is from Sándor Hermann's testimony:

> The young SS had their fun with us. On holidays, when they were drunk—or even sober—they picked out some Jew whom they disliked because of his nose and played target practice. They always hit their target. . . . The names of the dead were not written down or otherwise recorded. They were thrown into a common pit.[16]

Any prisoner attempting to escape was also executed.

In February 1945 the Todt Organization had 160, and the SS 240 members at Fertörákos. The Hungarian Labor Service companies 954/1 and 954/2 were there too. In early March their membership grew further, so that the Hungarian military units now consisted of 2,150 people. The number of the labor servicemen was about 1,200 to 1,400.[17]

The extremely violent and rapid evacuation of Fertőrákos started on March 27. Prisoners unable to work or too weak to proceed any further on foot were killed by the SS. The columns started off along Lake Fertő toward Mauthausen during the night of the 27th and 28th. The number of the Fertőrákos victims can be put at around 400, 240 of whom were buried in the Jewish cemetery of Rákoskeresztúr in Budapest after their exhumation in 1946; the identity of 163 of them is unknown.[18]

Hungarian Jews were transferred into the camp to work on the fortifications at Somfalva (Schattendorf) in the neighborhood of the Austrian Cinfalva and the Hungarian Ágfalva in early 1945. Their composition was rather mixed: some of them came from Komárom, from the concentration camps of Györ, from Jewish groups collected in the brickyards and barracks of Sopron and from the remnants of the erstwhile labor service companies. The Somfalva camp was located in the empty building of the village school.

Local work on the fortifications was stepped up in mid–January. A network of approaches and in some places anti–tank trenches were built under the supervision of the Todt Organization. The ragged prisoners worked in rain and snow, and mud. In the morning they were given small rations of "black coffee" (usually grape seeds), bread, and thin soup.

Because of the stepped–up work the SA guards treated the forced laborers of Somfalva "tolerably." No records survive about brutalities and executions. According to the opinion of a number of people the treatment was influenced by the Germans' interest in retaining the prisoners' capacity to work. Spotted fever, however, did not spare the laborers. On March 28, 1945 the sick were left behind and about 300 people were marched off to Mauthausen under SA supervision.[19]

The first group arrived at Agfalva camp, in the south section of the Niederdonau Defense Line, in early December 1944. They came via Hegyeshalom and Sopron. The German staff in control of the fortifications settled in the village with "120 persons for the time being." They intended eventually to concentrate 1,200 Jewish workers there.[20] Some of the prisoners had already been to the Ukraine and the Carpathians. They constructed roads, dug shelters, and transported ammunition; or else they pulled and pushed the horse–drawn "wagons" lagging behind on the steep slopes of the passes. Their interim station was the brickyard of Kassa, where a reception camp was set up, and the prisoners reached the foothills of the Alps after a two–week train journey.

The majority of the laborers of Ágfalva had been seized in Budapest. The camp was divided into groups of 50, headed by a "Jupo" (*Judepolizist;* Jewish police), appointed from among the prisoners by the SA, and with whom the SA would communicate for the most part. Again rations were slim.

At dawn, the labor groups, the sick and the well alike, stood in line for roll call along the road nearest to their own barn. Even the dead had to be carried by the comrades. According to the register of

Agfalva the first two deaths occurred on December 11, 1944; one was caused by "a shot penetrating the skull." The other was caused by "a shot penetrating the lungs."[21]

By late January 1945 typhus was already raging among the exhausted men dressed in rags and living in squalid conditions. On February 8, 120 cases of typhus were registered.[22] From then on, the Germans began to isolate the suffering prisoners out of fear for the health of their own soldiers. These unfortunates were totally abandoned.

On February 20 the Ágfalva camp still had 685 inmates. The novelist Tibor Székely died there. The reporter János Elek was also a prisoner, as was the journalist Ferenc Doros, who died there at the age of 33.

In early March there were six smaller German units with 442 men at Ágfalva. The number of workers at the trenches was 600, and that of the five different Hungarian units was 570.[23] The labor camp was evacuated around March 26. On May 18, 1945 the notary of Ágfalva reported that "altogether 591 labor servicemen died" in the village.[24] During the course of later exhumations the corpses of 820 prisoners were found at the fence of the local cemetery and along the railway line leading to Sopron; the identity of 224 of them remains unknown.[25]

Hardly any documents exist about the fate of the Jewish labor servicemen who had to work in the city of Sopron, which was actually more of a way station along the German–Hungarian frontier. Some buildings of the Lenk and Steiner Brickyard in the Pozsony district of the city, the farm of Sopronpuszta, the Jacobi factory, and the university hostel, then under construction, served as concentration centers and quarters. The Germans used the south railway station of Sopron as a reception and distribution point for the human shipments arriving from Zurány beyond the border, from Hegyeshalom, and from the *Felvidék* (Upper Province).

The labor servicemen and prisoners of the labor camps around Sopron worked on the shipments at the military food depots of Sopron, unloaded and reloaded freight cars, restored railway lines and equipment after bombings, and cleared away the ruins and snow from the roads. They also buried the corpses.

With the approach of the front, more and more labor service units were marched through Sopron for work in the German Reich. The writer Géza Hegedüs was a member of one of the columns in mid–February 1945. He spent two days in the brickyard of Sopron with the auxiliary labor service company 101/334 on their way to the concentration camps of Mauthausen and subsequently Günskirchen.[26] People suffering from typhus and frostbite, who were unable to endure the further ordeals and marches, were lying on the straw–covered floor of the low–ceilinged, doorless and windowless room that contained the oven. József Grätzer, the Hungarian king of crossword puzzles and secretary to Frigyes Kartinhy, the noted writer, died of typhus here.[27] He was known for having edited the bulky crossword column of *Szinházi Élet* [Theatrical Life].

The Todt Organization moved to Sopronbánfalva, 4 km north of Sopron in early November 1944. The laborers working on the fortifications immediately increased their output of wood cutting and stone quarrying. They used the lumber mills too. On December 2, SA guards escorted to Sopronbánfalva 1,000 people from Budapest.[28] They were members of the so–called protected labor service companies of the Hungarian Armed Forces. Deprived of their units and "protection," they were put in railway freight cars between November 27 and 29, 1944. They spent the first night in the open, forced to lay down, in groups of 50, in the mud of the main square.

The next day, after arrival, they were divided into labor units and sent off 6 km away up a hill (and this would become their daily routine) to fell trees, transport logs, and make planks. Soon, they had to dig trenches. In a few weeks, the now–emaciated laborers were felled by cold, their wounds, malnutrition, or lack of hygiene. Of a 57–member platoon, only six were still alive by the end of March.[29]

From the second month of the existence of the camp, the guards would execute two to six people daily, by revolver, the butt of their guns, or with clubs. The slaughtered, frozen pariahs were left unburied for days along the streets of the village. Mrs. Z. Magyar, a former resident of Sopron, recollects the scene as follows:

> I spent the last, most fateful four or five months in the rock cellars of the Carmelite monastery of Sopronbánfalva together with my parents and the inhabitants of the neighborhood. As the population of the Lövérek were seeking refuge in the rock cellars against he increasingly frequent air–raids, we often met the unfortunate labor servicemen carrying their bleeding, dead comrades on makeshift stretchers under cover, presumably to the common grave beyond the forest. At times we met three to four such groups until

we reached the monastery. . . .

The miserable labor servicemen were quietly asking for food from people hurrying toward the monastery. . . .

Only quietly mumbling we kept on repeating that food would be in the bushes. And there it was always as the inhabitants of the neighborhood were trying to share the little they had with their miserable fellow human beings.[30]

In mid-January 1945 the inmates suffered eight to ten dead daily. On January 26 the composer-conductor Sándor Venetianer (known by his stage name, Vándor) died of frostbite at the age of 43 in the Poropatich rolling mill.[31] On February 12 László Reiter, the 49-year-old graphic artist and writer, and the founder of the Amicus publishing house fell victim; on February 22 the 49-year-old writer Jenő Jób succumbed.[32] Skin diseases and lice, typhus and dysentery were common among the local population, while scarlet fever decimated the children.

On March 28 the defense line was still being built at Sopronbánfalva. The builders of the fortifications marched off even the civilian population increasingly reluctant to perform the obligatory military work. At night, however, the prisoners of the labor camp were made to form a column and the approximately 350 men still capable of walking were started off to the west. The sick captives were ordered put on carts by the SA guards and were transported to the Sopron brick works for "convalescence."

On March 29 the German military force mined some streets of the village and set up anti-aircraft guns. Resistance, however, had become meaningless because of the danger of encirclement, so the German and Hungarian military units quickly left the Sopronbánfalva section of the Reich defense line. The fortifications took the lives of 532 Jewish prisoners at Sopronbánfalva.[33]

The camp of Balf was considered to be one of the biggest labor camps of the region. It consisted of barns behind the houses, which were often wet because of ground water. Their floors were covered by damp straw. The first major contingent of about 1,000 servicemen arrived at Balf through Sopron and Fertőrákos early in December 1944. These people, including a number of well-known Hungarian writers and artists, were practically kidnapped from Budapest by Eichmann's *Sonderkommando* with the help of the Arrow Cross leaders, who even ignored their own international obligations.

At Balf and its vicinity, work on the fortifications was supervised by SS–*Sturmbannführer* Berghofer, transferred here from Kismarton (Eisenstadt), commander of the Stellungsbau, and *Ortskommandant* Fröhlich and his deputy Kutnik, while the technical works were controlled by chief engineer Eberth, head of the Todt Organization. The Gestapo and ranking Nazis and SS members found quarters in the excellent baths facilities of Balf.

A number of Hungarian writers, poets, and journalists died at Balf. On December 16 Antal Szerb wrote the following:

> Generally speaking the place where we are now, Balf, is a cursed place and our life is very bad in all respects. And by now I have no other hope left but that the war would end before long; this is what still keeps up my spirit.[34]

However, his hope did not materialize: Arrow Cross guards beat him to death on January 27, 1945. Soon afterward, the essayist Gábor Halász and the journalist Dénes (Deutsch) Ivor met their tragic fate.[35]

The first death of a labor serviceman was recorded on November 21, 1944.[36] By January, the general lack of hygiene, infections, and famine had taken their toll. In early February it had to be recognized that typhoid fever had infested the camp. The only help available was their doctor, a fellow–prisoner, who could exempt them from the daily drudgery. Those who had infectious diseases—their number can be estimated at around 400 by the records of 1945—were transported to Ilonamajor near Hidegség, where the SS executed them.

By March 1945 typhus was claiming twenty to thirty victims a day. On March 8 György Sárközi, one of the leaders of the movement of populist writers, lost his life.[37] Lajos Gosztonyi, a journalist of the social democratic *Népszava* [People's Voice], was dragged away from the Felvidék to Balf. The journalist Jenő Komlós and the teacher Bertalan Szikla died there as well.

In March the pace had to be stepped up because of the approaching Soviet army. Almost 2,000 men were in the village on the shore of Lake Fertő as members of the German units and there were 326 people in the Stellungsbau and pioneer units.[38] Evacuation was ordered on March 27 and the labor servicemen were marched off to the west.

At Balf the sick were left without nursing, medicines, or food in the numbered, so–callled sick barns. On March 31 an SS military police unit collected those still able to walk and drove about 185 people to the outskirts of the village, to Teknő Street, and shot them.[39]

At Harka (Magyarfalva since 1947), near the border, the remnants of the labor servicemen from the front and Jewish girls and women called up in October 1944 in Budapest were at work. Previously, they had to report to the brickyard of Óbuda and were subsequently marched off to Hegyeshalom and Zurány, leaving behind a number of victims on the way.

In late December the number of inmates at Harka reached 1,800.[40] In the ceaseless drudgery at the fortifications the laborers, who were forbidden to use the wells, were soon infested by lice. An epidemic of spotted fever promptly broke out, and hundreds died of starvation.

Nevertheless, productivity had to be kept up. At Harka, this was usually assured by beating the "recalcitrant." It was under those conditions that the actor György Nagy lost his life at the age of 40, on January 8, 1945. The 36–year–old Ervin Vándor, foreign correspondent of the *Pester Lloyd* also died there.[41]

On February 12, 1,068 cases of typhus were reported from the camps of the Sopron region. Of them, 343 labor servicemen and two civilians were from Harka.[42] One day later Miklós Vető, a contributor to *Népszava,* was among those who were thrown into a pit, along with the other typhus–infected victims. The poet, 25, was brought to Harka after a long period in hiding, during which time he lost two of his companions.

On March 29 the Germans ordered the evacuation of Harka. Those laborers still capable of work were gathered in the center of the village and marched off to Mauthausen. According to the memoir of Tibor Barabás, the trench workers left behind went into hiding. By March 31, they had already heard about the massacre of Balf by the SS.[43] In the confusion of the evacuation they were not executed, but 650 of the prisoners of the Harka camp would not live to see its liberation on April 1.[44]

Initially, trench workers arrived at the camp of Kópháza from among the women of Budapest. They were immediately sent to dig trenches. However, the work proved to be too hard, and 1,200 people were therefore transferred to the German Reich on December 18. They were replaced by about a thousand men who had been auxiliary labor servicemen of the Hungarian army, and the camp was increased to 1,800 men by the beginning of 1945.[45]

The prisoners of Kópháza were made to work from dawn to dusk. Several kilometers from the village they had daily to dig out at least two cubic meters of frozen earth, to make obstacles, and to clear approaches. The daily misery of trench digging was complemented by punishments thought up by the guards. Some prisoners were shut into ice pits without blankets or food for several days, after they had been beaten with a stick by the SS commander as additional punishment. Very few survived.

Dr. Endre Csatkai, a cultural historian, was a prisoner at Kópháza. Dr. Gyula Mérei, professor of history, arrived here as a member of Labor Service Company No. 101/12. János Honti, a folklorist, fell victim at the age of 34. Dr. J. Mohácsi was among those who committed suicide; she jumped into a well.[46] Her husband, a writer, poet, and translator, died in the freight car deporting him on July 8, 1944.

In early March 1945, 1,374 German soldiers were relocated to the village. Another thousand were stationed there for the hoped-for *Volksturm*, the "popular uprising" the Germans had planned as a last-ditch stand. There were another 135 men attached to the *Pionier Abteilung*.[47] On March 28 and 29, the Germans abandoned all their previous plans. They evacuated Kópháza, near Sopron. The SS marched off about 1,000 prisoners still capable of walking. The fortifications took the lives of 620 prisoners.[48]

At Nagycenk the 2,600 laborers were quartered in the machine sheds of a sugar mill and in a labor camp of barracks and barns. The SS placed labor servicemen from Carpatho-Ruthenia—their train was at the Nagycenk railway station—and Soviet prisoners of war at the disposal of the organization building the fortifications. The prisoners were building railway lines in the erstwhile sugar mill and at the railway station, where they dug approaches, anti-tank trenches, and obstacles.

As usual, death was the almost inevitable lot of the Jewish laborers. Within weeks dozens were carried off into the common grave 1.5 km away in Farkasverem.

From early 1945 a number of people fell victim to typhus. Already on February 8, 600 cases were reported.[49] Six days later, Dr. Hagen, the German medical officer, reported that "800 of the 1,200 Jews of Nagycenk fell ill of suspected spotted fever and 28 of them had died."[50] The February 16 note of the deputy prefect of Sopron County did not speak of any improvement.

Thd deaths of 864 prisoners were registered at Nagycenk until February 25. After that date, the registration was abandoned.

On March 27 and 28 the evacuation of the Nagycenk labor camp began. On the afternoon of the 30th SS soldiers drove those prisoners unable to walk into their quarters and set fire to the barracks. Some broke out, but were mowed down by the guns of the SS. Others who escaped but recaptured were also shot. The death toll was 244.[51]

Nagycenk was liberated the next day. The 1,180 victims of fascism there at Nagycenk were represented by the crooked line of burnt human corpses among the ruins surrounding the sugar mill.

At Hidegség, on the shore of Lake Fertő, the first arrivals were mostly women. Many of them, as elsewhere, became emaciated.[52] The prisoners secretly exchanged their belongings for food, which covered only a fragment of their caloric needs.

On December 28, 1944 the sick were isolated and 63 of them (including *Jupos*) were executed before the rest were put into railway trucks.[53] Those who were still suited for work were taken to Bergen–Belsen by the Germans; they were replaced by men brought from the Kassa brickyard. The engineer István Horváth arrived at Hidegség with remnants of Labor Service Company No. 108/34. As a survivor he gave a report of camp life, of the fate of the prisoners of Hidegség:

> Typhus, utter exhaustion, frost, and shots destroyed hundreds of innocent people, and nobody knew when his turn would come, when would he be hit by a lethal bullet. We were sunk to the level of a vegetating way of life, just like animals. We went if we had to and were driven, and those who could not keep up and sat down, were shot dead. We had to dig trenches and people froze to death in the trenches. There was straw sickness as well. It meant that apathetic and indifferent people who felt that as human beings they were unable to continue this beastly life, simply dug themselves into the straw and lay there apathetically, until they died.[54]

Reporting about the situation on March 2, 1945, Dr. Hagen acknowledged that there was a "larger number" of typhus cases at Hidegeség, and that it had spread to the population of the small village by the labor servicemen.[55] A few days later the health situation of the military units was assessed, but no further reports were issued about the number and fate of the prisoners working on the fortifications.

When the camp at Hidegeség was evacuated on March 28, about 400 laborers were still able to walk. Earlier, 200 or 300 were buried in a common grave. Medical student Ervin J. Heller, who returned from Günskirchen later on, remembered that:

> There are horribly mutilitated corpses. People destroyed by pick–axe, or shot in the face, who were murdered by Hungarian SS, naturally without any reason. The Hunyadi anti–tank grenadiers were the assassins. Boys of 17 and 20, who killed without a wink, out of joy.[56]

In early November 1944, 600 women were compelled by SS troops to do labor service and earmarked for deportation from the Hungarian capital. They were sent to the emptied stables of Ilonamajor (Ilkamajor), belonging to Hidegség. They dug approaches, trenches, and did the earth work of anti–tank structures under the supervision of armed German guards and Hungarian "Jew supervisors" called up in mid–November from the neighboring villages.

As their output did not reach the standard demanded by the builders, Eichmann's *Sonderkommando* succeeded in acquiring suitable male labor in Budapest by laying their hands on the "protected" companies, and they were replaced by labor servicemen transferred from the eastern front. In the second half of December the female prisoners kept in the farm were transported beyond the border—like their counterparts at Harka and Kópháza–presumably to Lichtenwörth near Wiener–Neustadt.

In late December 400 male laborers arrived from Kassa.[57] Thus the total number of prisoners rose to 700 or 800. According to the later testimony of witnesses recorded by the people's courts, the machine guns of the SS killed a number of people along the forest near Ilonamajor from the middle of January 1945 on. Around February 10 the Germans transferred the inhabitants of the farm to Hidegség and the road leading to the farm was closed down by German guards. SS "target practice" announced in advanced drumbeats, thinned the ranks of the prisoners by eight to ten lives each day.[58]

The ghastly crimes of the SS guards of Ilonamajor was somewhat exposed as a result of the people's court procedures. Eyewitnesses disclosed events that proved how deliberately planned and extensive the massacres had been: 1,286 people were murdered there. Today, there is no trace of what occurred.[59]

The village of Sopronkeresztúr (Deutschkreutz) south of Kópháza was much more fortified than the neighboring places of the Reich defense line. Its outskirts were surrounded by anti–tank trenches and approaches. Five thousand eastern workers (*Ostarbeiter*), two thousand Hungarian Jews, Poles, and Ukrainians, and thirty French prisoners worked on the fortifications according to the data of the

Austrian researcher Leopold Banny.[60]

On November 26, 1944, 1,500 Hungarian women deportees arrived at Sopronkeresztúr. The girls and women of the capital were quartered in the lofts of the sheep-folds open to the snow. They did agricultural work for the Esterházy estate. According to an extant list of names, 95 persons died in December.[61]

In the last days of December the majority of the Hungarian women were transported to the west and were replaced by men. They had to work at the fortifications and most of them had to produce the building materials themselves. The *Bauleitung* was not choosy about the materials employed. They used the tombstones of the cemetery of the liquidated local Jewish community for the building of defense walls and roadblocks.

The most feared person in the camp was SS corporal *Rottenführer* Scherer. He evoked terror by his brutal behavior wherever he turned up. Johann Posch, who worked as the gravedigger of the camp, witnessed several of his murders. In his official testimony after the war he also stated that Scherer personally supervised the burial of the prisoners he shot or beat to death. If any of them still showed signs of life, Scherer immediately used his gun. According to Posch, it was a practice for quite some time to put the corpses of 14 Hungarian Jews shot in the head on the cart carrying the dead on every second day. It also happened that the trench workers ordered to bury the dead were also shot by Scherer, with the participation of two SS guards, after they completed their sad labor.[62]

The number of Hungarian victims of the fortifications at Sopronkeresztúr reached 284 by the end of 1944. Their grave was not found until 1974. László Berend, a poet and short story writer, was among them.[63] Altogether, 650 Hungarian Jewish deportees lost their lives at Sopronkeresztúr.[64]

Here is a summary of the deaths at the camps: Ágfalva, 820; Angyalmalom (Felixdorf), 1,750; Balf, 185; Deutschkreutz, 650; Donnerskirchen, 500; Engerau, 460; Fertőrákos, 400; Harka, 650; Hidegség, 300; Ilonamajor, 1,286; Kópháza, 620; Nagycenk, 1,180; Schattendorf, unknown; Siegendorf, 300; Sopron, 120; and Sopronbánfalva, 532.

A new series of physical and psychic torments were to come for the trench workers still able to walk and work in the last weeks of March 1945. Most of them were evacuated from the border regions of Györ–Moson–Sopron County on foot, although some were transported by train or barge. The marching columns were gathered mainly at Királyhida from the North section of the Niederdonau fortifications. The first point of concentration of the columns of the labor camps of the Middle and South sections was Szentmargitbánya (Saint Margareth) opposite Fertőrákos. Because of the air–raids the columns usually had to march non–stop from 6:00 p.m. until 8:00 a.m.

The columns of the liquidated camps reached their destination, the concentration camp of Mauthausen, within 15 to 20 days, while suffering the renewed attacks of the SS near the inhabited areas. People travelling along these routes today are reminded of their heavy losses by tombs and moving memorials. Some groups were sent, not to the overcrowded Mauthausen camp, but even farther away, to the semi–finished, so–called Weldlager near Günskirchen.[65]

These camps were liberated by American troops on May 4 and 5, 1945. Until then, thousands more fell victim to the SS terror, and hundreds more were snatched away by death from emaciation, disease, and injury during their first weeks of freedom.

Notes

1 Personal communication by Dr. László Fogarassy, a researcher living in Bratislava.

2 *Dokumentationsarchiv des österreichischen Widerstandes*—DÖW [Archives of the Austrian Resistance], Vienna. Doc. E. 20 967.

3 *Ibid.*

4 Recollections of András Roth of Szeged, a former inmate of Engerau.

5 Szabolcs Szita, *Haláleröd. A munkaszolgálat és a hadimunka 1944–1945. évi történetéhez* [Death Fort. To the History of Labor Service and Military Work in 1944–45]. Budapest, 1989, pp. 126–28.

6 *Dejiny Bratislavy. Obzor,* Bratislava, 1978, p. 392.

7 *Widerstand und Verfolgung im Burgenland, 1934–1945. Eine Dokumentation* [Resistance and Persecution in the Burgenland, 1934–45. A Documentation]. Vienna, 1983, p. 335.

8 *Ibid.*, pp. 333–34.

9 Statement no. 605 recorded by the National Committee for the Care of Deportees (*A Deportáltakat Gondozó Országos Bi-*

zottság—DEGOB) in 1945–46. Deposited at the Jewish National Museum (*Országos Zsidó Muzeum*), Budapest. (Cited hereafter as *DEGOB*.)

10 *DEGOB* statements no. 360, 467, 766, and 2084.

11 Szabolcs Szita, *Holocaust az Alpok előtt* [Holocaust in Front of the Alps]. Győr, 1983, p. 87.

12 *Ibid.*

13 *DEGOB* statement no. 1143.

14 Szabolcs Szita, *Holocaust az Alpok elött, op. cit.*, p. 67.

15 István Dobi, *Vallomás és történelem* [Testimony and History]. Budapest, 1962, vol. 2, pp. 361–62.

16 *DEGOB* statements no. 1188 and 1191.

17 Jenő Lévai, *Fekete könyv a magyar zsidóság szenvedéseiről* [Black Book on the Sufferings of Hungarian Jewry]. Budapest, 1946, p. 275.

18 Szabolcs Szita, *Holocaust az Alpok elött, op. cit.*, p. 69.

19 *DEGOB* statements no. 741, 840, 1155, 1488, and 1489.

20 Elek Karsai and Magda Somlyai, *Sorsforduló. Iratok Magyarország felszabadulásának történetéhez 1944 szeptember–1945 április* [Turn of Destiny. Documents on the History of Hungary's Liberation, September 1944–April 1945]. Budapest, 1970, vol. 1, p. 274.

21 Elek Karsai, *Fegyvertelenül álltak az aknamezökön . . . Dokumentumok a munkaszolgálat történetéhez Magyarországon* [They Stood Unarmed on the Mine Fields . . . Documents on the History of the Labor Service System in Hungary]. Budapest, 1962, vol. 2, p. 712.

22 *Soproni Levéltár* [Archives of Sopron]. Documentary Collection of the Deputy Prefect. Documents 1945–845 (1970) and III.100/942. (Cited hereafter as *Soproni Levéltár.*

23 *Ibid.* Sopron District Officer's Collection, Doc. 5682/1944.

24 Elek Karsai, *Fegyvertelen álltak az aknamezökön, op. cit.*, vol. 2, p. 701.

25 *Soproni Levéltár*, Doc. 5555/1944. (Deputy Prefect's Collection.)

26 Géza Hegedüs, *A sötétség utolsó órái* [The Last Hours of Darkness]. Budapest, 1955, pp. 45–48. See also his *Vallomások egy városról* [Confessions About a City]. Budapest, 1978, pp. 73–76.

27 Szabolcs Szita, *Haláleröd, op. cit.*, pp. 165–66.

28 *DEGOB* statements no. 285, 2894, and 2919.

29 *Ibid.*, Statements no. 2851 and 2919.

[30] Personal communication to this author, dated March 9, 1989.

[31] *Soproni Levéltár*. Death register of Sopronbánfalva, No. 1945/14.

[32] *Ibid.*, No. 1945/198.

[33] *Ibid.*, Deputy Prefect's Documents No. 5555/1948.

[34] Antal Szerb, Mrs., "Szerb Antal utolsó hónapjai" [Antal Szerb's Last Months]. *Irodalomtörténet* [Literary History], Budapest, 1959, pp. 449–52.

[35] Szabolcs Szita, *Holocaust az Alpok elött, op. cit.*, pp. 62, 116.

[36] *Soproni Levéltár*, Death register of Kópháza, No. 1944/41.

[37] Szabolcs Szita, *Holocaust az Alpok elött, op. cit.*, pp. 63, 117.

[38] *Soproni Levéltár*, Sopron District Officer's Documents, No. 5682/1944.

[39] Szabolcs Szita, *Holocaust az Alpok elött, op. cit.*, pp. 64, 117–18.

[40] *DEGOB* statement no. 3017.

[41] Imre Kömüves, *A magyar sajtó mártirjai* [The Martyrs of the Hungarian Press]. Budapest, 1981, p. 99.

[42] Elek Karsai and Magda Somlyai, *Sorsforduló, op. cit.*, vol. 2, p. 232.

[43] Tibor Barabás, *Szerelmem, Eszti* [Eszti, My Love]. Budapest, 1946, p. 64.

[44] *Soproni Levéltár*, Deputy Prefect's Documents, no. 5555/1948.

[45] *DEGOB* statements, no. 432, 1476, 2918.

[46] *Soproni Levéltár*, Death register of Kópháza, no. 1944/62.

[47] *Ibid.*, Sopron District Officer's Documents, no. 5682/1944.

[48] *Ibid.*, Deputy Prefect's Document, no. 5682/1944.

[49] *Ibid.*, No. III.100/9.

[50] *Ibid.*

[51] Elek Karsai, *Fegyvertelen álltak az aknamezőkön, op. cit.*, vol. 2, p. 702.

[52] *DEGOB* statements no. 1926, 3329.

[53] *Ibid.*, statements no. 3329, 3408, 3413, 3467.

[54] *Ibid.*, statement no. 2467.

[55] *Soproni Levéltár*, III.100/942.

[56] *DEGOB* statement no. 3122.

[57] *Soproni Levéltár*, People's Court Case 42/1947. (Testimony of László Ausspitz.)

[58] *Ibid.*

[59] The names of 923 victims are known from the registers. *Soproni Levéltár*, Deputy Prefect's Documents, no. 5555/1948.

[60] Leopold Banny, *Krieg im Burgenland* [War in the Burgenland]. Eisenstadt, 1983, vol. 1, p. 227.

[61] Leopold Banny, *Schild im Osten* [Shield in the East]. Eisenstadt, 1985, pp. 150–57.

[62] *Dokumentationsarchiv des österreichischen Widerstandes, op. cit.*, Doc. No. 3967/61.

[63] Szabolcs Szita, *Holocaust az Alpok elött, op. cit.*, p. 89.

[64] Leopold Banny, *Schild im Osten, op. cit.*, p. 157.

[65] Szabolcs Szita, *Haláleröd, op. cit.*, pp. 115–223.

THE HESSISCH LICHTENAU SUB–CAMP OF THE BUCHENWALD CONCENTRATION CAMP, 1944–45

A Documentation

Dieter Vaupel

Translated by Maida Pollock

Establishment of the Concentration Camp Sub–Camp

The Hessisch Lichtenau commando, a Sub–Camp for Female Prisoners of the Concentration Camp Buchenwald, was first mentioned in files on August 1, 1944.[1] It then contained 1,002 prisoners, nearly all of whom were Hungarian Jewish women, with a sprinkling of three Slovaks and three Yugoslavs. There were also one Romanian and one Pole. From the list of new additions from Auschwitz[2] one learns that the ages of the women ranged from 15 to 49. Many were seamstresses, tailors, and hairdressers; but there were also teachers, educators, photographers, pharmacists, nurses, clerks, and a large number of students. Several mothers with daughters or other relatives were housed in "Camp Clubhouse" in Hessisch Lichtenau.

On September 19, 1944, the women were registered through the political branch of Buchenwald—as was customary—and provided with consecutive numbers, in this case 20,001 to 21,003.[3]

The girls and women were put to work in the munitions factory—now the Lichtenau suburb of Hirschhagen. The employer was the "Hessisch Lichtenau Factory Corporation for the Utilization of Chemical Products" (*Fabrik Hessisch Lichtenau Gesellschaft mit beschränkter Haftung (GmbH) zur Verwertung chemischer Erzeugnisse— "Verwert-Chemie"*).[4]

Karl Sommer, at the time Deputy Director of the Economic and Administrative Headquarters of the SS (*Wirtschafts-Verwaltungshauptamt—WVHA*), reported as follows to the Nuremberg Military Tribunal (1947) on the use of concentration camp inmates in industry.

> The employment of concentration camp prisoners in German industry began in the months August–September 1942. This happened as a result of pressure from the Ministry of Defense (*Rüstungsministerium*) which by this means wanted to enable industries to achieve their prescribed production quotas. . . . The number of allocated prisoners varied with each firm. No allocations were made unless the firm could use at least 500 concentration camp inmates. . . . At the time of peak employment of allocated personnel in the entire German industry, 500,000 concentration camp inmates were at work.
>
> The inmates who were put at the disposal of an industrial enterprise were housed in specially adapted camps at the factory sites. Such camps were designated as work–camps.[5]

The stream of prisoners–of–war who could be allocated to the defense industry as forced labor diminished after 1943 as a result of the defeat of the German 6th Army at Stalingrad. Since at the same time armament production was to be greatly boosted, the worker shortage in industries manufacturing essential war materials grew ever larger.

The principles of Jewish policy (*Judenpolitik*) that had been established in 1942 were suspended by Hitler in April 1944, when he ordered that 100,000 Hungarian Jews be brought to Germany as a labor force.[6] At first they were to be used solely for the building of six great bunkers.[7] A short time later, they were put at the disposal of armament industries, as long as these provided appropriate accommodations. In a letter to Goebbels on August 7, 1944, Waeger, the Plenipotentiary of Total War Preparedness (*Reichsbevollmächtigter für den totalen Kriegseinsatz*) outlined the plan:

> Following a decision by the Führer, it is known that a large number of Hungarian Jews have been placed into the German war economy during the last few weeks. Thus far, the experiences are quite good, so I would consider it of great value if those Hungarian Jews not yet allocated were immediately put at the armament industry's disposal.[8]

In a file entry to Defense Minister Speer, Waeger writes on the employment of Jews:

> Naturally, the use of these Hungarian Jews throughout Germany also contradicts my feelings. Under no circumstances, however, can we dispense with such an emergency action at the moment. In addition, the concentration camp-like accommodations of the Jews assures that neither the feelings of the German population will be offended, nor can the Jews cause any kind of harm.[9]

About the Munitions Factory Hessisch Lichtenau

The underlying reason for the establishment of a Concentration Camp Sub-Camp in Hessisch Lichtenau was the fact that one of the largest munitions factories of the German Reich was located there. Preparations for war had begun with the building of the munitions factory in 1936. In the course of these preparations a search had been made throughout Germany for locations. The area of the present Lichtenau suburb of Hirschhagen had several advantages: a favorable transportation network, no proximity to a large city, dense, mixed forestation, trouble-free energy supply through nearby softcoal mines, and a labor pool from the loosely structured labor force in the area.[10] In addition, Mayor Göbel of Lichtenau, also the District Leader of the Nazi party, was a man upon whom the National Socialists could rely.

The factory was erected by the Dynamite Nobel Company (DAG), with headquarters at Troisdorf, at the cost of about 100 million marks, under orders from the Army Weapons Bureau (*Heereswaffenamt*). The major stockholder of DAG was I. G. Farben,[11] with a share of 61 percent. Officially, the works belonged to the "Corporation for the Utilization of Chemical Products," which was wholly owned by DAG. Permanent buildings, as well as the property, belonged to Montan AG, a federally owned company.[12]

After a two-year construction period, the Hessich Lichtenau works were put into operation on June 1, 1938. It was the second of what would become 27 munitions factories. The Lichtenau population—well aware of the factory's existence—referred to it as the "Muna" or the "Moor's head factory."

Two types of explosives were produced: trinitrotoluol and picric acid. Trinitrotoluol, or TNT, is obtained from toluon, a methylbenzol and sulphuric acid, in several production steps.[13]

TNT was bottled in liquid state. For this purpose, it had to be heated in kettles to temperatures of from 90° to 120° C. At the bottling stations it was poured into "grenades, mines, and (very likely also) bombs."[14]

Pikrin, or picric acid (trinitrophenol) is formed by the heating of saltpeter and phenol.

> In various manufacturing steps, the picric acid was cooked, washed, dried, and then pulverized. Before finishing, this explosive—as opposed to TNT—was not liquified but bottled in granular form. Picric acid served as a propellent for bullets shot from cartridges, i.e., rifle ammunition. In . . . compression buildings this explosive was filled into cartridge cases and compressed under high pressure.[15]

The production of pikrin did not start until the beginning of 1940; until then only TNT was produced. Originally, the intention was to prepare a site for the production of a third explosive, nitropenta; however, this project was abandoned at the end of 1940.

Production output grew considerably during the war years: fiscal 1939–40 saw the production of 5,500 tons of TNT which increased to 29,170 tons in fiscal 1942–43.[16] There was an even greater increase in pikrin production: from 156 tons (1939–1940) to 2,074 tons (1944–45).[17] Thus, the factory was one of the three largest manufacturers of explosives in all Germany. Of the considerable profit, 50 percent—administered from Hessisch Lichtenau—was channeled to the federally owned Montan AG, owner of the property of the Hessisch Lichtenau works.

The factory area covered about 575 acres (233 hectares) with 399 workshops erected on it by the end of the war. The unfenced territory was crisscrossed by a wide network of roads and had its own rail connection (35 kilometers of track) and its own station, as well as a cable railway to the Hirschberg mine. Great emphasis was placed on camouflaging the area (roof plantings, underground bunkers, masking nets, etc.).[18] There were elaborate security regulations and safety controls as well as factory security. Gestapo and SS personnel acted as enforcers of these regulations.

At first, a conscripted and volunteer labor force from the area was drawn for work in the "Muna." As the war years progressed, however, increasing numbers of "volunteers" from occupied territories, prisoners-of-war, and forced laborers were put to work in Hirschhagen. The workers (men and women) came from Belgium, Bulgaria, Czechoslovakia, Hungary, the Netherlands, Poland, Romania, Spain, the USSR, and Yugoslavia. The size of the work crews grew steadily. In April 1939 the Verwert–Chemie reported around 750 workers and employees; in April 1941 there were 3,100; at the beginning of 1945 there were 4,400.[19] Added to these, in 1945, were approximately 800 concentration camp prisoners (under the authority of the SS),[20] 800 to 1,000 people in federal labor service, and 2,000 construction workers,[21] who worked on the terrain and were employed by various construction firms.

Because most of the work consisted of "light"—but at the same time very dangerous—labor, the proportion of women workers was very high, even though all the men were soldiers. At the start of the war women made up one–seventh of the labor force; this proportion grew to more than one–half by 1945: 2,300 women.[22]

Working conditions in the factory were as follows:

> Work in Hirschhagen was arranged not only according to physically light and heavy but also—first and foremost—into dangerous and less dangerous activities. Of course, even the less dangerous work–places were exposed to the chemically poisoned air and to the danger of explosions. . . . Considered as dangerous were the TNT and picric acid operations buildings, . . . the bottling stations, and the compression buildings. In these, the men and women came in direct contact with chemicals and/or the buildings were especially vulnerable to the danger of explosion.[23]

While the factory was in operation, several major accidents occurred with the loss of over 200 lives.[24]

In order to accommodate the labor force, a ring of camps (*Lager*) was established around the factory: "Camp Clubhouse," Camps Föhren, Herzog, Teichhof, Lenoir, Settlement Fürstenhagen, Camps Friedrichs- brück, Esche, Steinbach, and Waldhof. The camps, which consisted of wooden barracks, were torn down after the war—some not until the fifties—while the ones built of stone, such as Waldhof and Herzog, serve as general housing today.[25]

About the Origins of the Concentration Camp Prisoners

As mentioned before, the women housed in "Camp Clubhouse" were, with few exceptions, Hungarian Jews. It is therefore important to examine the specific fate of the Jews of Hungary.

Until 1944, Hungary was the only European country with its Jewish congregations almost intact. About 725,000 Jews survived here until May of that year.

> They were killed during Hitler's last year, surrounded by the world of the Axis whose downfall was already unavoidable. In no other country . . . did the Final Solution start so late. Hungary was the only country where the perpetrators of the deed knew from the beginning that the war was lost. The Hungarian Jews were almost the only ones who were warned at a time when their congregations were still intact, and they knew exactly what awaited them. Finally, the Hungarian mass deportations were also unique in that they could not be hidden from the rest of the world; they were carried out quite openly in plain view of the entire world.[26]

At the crucial moment, the Hungarian government was incapable of a determined resistance to the German pressure. From the beginning of 1938, pro–German party hacks and puppet collaborators were interspersed in the succession of Prime Ministers.[27] Therefore, the course of the annihilation process was predictable: "Periods of almost complete calm alternated with hectic phases of destruction."[28] The Jews, heavily engaged in commerce and the professions, were indispensable for the normal flow of the economy and should simply be called Hungary's middle class.[29] As a result, the elimination of the Jews from the Hungarian economy caused enormous difficulties which were only gradually overcome by the authorities.

A unique feature of the Hungarian policy toward Jews was the inclusion of Jewish men in the Hungarian army as forced labor.[30] At its height, there were 80,000 workers in this program,[31] many of whom worked side by side with German soldiers at the front.

The Kállay government came under massive pressure from 1942 on to proceed with the deportation of Jews, but continued to resist.[32] Admiral Miklós Horthy, the Hungarian Regent, also resisted the constantly reiterated German demands for a while, for politically calculated reasons.[33]

The dam burst when the Germans managed to establish a Hungarian government under Prime Minister Döme Sztójay on March 22, 1944, and at the same time empowered a special command under Eichmann which was to set in motion the Final Solution in Hungary. By clever manipulation of the Jewish community leaders—

who were ordered to form a Jewish Council—Eichmann succeeded in exploiting them for his plans of annihilation. In the following weeks, thousands of Jews from the provinces were herded into ghettos (in Kolozsvár, Pincehely, Kaposvár, Dombovár, Kerecsend, Szatmár, etc.) and shortly thereafter packed into cattle cars and deported to Auschwitz. Between May 15 and July 9, 1944, 437,402 Jews were deported from Hungary.[34]

The girls and women, requisitioned by the munitions factory and taken to Hessisch Lichtenau, were selected in Auschwitz for forced labor and shipped to Lichtenau in freight trains.[35]

Klara S. states: "On the first of July 1944, I was transferred from my hometown of Tab to the ghetto of Kaposvár. A few days later I was deported from Kaposvár to the concentration camp Auschwitz. After about three weeks I was transferred with a group of about 1,000 prisoners to Hessisch Lichtenau, guarded by SS men."[36]

Reinhard Kühnl writes: "In Auschwitz all their belongings were taken away, in place of their own clothes they received a single, sack–like garment of the roughest material and wooden clogs with cloth tops. Their heads were partially shaven. Many of their family members were gassed at Auschwitz."[37]

In the summer of 1944 alone, close to 400,000 Hungarian Jews were sent to the gas chambers of Auschwitz. The rest, less than 20 percent of the total deported, were selected as "fit for labor."[38] According to Rudolf Höss, Commanding Officer of Auschwitz, these were used for "slave labor in industry."[39]

One of the women, who was forced to work in the munitions factory "Verwert–Chemie" in the town of Allendorf (similar to the Jewish women in Hessisch Lichtenau), reports on the selection process in Auschwitz:[40]

> Though we were as yet unaware of the gas chambers, we did know that in order to survive we had to try to get out of the hell called Auschwitz. Dr. Mengele was once more in charge of the selection process. My daughter and my sister were assigned for labor. Because of my thinness and weak condition, I was turned away. I tried to sneak to the other side and join my daughter but I was grabbed and beaten by Mengele himself. I defended myself as best I could. . . . Later, while the selection was still in progress, I attached myself to another row and managed somehow to join the transport.

The same woman reports on the freight transport to the sub-camp.[41] "We traveled many days. I am not familiar with the exact route. For many days we were sidetracked as the rails were needed by the military, we were bombed and the tracks destroyed."

The coordination of the sub-camps with the Buchenwald concentration camp does not give a clear picture of the actual origins of the prisoners. From 1944 on, the "delivery" of the men and women started mostly from Auschwitz, but "the sub-camps, which were in Buchenwald's geographic proximity, were placed under its command."[42] The prisoner transports were delivered directly to the sub-camps in freight trains. The designation "Sub-Camp Buchenwald" was of purely administrative significance, especially in the case of those with female prisoners. With few exceptions, women were taken directly to the various sub-camps without a detour to Buchenwald. In January 1945, the distribution point at Buchenwald accounted for a total of 21 sub-camps with 25,393 female prisoners. At this time, the total of Buchenwald sub-camp inmates numbered 75,000.[43]

The "Camp Clubhouse"

The Jewish women, assigned to the Hessisch Lichtenau Munitions Factory as forced labor, were housed in "Camp Clubhouse" at the edge of town.[44]

This camp, also called "Camp South," was the first one erected by the factory. It was built from 1938 to 1940 in three phases.[45] The owner was not Montan AG, as in the case of the other camps, but the town of Hessisch Lichtenau.[46] The name "clubhouse" refers to the neighboring Auguste-Viktoria-Home, popularly called "the clubhouse." The home was erected in 1913 as the Lutheran community house; it served later as kindergarten, elementary school, and cultural center. Children went to school there in 1944–45 while Jewish women were imprisoned next door.

Mrs. S., who was 32 years old in 1944 and conscripted for service as a lay teacher in Hessisch Lichtenau, writes: "When we were outside with the students, the Jewish women came to the fence and begged."[47]

The camp consisted of a total of 23 buildings, almost all of wooden construction. Only two buildings, or parts thereof, were more solidly built: the furnace room and a storage house.[48] The camp consisted of the following buildings:[49]

10 barracks for living quarters (between 240 and 300 square meters each)
2 administration (business) barracks
3 toilet barracks
2 washroom barracks
6 storage barracks or sheds

These buildings occupied the grounds of a former nursery between Heinrich Street and Hopfelder Street. The wooden barracks were heated by a central system; only the kitchen had an open fire. The camp was planned to house 700 people.[50] Later this number increased to more than 1,000 occupants.

At first, the camp was used to house German and foreign construction workers; soon French factory workers were added.

In the summer of 1944, a section of the camp was put at the disposal of the SS for the housing of female concentration camp prisoners, mostly Hungarian Jews.[51] The transfer to the SS was made by the Verwert–Chemie, and from August 2, 1944 between 790 and 1,000 Jewish women were placed in this special section under most crowded conditions. The rest of the barracks was occupied by foreign workers until the war's end.

In order to produce concentration camp–like quarters, the SS rearranged the section transferred to them. A chain–link and barbed wire fence was erected,[52] with lights on all four corners for better guarding at night.[53] There are conflicting statements as to the existence of guard towers. Also, it is still unclear whether a gallows existed on the roll call area of the camp.[54]

Lenke Löwinger describes her arrival in Hessisch Lichtenau:

> I saw two camps surrounded by barbed wire, one was empty, the other had several prisoners in it. Later I heard that these were of French origin. Our group was led into the empty camp. We were placed in wooden barracks.[55]

The main entrance faced Heinrich Street; there was also a passage on Hopfelder Street for the guards' use. The section transferred to the SS consisted of a kitchen, a bath, a laundry, storage spaces for food and clothing, a building for the segregation of the sick, and one for the SS guard personnel—beside the living quarters.[56] The office of the SS clerical staff was located outside the camp's territory.[57]

At the war's end, American soldiers and Poles were billeted in the camp. It became a refugee camp after the spring of 1946.[58] Later, single barracks were rented to local business enterprises, including a horsemeat butcher shop. The Lichtenau *Realgymnasium* (secondary school, emphasizing science), was housed in one area of the camp in the years following the war. The last wooden barracks were torn down in the mid–1950s, some of them to be rebuilt elsewhere. Thus, hundreds of young people slept in the Youth Hostel at *Grosse Steine* in Reichenbach, built from the barracks that once served as the prison of the Jewish women. At present, the elementary school of Hessisch Lichtenau, the advanced classes of the Freiherr vom Stein school, and the kindergarten occupy the grounds.

Living Conditions in the Camp

Food for the prisoners—all performing heavy labor—consisted of watery soup with turnips or white cabbage and 50 grams of bread a day.[59] Occasionally, a few pieces of potato were added. Buchenwald Concentration Camp was the supplier of provisions.[60] A few women knitted and sewed for Germans after work at the factory and received food for this service, as the normal fare was not sufficient.

During the first years of the munitions factory's operation, women workers who were exposed to particularly poisonous vapors at work received a so–called "poison allowance": a loaf of bread, half a pound of butter, half a pound of sausage, and a quarter pound of coffee beans per week, as well as a daily ration of pills and milk.[61] These "advantages" ceased during 1944–45 for the Jewish women as well as all others.

In the beginning, hygienic conditions in "Camp Clubhouse" were clearly better than those in Auschwitz; as time went by, they got worse and worse, mostly because of severe overcrowding.[62] This deterioration was also reported by the women who had to scrub the barracks after the war and rid them of bedbugs and other vermin. There were several attempts at delousing the prisoners. Only once in a while did the women receive a sliver of soap.[63] The barracks were cold and damp; rats were everywhere. The women slept on plain wooden bunks; each had a wool blanket for the night.

> I remember they told me that Saturday was laundry day. They had to wash all their clothes then but had nothing to change into, because everything they owned was on their backs. That's why they wrapped themselves in their blankets.[64]

Conditions must have been unbearably cramped when one considers that the entire camp had been planned for 700 people, while now one section "housed" 1,000.

Undoubtedly, the SS calculated that the women didn't "need" individual sleeping places because of the factory's 24–hour operation. Thus, added to the work–shifts at the factory were the sleep–shifts in the camp. Concentration camp–like living conditions meant that "Camp Clubhouse" had the same tightly packed conditions as the concentration camps of Auschwitz, Buchenwald, Bergen–Belsen, and others.

The women in Hessisch Lichtenau had no adequate clothing, let alone for winter conditions. They were wrapped in rags, their bare feet in wooden clogs which they received in Auschwitz. They wrapped newspapers and rags around their legs and wore their blankets for protection against the cold. When the leadership of the Social and Economic Departments of the munitions factory became aware of these conditions—which also threatened the working ability of the women—they supplied them with "a coat and two pairs of wool stockings,"[65] as reported by a former leader of these departments in a conversation.

All the women had clean–shaven heads; many—like other workers who also came in contact with pikrin—were colored yellowish–green in face and body through handling chemicals.

Medical care was undertaken by Dr. Fuckert, company physician of the factory, as well as by the Italian "prisoner doctor" Luciana Nissim and the dentist Else Cserepfalvi. In addition, two women prisoners were designated as nurses, Maria Lieber and Eva Lenczner, a former medical student.[66] Dr. Nissim and the two nurses were assigned to the sub–camp on August 31, 1944, one month after its establishment.[67] The doctors and nurses, with no medication at their disposal,[68] had more than enough to do, as attested by—among other reports—a document signed by Camp Commander Schäfer: on March 22, 1945, the sick list consisted of 36 patients—25 convalescents and 11 women under dental care.[69]

The women avoided the sickroom whenever possible. This is shown in several statements from the investigative files of the State Government in Kassel. Esther Fuchs: "I, for one, did not go to the sickroom when I felt sick because I did not want to be deported elsewhere."[70]

The Path to Work

The women had to walk at least two kilometers—some of them

five kilometers—to work every day. They were led, under guard, from "Camp Clubhouse" either through Biegen Street or Desseler Street to the railroad stop Hessisch Lichtenau, or they had to walk the entire distance to the munitions factory. In addition to working time, they spent about three hours getting to and from the factory.

"As they were led out the camp entrance on Heinrich Street they were made to sing, SS women went in front and back and on the sides. They had whips and drove the women, hitting at their legs and shouting 'Move, move!' "[71]

Many had to walk to work barefoot, some had wooden shoes.

"During the winter, whenever the women had to stand around, some of them knocked their shoes together to keep their feet warm. Then the SS women would come and hit them on the legs with sticks."[72]

Sabine Gross and Esther Fuchs report in their letters[73] about the arduous path to work. The women were herded to work regardless of weather conditions, accompanied by abuses, beatings, and kickings.

One group traveled in a "special train" from Hessisch Lichtenau to Fürstenhagen station (one locomotive with at least three modified freight cars); from there they had to walk the rest of the way to work. Boarding the freight cars was difficult because they had no steps—unlike passenger trains. If the women didn't board fast enough, the guards drove them on with clubs—according to eyewitnesses.

Mr. T., 55 years old, on the arrival of the women at Fürstenhagen station, writes:

> There was a footpath, about 2–1/2 meters wide, which led from the Fürstenhagen station toward the munitions factory. One day in the summer of 1944, when I was 11 years old, I stood on this path when about 100 Jewish women were led past. They climbed up the path. They were young, slim women with shorn heads, dressed alike. Today I would say that one could tell from their looks that they were specially selected to perform heavy and dangerous labor. I knew one of the guards; he came from Rommerode and used to do some butchering for us. I started to talk to him but he told me not to talk to him or to the women either. I couldn't understand this as a child. It was an oppressive atmosphere and I was aware that something was wrong. This picture made a deep impression on me. To this day I see the women climbing up the path.[74]

The Jewish women were divided into several—presumably of differing sizes from time to time—for the road work. There were several ways to work and single groups of women worked in different places (i.e., filling stations, outside work, work on construction companies).

The various paths to work can be seen from the survey sketch.[75]

1. Footpath from "Camp Clubhouse" through Desseler Street/Post Street/Mühlweg to the munitions factory.
2. Footpath to railroad stop or station Hessisch Lichtenau (H/L)—by train to below Lager Teichhof—footpath to factory.
3. Footpath to railroad stop or station H/L—by train to Fürstenhagen—footpath to munitions factory.
4. Footpath to railroad stop or station H/L—by train to Eschenstruth—footpath to factory (western section/Helsa Gate).
5. Footpath to railroad stop or station H/L—by train to Helsa—footpath to the Herges Brook valley.
6. Footpath to railroad stop or station H/L—by train through Walburg/Velmeden/Steinholz to the munitions factory.

In addition, one group of women had to walk to a Lichtenau/Fürstenhagen construction firm.

A large number of the women remained in camp while the others went to work, as the factory operated in three shifts. The various paths to the workplaces also explains the work force of 1,000, which has been questioned by some witnesses. The reason is that the inhabitants of Hessisch Lichtenau and Fürstenhagen, and the factory workers, saw only a single group of women most of the time. To be sure, people living on Biegen Street reported that several groups were led through the streets, one after the other.

Working Conditions in the Munitions Factory

The working time for the Jewish women on the day shift was 10–1/2 hours daily—from six in the morning to five in the evening, with a midday break from eleven–thirty to noon,[76] while all others had to work only eight hours. The majority of the women worked in a three–shift pattern. Saturdays and Sundays were also workdays. In addition to the 8–hour shifts, the women had to perform work on the factory grounds (described later) two to four hours daily. Added to this was the trip to and from work.

The women performed not only dangerous[77] but also physically heavy labor. They were included in various operations of the factory.

One was in the manufacture of explosives. Mrs. K. writes, in a letter of January 1, 1984:

> The powder was cooked during the night in the small bunkers and weighed during the day. . . . Every morning, around 7 o'clock, whole columns of Hungarian Jewish women arrived . . . in grey smocks, smoothly shaven heads, barefoot or in wooden clogs, and then the weighing began. Other groups had to cook the powder at night; all who did this were doomed because the liver and pancreas were inevitably attacked.[78]

Women were also required to perform clean–up work on the factory grounds and work in the forest, as well as loading and unloading railroad carriages at Fürstenhagen station or loading work at the factory. They also were engaged in excavation work, such as digging ditches and pits (i.e., the cascades of Helsa), and in the construction of an aqueduct from the Helsa pump to the munitions factory.

Mr. H. recalls the following:

> I was only a child then. I observed that Jewish women were brought to Helsa by train. They came in freight trains, maybe three or four carriages long. There was a total of maybe 60 or 100 women. They went to the Herges Brook Valley to work there. They had to lay an aqueduct from the Helsa pump to the munitions factory. This happened in the fall and winter of 1944. My parents had a piece of property in the Herges Brook Valley and the women worked on the neighboring property, and that's why I know this so well. The grown–ups told us children we shouldn't look, this was not for children.[79]

In addition, some of the women were put to work on construction projects which were carried out on behalf of the munitions factory. A Lichtenau construction firm had thirty women at its disposal in the cement works alone. Mrs. Sabine Gross writes about her work with a construction company in Fürstenhagen: she had to carry heavy cement slabs daily from early morning until the afternoon and she still feels the results of this heavy labor.[80]

Mainly, however, the women were employed in the filling stations and bottling bunkers of the munitions factory. The performance of the Jewish women in the filling stations was praised by the mobilization inspectors in Kassel on August 16, 1944 and rated "very good."[81]

A former factory worker reports on the work routine in the filling stations, where grenades and mines were filled with TNT:

> The filling stations consisted of two large chambers which were linked by a connecting tunnel. The raw materials were delivered to the front section, unpacked, screwed apart and filled with the liquid explosive. The filled bombs were placed on carriages and shipped through the cooling tunnel, "tails" toward the outside, directly to the back section. The tunnel was a many–angled, concrete structure to contain an eventual explosion. The bombs were supposed to cool in this connecting tunnel.[82]
>
> There was a lot to do in the back section: the bombs had to be cleaned of powder remnants, the mirror, the powder surfaces were rubbed smooth, then came the 'perfume'—that was beeswax or something similar to coat them to prevent dampness from seeping in. Then the 'tails' were put on and screwed in.

The actual filling of the shells was done by Germans. The Jewish women did only preparatory work—as for example the unloading and screwing–apart of the shells—and they scraped clean the filled shells in the back section of the filling station. A woman from Hessisch Lichtenau who worked with the Jewish women in one of the filling stations said: "The Jewish women didn't fill the grenades, we mistrusted them."[83]

The production of TNT created the following health hazards:

> Well known were acute tissue poisoning through the absorption of nitro–compounds into uninjured skin, through direct touch or through the inhaling of vapor or dust containing nitro–particles, which resulted in excemas, anemias (the formation of methämoglobins) and liver damage.[84]

Many women came in contact with trinitrophenol (pikrin) in the bottling bunkers (compression buildings). In their work "Explosives from Hirschhagen," Wolfram König and Ulrich Schneider describe the production method as follows:

> The compression buildings consisted mostly of two sections. In the front section the shells were filled with pikrin by hand. The amounts of explosives had to be weighed most accurately as overfilling could have resulted in explosions during compression. This part of the building was separated from

> the actual filling-room by a thick concrete wall and had only a small opening for transports to it. The opening locked automatically with a heavy steel door during the compression process.
>
> Usually there were several presses in one filling station, separated from each other also by heavy steel/concrete walls. These presses compressed the picric acid simultaneously in several cartridges (12–24), under a pressure of from 100 to 200 *atü*.
>
> . . . Almost every compression building had a "finishing building" assigned to it where the pressed cartridges were (probably) made live.[85]

Pikrin, hand filled in the compression buildings, contains extremely poisonous yellow crystals, whose vapor invades the body through breathing and through the skin. They cause liver poisoning with severe jaundice and irreparable lung damage. A discoloration of the skin and hair appears—from yellowish-green to bronze; as a result, the women who had these signs of illness were called "canaries" by the population. Somewhat later weakness is observed but the patient still has no pain. In many workers (men and women) liver poisoning was so advanced that the sickness resulted in death.[86] Death certificates in the town records of Hessisch Lichtenau often list "lung tuberculosis" or simply "died in camp" as the cause of death.[87]

While there were many small explosions (spontaneous combustions) in the bottling bunkers, they only rarely resulted in serious damage. At the filling stations, however, during the process of bottling TNT, dangerous explosions occurred, resulting in many deaths and serious injuries.[88] How many deaths occurred among members of the sub-camp as a result of such accidents in the factory is difficult to ascertain. The principal state archive of Hesse records 150 victims;[89] this number, however, cannot be verified by any other record. Companies which employed concentration camp prisoners were not obligated to report causes of deaths. The diminished number of inmates was reported only to the main camp, so that a new shipment of prisoners could be received.[90] This is evident from a communication of October 24, 1944, signed by the camp commander and sent to the Buchenwald concentration camp, in which the deaths of five prisoners are reported—among them two teenagers, one 16 and the other 17—and "duly noted in the attached"[91]; but no causes of deaths are mentioned. A former aide to SS women, Mrs. N. notes: "I remember that one night first one girl and then another died. According to the rules, these girls were buried in wooden caskets in Hessisch Lichtenau."[92]

Bunker explosions were frequent after the war started, because safety regulations were somewhat reduced in order to achieve greater production, and at the same time more and more qualified men were drafted into the armed services.

In the factory where the Jewish women worked in the same sections with Germans, it was forbidden—on pain of death—to establish contact with the Jewish prisoners. Despite this—according to interviews—contacts did occur in the factory and there were a few people, especially among those who had to perform the same dangerous work, who gave food to the Jewish women, endangering their own lives.

Undoubtedly, the largest financial gain from the use of concentration camp prisoners in industry accrued to the SS. But the employment of prisoners was also a profitable business for the DAG and its principal stockholder, I. G. Farben, as the prisoners were the cheapest labor. The company paid the SS a fixed amount per "delivered" concentration camp prisoner per day. For the women in Hessisch Lichtenau, placed as unskilled labor (prisoner work–aides),[93] they received four Reichsmarks.[94] The prisoners themselves received nothing for their labor. Accounting was transacted directly between the administration of the Hessisch Lichtenau factory and the SS business administration. Auschwitz appears undisguised as the "supplier" of the work force, which was in constant danger of being returned to Auschwitz to be annihilated.[95]

Despite everything, the condition of the concentration camp inmates employed by the Hessisch Lichtenau munitions factory was more favorable than that of the men and women working directly under the control of a concentration camp. During the time they spent in the factory, at least, the prisoners were removed from the direct interference of the SS and received their instructions from factory bosses and foremen. Benjamin B. Ferencz writes:

> It is true that many of the inmates were eager to leave the concentration camp to work in war production. But it was not because they desired to help Hitler's war effort or to

enjoy the benefits of such employment. It was because their only alternative was the gas chamber.

It cannot be denied that the lives of many inmates were indirectly saved by virtue of the fact that they were employed in vital war work. But there is very little moral credit due to a company whose motivation in using the inmates was not to save the prisoners' lives but to serve corporate or national purposes. Had Germany won the war, the fate of the Jews would have been sealed. Concentration camp inmates were put to work by German industry not to save them but to save Germany. Victory for Germany meant defeat for the inmates and death for the Jews.[96]

Population of the Sub-Camp

There is detailed information available on the total population figures of the sub-camp from the files of Weimar-Buchenwald and Auschwitz-Birkenau. On the average, there were 900 Jewish women in the women's camp, most of them enlisted to work in the munitions factory and some in a Lichtenau/Fürstenhagen construction company during the years 1944 and 1945.[97] At times, the population of "Camp Clubhouse" was larger. A list from the Buchenwald concentration

Table 1.
Arrivals and Departures in Hessisch Lichtenau

Date	Arrival	Departure	To/From	Date List Ready	Number of Prisoners
2/8/44	1,000	–	Auschwitz	9/20/44	1,000
8/4/44	–	1	+Eva Fischer		999
8/11/44	–	1	+Anna Kasztl		998
8/31/44	3	–	Auschwitz	10/10/44	1,001
9/24/44	–	1	+Edith Lederer		1,000
10/5/44	–	1	+Magda Horovitz		999
10/8/44	–	1	+Magda Mandel		998
10/27/44	–	206	Auschwitz	10/31/44	792
1/4/45	–	2	Bergen-Belsen	2/8/45	790

Source: Dieter Vaupel, *Das Aussenkommando Hess. Lichtenau des Konzentrationslager Buchenwald, 1944/45*. Kassel: Gesamthochschulbibliothek, 1984, p. 74.

camp of November 25, 1944, accounts for 1,003 prisoners, under the heading "Camp Population/Increases." The actual number comes to 792 prisoners at this time.[98] The last mention of the sub-camp Hessisch Lichtenau appears on March 23, 1945 in a file of the Buchenwald concentration camp, with a population of 790 (Table 1).[99] By March, the number of prisoners was reduced to 706;[100] the changes were duly recorded.[101]

The SS Guards

The SS guards and camp personnel consisted of 25 SS members, mostly older men unfit for military duty, and 40 SS women wardens.[102]

The SS women were selected from the munitions factory workers through its personnel office. In addition, as early as June 1944, mayors of surrounding communities were contacted and requested to designate "suitable" female personnel.[103] These were then transferred to the SS and subsequently given a short training course (from July 16 to August 3, 1944) in the concentration camp Ravensbrück before their assignment.[104] The women had no right to refuse this "selection." On July 15, 1944, one day before the start of the training course, they were informed in a letter from the Hessisch Lichtenau factory that "you are to participate in this course" and "participation is compulsory."[105] Some of the women, under consideration to be SS guards, were apparently returned from Ravensbrück because they were deemed unsuitable.[106]

A number of the SS women came from Hessisch Lichtenau and surroundings; many, however, came from far away and were previously conscripted for labor in the munitions factory: from Soest, Montabaur, Berlin, the Odenwald, Pfalz, and especially from the Frankfurt area.[107] At first, Liesel Herzberger was chief woman warden who, however, proved not to be "reliable enough" and was replaced by Anna Sieberhagen after three or four months. It was her duty to oversee the other SS women and to make sure that they went to work on time with their detachments. Also included in her duties was the listing of prisoners remaining in camp because of illness.[108] She, herself, always remained in camp.

One of the SS women describes her activities:

> As wardens, our task was to supervise the Jewish women and girls, both in the camp, where they lived, and also in

the workplace. It was not part of our duties to instruct or train the women in their work. This was the responsibility of the people at the plant.[109]

SS–Sturmscharführer Wilhelm ("Willi") Schäfer was camp commander during both 1944 and 1945. The rank *Sturmscharführer* was fairly rare in the SS. It was the equivalent of *Stabsfeldwebel* (staff sargeant–major) of the old Wehrmacht.[110] The service rank of *Sturmscharführer* was awarded only after many years of service and carried with it the highest pay of all noncommissioned officers. Wilhelm Schäfer came from Stettin, was married, and was then thirty–six years old (born 1908). "He was large, robust, wide–shouldered, thirty to forty years old, always appeared with a dog."[111]

His deputy was *SS–Oberscharführer* Neumann who arrived from the Buchenwald concentration camp some time after the establishment of the sub–camp and who took care to establish harsher conditions.[112] "Schäfer and Neumann stayed in camp all the time, except that once in a while Schäfer came on motorcycle to check on us at the workplace."[113]

The other SS men were mainly responsible for guarding the exterior of the area and partly for guarding the women on their way to work. Most of them came from the Leipzig area.[114]

The makeup of the SS guard personnel can be seen in Table 2.

Table 2.

Status Report on Health Personnel, Prisoners, and SS Guards in Hessisch Lichtenau: March 20, 1945

Hessisch Lichtenau
March 20, 1945

SS Commando
Vereinhaus Camp
(16) Hessisch Lichtenau
Telefon 286

By Courier

Waffen SS
Concentration Camp Bureau
Att: Camp Physician
(15) Weimar – Buchenwald

A. <u>Subject: Monthly Report on Prisoners</u>

a. Ambulatory treatment of prisoners 11
b. Stationary treatment of prisoners 58
c. No cases of death
d. No illnesses
e. Scheduled delousings have taken place

b. Subject: Health Force Report for the Prisoners Camp
a. Dr. Fuckert, Hessisch Lichtenau Factory

b. Prisoner Physician: Luciana Nissim	Prisoner No. 21001
Prisoner Dentist: Else Cserepfalvi	Prisoner No. 20136
c. Prisoner Nurse: Lencner	Prisoner No. 21002
Prisoner Nurse: Lieber	Prisoner No. 21003

c. 27 SS Guard Troops
1 SS Commando Leader
1 SS Administration Leader
1 SS Deputy Administration Leader
1 Cook
1 SS Commando Clerk
2 SS *Oberscharführer*
4 SS *Unterscharführer*
5 SS *Rottenführer*
10 SS *Sturmmänner*
1 SS *Schütze*
1 Nurse (SS Supervisor)
31 SS Women Supervisors

f. Jewish Prisoners 790

Note: *Sturmann* Walter Lange, born on May 15, 1887, in Threna, Grimma/Sa District, is in the Marburg Lazarett, Surgical Department, with a stomach ailment.

Schäfer, Commando Leader
SS Sturmscharführer

Source: Dieter Vaupel, *Das Aussenkommando Hess. Lichtenau des Konzentrationslager Buchenwald, 1944/45.* Kassel: Gesamthochschulbibliothek, 1984, p. 78.

The Terror of the SS

For a long time, there was very little known of the behavior of the SS guards toward concentration camp prisoners. Information was recently obtained from two letters by former prisoners.

In the minutes of the hearings of the District Attorney's office in Kassel, deputy camp leader *Oberscharführer* Neumann is described as especially sadistic, according to statements by Jewish women, but they give no further details of such sadistic behavior. Conditions worsened after his appearance, especially with regard to disciplinary measures and food.[115] A former secretary of the factory who worked in "Camp Clubhouse" in the same office with the clerk of the SS, says about Neumann:[116] "He was a pig . . . a typical bloodsucker."

It is also known that the women were methodically harassed by the SS, having to stand at roll call for hours—no matter what the weather—before they were allowed to return to the damp, cold, and overcrowded barracks. Inhabitants of the camp relate that some SS members were "very mean with the women."[117]

The prisoner Esther Fuchs reports details about the chicanery of the SS guards. She writes of daily cursings, such as "dirty Jew" or "dirty Jewish whores," beatings, and torments. She describes the entire SS personnel, including the women, as sadists, who tried to outdo each other in harassing the women in camp or on the way to work.[118]

The SS made very sure that there should be no contact established between the women and the population during the trip to work. Eyewitnesses agree the women were beaten with whips and cursed by the SS men and women when they didn't proceed fast enough or attracted attention in any way; even cudgels were used to hurry them in entering the freightcars which transported them to work.[119]

There were several deaths among the prisoners, according to evidence given by former concentration camp prisoners of the sub-camp:

1. In retaliation for the successful escape of two women from camp, two relatives of the escapees were to be shot. The executions were to have been carried out by SS men.[120]

Katarin Müller: "The two selected prisoners were made to face a wall—20 meters away, across from us. The camp commander's deputy ordered four soldiers there . . . to fire at the prisoners. I don't remember how often the SS soldier Neumann fired, but I know that the shots were fatal because later they brought out other prisoners who had to throw the bodies of the executed into a chalk pit. The pit was within the camp's area, next to the turnip field."[121]

2. An SS man allegedly shot at some women during a disturbance in connection with the distribution of clothing and fatally hit one or two of them.[122] Three Jewish women remark:

Katarin Müller: "Manci Pál, called "Kapo," distributed the clothing through a barrack window. The women prisoners standing in line got impatient and pressed forward in order to get their clothing sooner. The previously mentioned SS man Neumann was in charge and when he noticed the pushing, he fired into the line, killing a fifteen–year old prisoner."[123]

Margit Bachrach: "One day before the evacuation of the camp, I don't remember whether it was morning or afternoon, I heard a shot. I went to the other prisoners to find out what happened; I discovered that there was a distribution of clothing, and during the commotion created by the grabbing of dresses one of the soldiers of the guard fired into the group of prisoners and hit a young girl."[124]

Esther Glück: "Shortly before the camp's evacuation—perhaps one or two days before—there was a distribution of clothing. I was walking in that direction and on the way I heard a shot. I turned back immediately and later heard from other women that two prisoners—either sisters or good friends—were hit. I have no knowledge whether they were fatally wounded, but they were not among us at the evacuation of the camp."[125]

3. It is alleged that about one month before evacuation, several prisoners were hanged on the camp gallows. One of the inmates' reports is based on notes she made immediately after liberation in 1945:[126]

> I believe it was a month before the camp's evacuation that in the middle of one day work was stopped at our workplaces in the munitions factory. All of us had to return to camp, although it was during working hours. When we arrived back, I saw two or three women prisoners hanging from a gallows on the roll call place. They were already dead. All prisoners, as well as the entire camp personnel, stood in the place and we were informed why the prisoners were executed. I remember all right, but not today, who gave us this information and I also don't remember why the prisoners were executed.

This reported incident is strongly disputed by former members of the SS guard who also deny the existence of a gallows on the camp grounds.[127]

Part of the SS terrorism was the fact that the women had to live with the constant fear of being returned to Auschwitz–Birkenau to be annihilated—as were 206 of their fellow sufferers. The great selection, which took place at the end of October 1944 in Hessisch Lichtenau, makes the total inhumanity of the SS system of terror evident.

The "Transfer" to Auschwitz–Birkenau

The women's strength was rapidly exhausted by conditions in the camp and the factory, which is evident from the fact that as early as October 27, 1944—three months after the arrival of the Jewish women in Hessisch Lichtenau—206 of them were "transferred" back to Auschwitz–Birkenau. As the factory had no interest in other than able-bodied and healthy workers, these forced laborers were sent back to the deathcamp.

Those prisoners who were sick and unfit for labor, and their relatives, were sorted out in "Camp Clubhouse." The camp commander, as SS-*Oberscharführer*, and the head woman warden participated in this selection.[128] Transfer to Auschwitz was the equivalent of a death sentence, according to all available information to date. There are reports from more than 20 former prisoners in the state files of Kassel about the selection. Not one of the 206 women selected in Lichtenau were ever seen again by those reporting prisoners after the war. They were sent to Auschwitz from Hessisch Lichtenau by the SS to be annihilated. To this day, the survival of any member of this transport cannot be verified.[129]

One shudders at the practicality and businesslike detachment found in the correspondence between the "SS Command Camp Clubhouse Hessisch Lichtenau" and the "Administration of the Concentration Camp Weimar-Buchenwald."[130] The books were kept painfully accurately; everything had to be in order. Even the planned annihilation of human beings had to proceed according to regulation. The transfer list consists of four pages with the names of Jewish women; it was prepared for the sole purpose of having a record of who was to be sent to the deathcamp. It is significant that occupations are no longer listed—in contrast to the list of arrivals of September 19, 1944. The

Jewish women traveled four days to Auschwitz (from October 27–31, 1944), crammed together in a freight train.[131]

In 1969, survivors of the sub–camp Hessisch Lichtenau report on this selection as follows:

Towa Dukesz: "Two or three months after our arrival, during a roll call, the camp commander "Willi" sorted out several of our co–prisoners who were weaker and older. Before the sorting out, Willi informed us that these women would be sent to a better camp where they would not have to work. The group consisted of 200 women prisoners who were taken from the camp the next day. We were still in camp when we heard—I don't remember the source—that the 200 prisoners were taken to Auschwitz. There were several women in the group from Léva; none returned after liberation. I know this because I lived in Léva for one year after liberation."[132]

Ilona Mueller: "I do know that about 200 women prisoners were taken away from the camp at the end of 1944. Now that I think about it, the transporting may have taken place earlier than the end of the year. We were working in three shifts and when I returned from work one day I heard from one of the other prisoners that the sick and unfit inmates of the camp were taken away. Other prisoners joined the group, for example a daughter would join her sick mother—who was selected for the transport—or a mother went with her daughter, etc. I don't know who put the group together, I remember only that about 200 prisoners were taken away. It was rumored in camp that they were taken to Auschwitz. An acquaintance of mine, called Bözsi Benedek, who came from Tab, Hungary, was one of the group; after liberation I visited Tab and heard that she never returned."[133]

Klara Singer: "I believe it was January 1945 when one day I should have gone to work on the first shift. They held a roll call at six in the morning and at that time I was selected to join a group of about 300 prisoners because I had a fever. This group of 300 consisted of those inmates who were sick and stayed in the sickroom, or of those who were too weak to work in the factory. I don't know who gave the order. I didn't want to join this group because my friends were not included. So I plucked up enough courage and—as the camp commander passed me—I stepped out of the line and asked him to allow me to stay in the camp. We heard, namely, that this group would be taken away. I told the commander that I was healthy and fit for work. He consented, and another prisoner replaced me in the selection. As I was feverish I stayed in camp—the others went to work—and so I could see that the selected group of 300 women prisoners was led outside the camp. There were a few acquaintances from my home town of Tab in this group of 300, namely Bloch—Panni and Vera—[they were] twins [and] were with their mother. [There were also] Mrs. Elisabeth Gross, and Mrs. Donnenberg. I was in Tab after my liberation and there I heard that not one of the above-mentioned returned. I don't know what happened to the group of 300 after they left the camp, and I could discover nothing of their fate in Tab either."[134]

Terezia Farkas Berkowitz: "I remember . . . that a very young prisoner became ill and was put in the sickroom. When the order came that all prisoners in the sickroom would be taken away, the mother of the young woman came forward and said that she and her other two daughters would like to stay with the sick prisoner and wanted to join the transport. All four daughters and the mother were taken away and they never returned to the camp. I lived in Sajószentpeter before being taken to the ghetto of Salgótarján. The four sisters and their mother also lived in Sajószentpéter before deportation; when I returned there after liberation, I found out that none of them came back. The family's name was Frank but I don't recall the first names of the mother and her four daughters."[135]

Margit Bachrach: "I had been in the camp for a few months, I believe, when I found out—it was talked about in camp—that a transport of about 300 prisoner-women was taken away. This happened while I was working outside the camp. The way I heard it, those prisoners who were sick and unable to work were the ones taken away. But there were also healthy prisoners among them. I remember some of them from Tab, namely the girl Vera Bloch, who was slightly ill and was selected for the group with her healthy sister, Panni Bloch, for the transport. They were twins. The twin's healthy mother was also selected. Mrs. Janka Donnenberg, Gitta Kürschner—who were not sick—were also taken away. When I returned to my hometown of Tab after liberation, I found out that none of the above came back. Later—after the transport left the camp—I heard in camp that the transport was sent to a death camp."[136]

Elena Surkes: "I don't know exactly—was it the end of 1944 or the beginning of 1945—that one morning, at roll call, they sorted out 200 prisoners and later led them out of the camp. I know that the women were taken out of our lineup on the basis of a list. I don't remember exactly who carried out the selection at roll call. The evening before the selection we were told . . . that women prisoners, no longer fit for work, or sick, will be taken to another camp where work would be lighter. Those healthy prisoners who wish to remain with their family members may sign up voluntarily. I, too, wanted to sign up because I found out that my sister–in–law, Jolán Ciobanu, was included in the list. During the night the camp elder, Manci Pál, appeared in the barracks where I lived; she came to me and talked me out of going with the transport. She told me that SS officers arrived in camp from Auschwitz and that the transport will be taken to Auschwitz. . . . After the roll call we were led to work and the selected group stayed in camp. When we returned from work in the evening, the selected group was not there any more and, as we heard later, they were taken to Auschwitz and killed there. After my liberation, when I returned to Klausenburg (Kolozsvár), I discovered that my sister–in–law, Jolán Ciobanu and Mrs. Nezsi Farkas did not come back."[137]

Magdalena Reismann:" "I don't recall the date, but one day a transport of 200 prisoners was put together and taken away. The camp commander informed us, at an early morning roll call, that the sick and unfit women prisoners will be moved to another camp. In this camp—he told us—the work will be easier, it would be in a cardboard box factory. All the inhabitants of the sickroom were brought out and a prisoner, a doctor from Italy, put their names on a list. The number of the transport—200 prisoners—was still short of a few people and then the camp commander selected from the lineup those who would be taken away with the transport. . . . The transport left the camp the same day under guard by SS soldiers. These SS soldiers were not the ones who were with us at the camp. Before the transport was led away, I heard—on the camp grounds—the camp commander's furious shout at the group assembled for the transport: 'You will be taken to Birkenau.' When I returned to Klausenburg after liberation, I found out that one of the prisoners named Hirsch who also came from Klausenburg and who was in the transport, never returned."[138]

Miriam Gáti: "I do know that at the beginning of November 1944, as I was returning to camp from the night shift one early Sunday morning, I had to appear immediately at roll call. All of the camp's prisoners were present. . . . The camp commander appeared, in company with the *Unterscharführer* and the Kapo Manci Pál, and informed us that a group of prisoners will have to be taken from the camp to Auschwitz to be cured there. These would be the sick and those unfit for labor. The commander read the prisoners' names from a list, and those prisoners whose names were read had to leave our ranks. There were altogether 200 women prisoners, including the sick, who were called. Afterwards we left the roll call place. As it was Sunday, I changed shifts and left the camp at 11 a.m. in order to be able to start work at 2 p.m.; when I returned from work at night, the group destined for Auschwitz was no longer in the camp. The way I heard it later from other prisoners, the group left the camp on foot and went to Lichtenau station. I remember a few women who were taken away with this group, namely, Edith Fein from Dombovár, and Mrs. Kürschner from the village of Konyi (near Dombovár). I returned to Dombovár after my liberation and found out that the above mentioned people never returned."[139]

Lenke Löwinger: "There was a rumor in camp that the sick prisoners would be transferred to Auschwitz, and this information came from the camp elder. One day we were told that those of us who no longer felt strong enough for work should come forward in order to be transferred to a camp with light work. Some women signed up and these were taken away with the sick prisoners. We knew that the sick were taken to Auschwitz and—once when I was sick—I went to work in that condition in order to avoid confinement and a later transfer."[140]

Frieda Német: A selection remains in my memory, when about 200 women prisoners were selected and sent away from camp. I was sick at the time and was in the sickroom at the time of the selection. Other prisoners, my friends, came to the sickroom and informed me that the sick and pregnant prisoners would be taken away. I left the sickroom in order to avoid the selection; I suspected that nothing good would happen to the ones selected. I didn't know that they would be taken to Auschwitz, but I had an idea and a feeling; and when we were in Auschwitz I sometimes heard about the gassing of the sick."[141]

Esther Glück: "I remember a selection when 200 prisoners were taken away from the camp . . . as I had a foot injury I was in the so-called sickroom. A few days later my sister, Margit Roth, came to me and forced me to leave the sickroom after she found out that all sick prisoners who were staying there would be taken away. I left the sickroom, went to work. In fact, the prisoners from the sickroom were listed, and at roll call, in the morning, additional weak women were sorted out. Altogether—as rumor had it—200 prisoners were selected. We went to work and when we returned in the evening we heard that the transport was led away. . . . A woman prisoner, who came from a neighboring village, from Szomoja, named Fleischer, also was taken away; after my liberation I was again in Nowaj—where I lived before my deportation—and I learned there that neither the prisoner named Fleischer nor others who were in the transport ever returned."[142]

On January 4, 1945, two more women were sorted out as "unfit for labor" and sent back to Auschwitz. One of them, Aranka Kohn, because she was eight months pregnant,[143] the other, Rozsa Schüssler, "because of mental illness."[144] A woman, who was conscripted for work in the filling station at the time, reports the following about the pregnant prisoner:

> One day the supervisor of the Jewish women, Maria, told us that one of the girls was pregnant and asked if we knew anyone who could perform an abortion. There was a nurse who did such things, but she was in prison just then because she had been caught doing an abortion. So we couldn't help the girl. Shortly thereafter I brought her a body wrap from my mother. I know that she sang and danced at Christmas, despite her condition. She had two sisters, one could hardly tell them apart. . . . At the beginning of the following year the girl didn't appear with us anymore. I don't know what happened to her.[145]

From documents, it appears that neither of the two women was accepted at Auschwitz—reasons unknown. The "transport leader," and SS-*Oberscharführer*, took them through Oranienburg into the Bergen–Belsen concentration camp. On January 8, the prisoners (Nos. 20,452 and 20,789) were "delivered and retained,"[146] as reported in the in human language of the SS. Evidence from Jewish women who survived the period of forced labor in Hessisch Lichtenau is available on the selection and subsequent fate of the two women:

Klara Singer: "Similarly—I believe it was January 1945—three more prisoners were taken away from the camp. One was called Aranka and was pregnant, the other—name unknown—lost her mind, but who the third was I don't remember any more. I saw when the three women prisoners were led away under the guard of a woman warden and an SS soldier. . . . The sister of the pregnant woman told me—she slept next to me—that the warden assured her that her sister was in a good place where she could give birth to the child."[147]

Ilona Mueller: "I was together with my two sisters in the camp Hessisch Lichtenau, namely Aranka Steiner, née Kohn, and Mrs. Ibilea (now Miriam) Gáti, née Kohn. My sister Aranka was pregnant, and on January 4 the deputy commander of the camp and a woman warden appeared in our barracks and led away my sister. My other sister, Miriam Gáti, and I begged them not to take our sister away, but they explained that our pregnant sister cannot remain in camp. They took her away, together with another prisoner who probably became mentally ill in the camp. When the warden who took our sister away returned to camp after a few days she answered our questions by saying that our sister was taken to Bergen–Belsen. Our sister never returned."[148]

Miriam Gáti: "On January 2, 1945, my sister Aranka, together with another prisoner who came from North Hungary and was called Rózsi, were taken away from the camp. It was confirmed that my sister was pregnant, and the prisoner Rózsi became mentally ill in camp. The *Unterscharführer*, with an SS–woman, came to fetch my sister. . . . My sister and the prisoner Rózsi were taken away on a sled and were brought back the next day. My sister told me that they traveled by train and have returned because Auschwitz didn't exist any more. But on January 4, 1945 my sister Aranka and the mentally ill woman were again taken away on a sled by the *Unterscharführer* and the above mentioned SS–woman; I have never seen her since. The SS–woman returned about a week later and told me personally that my sister was taken to Bergen–Belsen."[149]

Towa Dukesz: "Two more prisoners, acquaintances from Léva, were taken away later, we know nothing of their fate, either. Both were sent away under guard to [place name illegible] after the transport of the group of 200 women. One woman was pregnant, the other mentally disturbed. This mentally disturbed woman came from the vicinity of Léva and I know that she did not come back after liberation."[150]

Whether there were further selections in the sub–camp Hessisch Lichtenau cannot be unequivocally established at this time. Allusions to them are given in the statement by Terezia Farkas Berkowitz, among others:[151]

> Several times, at roll call, the camp commander and other SS–men and women who accompanied him, selected from the lineup prisoners who were sick, weak, or unfit for work. They were taken to the sickroom and we never saw them again. I don't know what happened to them, but it was rumored in camp that they were transported away.

Evacuation and Liberation

Toward the end of the war the SS was determined not to allow any concentration camp prisoners to fall into enemy hands, in order to prevent witnesses of the crimes committed from speaking out. Liberation by the Allied armies became a race against the plans for evacuation and annihilation by the SS.[152]

During the last days before evacuation three women escaped from "Camp Clubhouse."[153] It was reported that under cover of darkness they dug under the barbed wire fence with bare hands and took flight through the woods in the direction of Glimmerode/Reichenbach. The guards searched for them but they were not discovered. They hid in the woods until they were certain that the American troops occupied Hessisch Lichtenau. This happened on April 2, 1945. The three Jewish women lived with a family in Fürstenhagen until May 15, 1945.

On March 29, 1945, when the Americans already had reached Melsungen—15 kilometers away—the surviving inmates of Hessisch Lichtenau were evacuated.[154]

"One day before the evacuation the Jewish women were terribly excited and screamed and cried. When I went near the fence they said quite openly: 'We are done for!' "[155]

"The next day they were driven in the direction of Walburg. One of the women was shot at. What happened to her later, I don't know."

Next, the women were transported to Leipzig by rail, guarded by several members of the SS. The trip took five days. They stayed two days in Camp Leipzig-Schönau and a week in Camp Leipzig-Thekla. Afterward came an approximately two-week long evacuation march which was joined by other evacuated groups guarded by German soldiers. According to survivors, many prisoners who were unable to continue on this march were shot by the SS. An eighteen-year-old woman from the sub-camp Hessisch Lichtenau was killed by an SS man for having stolen a few potatoes for food. A few concentration camp prisoners were able to escape during the evacuation march. Members of the SS guard also deserted the transport, among them—supposedly—the camp commander Schäfer.[156] The evacuation march ended in Wurzen; there the surviving Jewish women were liberated by American troops on April 25, 1945.[157] Some of the SS men and women, who were still with the transport, were imprisoned by the Americans.

Survivors report on the evacuation march:

We had to work in the munitions factory until March 29. We were taken away ahead of the approaching Americans. We reached the aircraft factory Thekla near Dresden where we stayed a few days, until we started on the death march which led from Thekla through Leipzig to Wurzen; those who survived were liberated here by U.S. troops on April 25, 1945.[158]

As I explained before, the camp was evacuated at the end of March or the beginning of April. All the camp's inhabitants, SS soldiers, prisoners, left the camp. We formed a marching column and were driven through fields, woods, and different places. I was liberated in Wurzen on April 27, 1945. Other prisoner groups joined our column during the march. I remember that many prisoners who couldn't go on were shot dead. Names of the killers and victims are not known to me.[159]

We marched day and night and crossed the Elbe a few times.[160]

As I explained before, the camp was evacuated [on] April 25, 1945. All the camp's prisoners formed a column and—led by the camp commander and the entire camp personnel—we marched in a direction unknown to me. . . . We were driven through fields, woods, and villages—with unfamiliar names. . . . Once we spent a night in a barn and I could not continue in the morning because of exhaustion and sickness. Together with others—about ten women prisoners—I stayed back and let the column march on. On May 8, 1945, I was liberated here by the Russians. As I recall, the place where I stayed behind was called Treplitz.[161]

I think it was the middle of March 1945 when the camp was evacuated. The entire camp was evacuated and for about four weeks we were forced to travel by rail and on foot through various places, without a definite route, and guarded by the whole camp personnel. We were warned that anybody who lagged behind the column would simply be shot.[162]

The camp Hessisch Lichtenau was evacuated at the end of March or the beginning of April. We left the camp together with the camp commander and SS men and women. For about three weeks we were driven through meadows, fields, and woods, and on April 24, 1945 I was liberated in Wurzen. I stayed in Wurzen for two or three weeks, where the Russians took us over. The camp commander and the SS men and women disappeared during the march.[163]

The SS women threatened us that anybody leaving the column would be shot during the march but I was not an eyewitness.[164]

Many women prisoners, who could not continue the march, lagged behind the column and I am sure that those who were unable to hide were seized and shot by the SS soldiers. I was eyewitness when a woman prisoner named Tepper, who came from Ózd, was shot dead by an SS soldier because she stole a few potatoes from a barn. I saw her corpse was dragged away by other prisoners to be buried.[165]

About a week before April 25, 1945 we took a rest at a farm. The farmer was just cooking potatoes for his pigs and one of our co–prisoners, a young girl—perhaps eighteen years old—who came from Ózd, tried to steal one of the potatoes. I don't remember her name, but I know that she had two sisters in camp. As she was trying to steal, she was noticed by the *Unterscharführer*; he pulled his pistol from his holster and fired at her. She died immediately from the shot. This happened in front of me, at a distance of 3–4 meters. When the victim fell to the ground, the *Unterscharführer* said: "Take the trash to the trash–heap." After this murder the *Unterscharführer* disappeared, i.e., I never saw him again.[166]

Once a girl was shot during the march. She took one or more potatoes from a pigsty in a village . . . to eat. This was discovered by one of the guards. We were resting at the time in the courtyard of a farm. The guard shot the girl immediately. I have seen this. . . . We dug a grave for the girl in the courtyard and buried her.[167]

A few days before the liberation we rested in a farmyard. We noticed that the farmer brought out some potatoes to feed the animals. We ran to him—we were starved—to get some potatoes. Suddenly an SS soldier appeared and all of us ran away. One woman prisoner did not succeed in running away, the SS soldier fired at her; we saw this while running. The SS soldier approached the woman who was already lying on the ground, raised her head and—when he saw that she was dead—gave an order for roll call. I don't remember the killer's name but he had come with us from Lichtenau. About the victim, I know only that she was with us in camp with two of her sisters.[168]

I remember that one day during our march—when we stopped to rest—a woman prisoner tried to steal some potatoes. One of the SS soldiers—I don't know any longer who he was—fired at her; she collapsed and died almost immediately.[169]

The entire camp was evacuated, we marched two or three weeks under the camp commander's guard and crossed the Elbe. One day during the march, when we were resting in a barn, I heard a shot and when I turned in the direction of the shot I saw a soldier of the guard personnel with his weapon in his hand. Not far from the soldier I noticed a woman prisoner lying on the ground. The soldier yelled to us: "Take this trash away from here." Other women prisoners carried the dead woman away. I felt so sick that I went back in the barn, and I don't know what happened afterwards. As I heard later, the soldier fired at the prisoner because she had stolen a potato. We were constantly threatened during our march that anyone who stayed behind the column would be shot. I heard a few shots during the march, but I don't know why these were fired.[170]

I know from hearsay that during our march—when we stopped to rest near a playing field—a woman prisoner called Marika [last name unknown], a pharmacist from Targu, was shot and killed. Details of the murder are not known to me. I do know that she marched with us—with our group—and that she wanted to fetch some water. When we left the playing field she was no longer with us.[171]

Reactions of Lichtenau Citizens

Although the population of Lichtenau was not allowed to establish any contact with the Jewish women—who were heavily guarded—it could observe their pitiful condition when the women had to go to work. Reaction to the Jewish women, as far as this is still possible to reconstruct, often consisted of pretending not to notice them. In other cases, townspeople actually made fun of their peculiar appearance (shaved heads, rags for clothes, emaciated condition, tinted faces and bodies).

Reactions to the first reports in the local section of the *Hessische Niedersächsische Allgemeine* about the sub–camp[172] clearly showed that there were a great many people in Lichtenau and surroundings who felt inner sympathy with the fate of the Jewish women. There were a few others who tried—in spite of threats of the harshest punishment—to sneak some food to them, or give them clothing. Mrs. H., (now 83 years old), a resident of Hopfelder Street, relates:[173]

> I often went to the fence and threw them something: pieces of clothing, shoes, and above all, food—mostly when it was dark. I had to be careful because the guards were constantly patrolling around the fence.
>
> Some of the men were quite reasonable, but there was one among them who even threatened to shoot me dead. I wouldn't be the first one, he said.
>
> Saturdays I sometimes baked a cake for the women, packed it in shoeboxes, tied it up and threw it over the fence. I bribed the guards with the cake beforehand. . . .
>
> When there were no guards nearby, we sometimes talked over the fence. Women who spoke German said: "We have committed no crime." One of them told me: "I have three blonde sons, who knows what's happening to them. They are probably dead by now!" I tried to comfort her.

Other contemporary witnesses report that there were men and women workers in the munitions factory who—at the risk of their lives—gave the Jewish women something to eat during unobserved moments.

Without the help of a few from the Lichtenau population and from the workers in the factory it is certain that some of the women would not have survived their stay in the camp.

Did Memory Stop in 1945?

After the war, the history of the "Camp Clubhouse" was ignored by both the local historians and the municipal politicians. The Guide to Prison Locations of the International Tracing Service[174] has shown a camp in Hessisch Lichtenau since 1969, but nobody took notice of this in Lichtenau. The lack of public awareness is best demonstrated by the absence of a memorial tablet on the school grounds between Heinrich and Hopfelder Streets.

The following is ascertainable of the legal proceedings after 1945: both female and male members of the SS guard personnel were interned in camps after the war's end. The SS woman Mrs. Herzberger, as well as camp commander Schäfer and the SS-*Oberscharführer* Zorbach, were imprisoned for a total of twenty-five months in Schwarzborn, Ludwigsburg, and Darmstadt, respectively.[175] The SS woman Mrs. Sieberhagen was detained from June 1945 to February 1, 1948 in the Allied detention camps of Schwarzenborn, Ludwigsburg, Dachau, and Augsburg.[176] Others got away scot-free, and were denazified without legal proceedings against them.[177] In 1946, the Americans examined the incidents of "Camp Clubhouse." The hearings were held in Bad Homburg. However, the witnesses questioned were apparently not willing to give evidence, so no prosecution resulted.[178]

A more detailed attempt at judicial proceedings has been made since 1966, when Hessisch Lichtenau surfaced in connection with investigations in Buchenwald. Preliminary inquiries "for the killing of prisoners in the sub-camp Hess Lichtenau"[179] were conducted by the Center of Federal Judicial Administration for the Interpretation of Nazi Crimes until 1974. Former concentration camp prisoners, who now live in Israel, Czechoslovakia, the United States, and Canada, were questioned. Until 1976, the inquiries were conducted by the Public Prosecutor's Office in Kassel, which also interrogated former members of the SS guard. The investigations were suspended because the identity of those chiefly responsible—camp commander Schäfer and his deputy, Neumann—could not be documented, and detailed accounts required for an inquiry which would have led to further clarifications were no longer verifiable.[180] According to the District Attorney who presided over these investigations, a reopening of these proceedings is unlikely.

At the start of research in the summer and fall of 1983, it was difficult to obtain information about the sub-camp by questioning Lichtenau citizens, for reasons described above. The students, who initiated the study, and this writer had the impression that there was very little willingness by the population of Lichtenau to talk about the sub-camp, or about the years between 1933 and 1945 in general.

This situation changed only after the publication in the November 26, 1983 issue of the *Hessische Niedersächsische Allgemeine* of a report about the research which was based mostly on materials collected elsewhere.[181]

This report had wide repercussions and provided much material for discussion in Lichteanu's environs. The repercussions were also made evident by a profusion of telephone calls and letters. In part, these confirmed the results of the research up to that time, and even provided new information. Although the views expressed were overwhelmingly positive, there were a few callers who accused this researcher of trying to pick on the citizens of Lichtenau, asking why there was a wish to wallow in the past. One of the callers even said the women had it good in Hessisch Lichtenau and were glad to be allowed to work in the munitions factory. This caller may have had a point. After all it is better to be "allowed" to work than to perish in the gas chambers of Auschwitz.

The second of the more extensive newspaper reports of January 3, 1984,[182] which revealed to the public those findings of the Center of Federal Judicial Administration on the sub-camp that had been shown to this writer, elicited similar reactions as to the first one. This time, though, there were stronger and more direct threats from several callers. Thus, an older male, who introduced himself as an "SS-*Sturmbannführer*," made the suggestion that one "keep out of it" and not "wallow in the dirt." Another, extremely aggressive caller, who used the term, a "snot-nose" among others, pointed out that "those who dig in the dirt better watch out!"

All told, wide coverage in the local press[183] was instrumental in not permitting the memories of the Jewish women's fate to end in 1945. There are many people who are willing—after more than forty years—to remember and to share their experiences and observations with others, now that the subject is out in the open.

Fortunately, the town has also responded to the results of the investigations, and has announced its participation in further research. "We cannot sweep historical truth under the carpet," said the Mayor of Lichtenau, Ingo Geisler, in the *Hessische Niedersächsische Allgemeine* of January 11, 1984. In the meantime—after the first public discussions of the sub-camp were held in Feburary—the municipal council called for the establishment of a study group for completion of a detailed history of the munitions factory and the camps which belonged to it.

Notes

[1] Public Prosecutor's Office, Kassel. *Preliminary Investigations into the Suspicion of Murder in the Sub–Camp Hessisch Lichtenau of the Buchenwald Concentration Camp*, File no. 13JS395, p. 10. (Referred to hereafter as *Publ. Pros. Ks.*)

[2] *Archiv Auschwitz*, Doc. 144ff. (List of new arrivals, September 19, 1944.)

[3] *Ibid.*

[4] International Search Service, Arolsen. *Places of Imprisonment under the SS, 1933–1945.* (Referred to hereafter as *Prison Guide.*)

[5] Reinhard Kühnl, *German Fascism in Sources and Documents.* Köln: Pahl–Rugenstein Verlag, 1975, pp. 380ff. (Referred to hereafter as Kühnl).

[6] With respect to the situation of the Jews in Hungary, see section titled "About the Origins of the Concentration Camp Prisoners."

[7] Albert Speer, *The Slave State.* Stuttgart: Deutsche Verlangsanstalt (DVA), 1981, pp. 400ff. (Referred to hereafter as Speer.)

[8] *Ibid.*, p. 448.

[9] *Ibid.*

[10] Wolfram König and Ulrich Schneider, *Explosives of Hirschhagen.* Dissertation, School of Architecture, City and Environmental Planning, University of Kassel, 1983–84, p. 27. (Referred to hereafter as König and Schneider.)

[11] During the Nazi era, I. G. Farben owned 56 factories, producing all kinds of chemicals. According to Raul Hilberg, "I. G. Farben was not merely a business; it was a bureaucratic empire, and a major element in the machinery of annihilation." See his *Die Vernichtung des europäischen Juden. Die Gesamtgeschichte des Holocaust.* Berlin: Olle & Wolter, 1982, p. 623. (Referred to hereafter as Hilberg.) For further details on I. G. Farben, including wartime employment of slave labor and medical experiments conducted under its auspices, see Hilberg, pp. 628ff and 632. See also Renzo Vespignani, *After the Twenties: Fascism.* Berlin: Elefanten Press, 1976, pp. 117ff. (Referred to hereafter as Vespignani.)

[12] König and Schneider, pp. 26ff.

[13] *Ibid.*, pp. 49ff. These pages contain an exact description of the

procedure used.

14 *Ibid.*, p. 54.

15 *Ibid.*, pp. 56ff.

16 Werner Keller, *Munitions Factory Leaves Region a Poisonous Inheritance. Hessisch Niedersächsische Allgemeine (HNA)*, local section Werra–Meissner, March 9, 1984. (Referred to hereafter as Keller.)

17 *Ibid.*

18 To maintain camouflage at an optimum, the forty gardeners of the factory were employed full time. Gabriele Rothemann, *Pictures from Hirschhagen.* Research work at the University of Kassel, 1981, p. 8. (Referred to hereafter as Rothemann.)

19 Keller, *op. cit.*

20 Personnel report on prisoners at the local sub–camp Hessisch Lichtenau, January 8, 1945, Federal Archive Koblenz, NS 4/Bu 223.

21 This figure is based on information from Mr. F., former employee of the factory. (Conversation of October 28, 1983.)

22 Keller, *op. cit.*

23 König and Schneider, p. 78.

24 *Ibid.*, p. 91. See also footnote 88.

25 *Ibid.* For detailed description of individual camps, see pp. 39ff.

26 Hilberg, p. 542.

27 *Ibid.*

28 *Ibid.*, p. 543.

29 *Ibid.*, p. 546.

30 *Ibid.*, p. 543f.

31 *Ibid.*, p. 549.

32 *Ibid.*, p. 553.

33 *Ibid.*, p. 556.

34 *Ibid.*, p. 577.

35 *Publ. Pros. Ks.*

36 *Ibid.*, p. 74.

37 Kühnl, p. 367.

38 Wilhelm Van Kampen, *Holocaust.* Wiesbaden: Hessische Landeszentrale für politische Bildung, 1978.

39 *Ibid.*

40 Bernd Klewitz, *Sub–Camp Münchmühle/Allendorf.* Stadtallendorf, 1983. (Manuscript)

41 *Ibid.*

[42] International Camp Committee, *Buchenwald. Warning and Obligation.* Berlin: Deutscher Verlag der Wissenschaften, 1980, p. 14.

[43] Bernd Klewitz, *Sub-Camps of Hesse during the War.* Stadtallendorf, 1983. (Manuscript)

[44] International Search Service, Arolsen. Written communication of April 8, 1983. (Referred to hereafter as *International Search Service.*)

[45] Construction Deeds (Bauakten) Camp Clubhouse, Archives of Hessisch Lichtenau. (Referred to hereafter as *Constr. Deeds.*)

[46] Acceptance Report of the Trustees of Montan Industries, Inc. for Hesse, Frankfurt am Main, July 1, 1946, rider 8, p. 3. (Referred to hereaafter as *Accept. Report.*)

[47] Conversation with Mrs. S., December 2, 1983.

[48] *Constr. Deeds.*

[49] *Ibid.*

[50] *Accept. Report*, rider 12/III.

[51] Papers of the Factory Hessisch Lichtenau, November 21, 1946, p. 2.

[52] *Publ. Pros. Ks.*, p. 305.

[53] These statements are based on eyewitness reports.

[54] *Publ. Pros. Ks.*

[55] *Ibid.*, p. 72.

[56] *Ibid.*, pp. 305 and 356.

[57] *Ibid.*, p. 356.

[58] *Refugee Camp in Hessisch Lichtenau*, Werra–Bote, March 13, 1946.

[59] Written communication from Esther Fuchs, April 28, 1984.

[60] *Publ. Pros. Ks.*, p. 15.

[61] Rothemann, p. 14.

[62] Letter from Esther Fuchs.

[63] Ursula Krause–Schmidt, "Concentration Camps in Hessen" in *When the War Ended.* Hessen, 1945. Ulrich Schneider, *et al.*, Frankfurt: Röderberg–Verlag, 1980, p. 148. (Referred to hereafter as Krause–Schmidt.)

[64] Conversation with Mrs. A. who worked with Jewish women in the filling station, February 13, 1984.

[65] Conversation with Mr. F., October 28, 1983. According to later testimony by Dr. Praetorius, director of the factory, 500 pairs of leather shoes were acquired for the women (notes of Dr. Liebers,

Lichtenau, 1960, p. 1). There is no other evidence for this statement; it seems highly unlikely, as by this time even German soldiers could not be supplied with leather shoes.

66 *Publ. Pros. Ks.*, p. 11.

67 *Archiv Auschwitz*, Document 139. Correspondence, September 6, 1944.

68 *Publ. Pros. Ks.*, p. 145.

69 *Ibid.*, p. 11.

70 *Ibid.*

71 Conversation with Mrs. H., former neighbor of Camp Clubhouse on Hopfelder Street, October 26, 1983.

72 Conversation with Mrs. B., October 26, 1983.

73 Letters to the author from Sabine Gross (March 2, 1984) and Esther Fuchs (April 24, 1984).

74 Conversation with Mrs. T., November 30, 1983.

75 Description of routes is based on reports by contemporary witnesses. It must be remembered, however, that some roads (especially nos. 2 and 4) were seldom used; others (nos. 3 and 5) were used almost daily.

76 *Publ. Pros. Ks.*, p. 17.

77 Files of the factory, November 21, 1946, p. 2.

78 Written communication from Mrs. K., January 3, 1984.

79 Conversation with Mrs. H., January 3, 1984.

80 Written communication from Sabine Gross, March 2, 1984.

81 Military Archive, Freiburg, *War Diaries 1944 of the Mobilization Inspection IX Kassel*, p. 15.

82 Conversation with Mrs. K., October 27, 1983 (conducted by König and Schneider).

83 Conversation with Mrs. G., November 26, 1983.

84 Opinion of Hygieninstitut Gelsenkirchen, September 11, 1975.

85 König and Schneider, p. 57.

86 Rothemann, p. 22.

87 Information protection prevented access to the state files. However, I did receive summarized information on dates and causes of deaths, as well as age and origin of the dead.

88 Some of these accidents are listed in the *War Diaries of the Mobilization Inspection IX Kassel* (in the Military Archive of Freiburg). The number of victims can be ascertained also from church records and from the State Registrar's files. Only 200

are mentioned here; in addition there are those who died outside (in the area hospitals), and those not registered in Hessisch Lichtenau (the dead of the Sub–Camp).

89 Written communication from the Main Archive of Hesse, Wiesbaden, April 20, 1983.

90 Kühnl, p. 377.

91 *Publ. Pros. Ks.*, p. 10.

92 *Ibid.*, p. 351. Whether the two girls were buried in Hessisch Lichtenau could not be ascertained to date.

93 *Ibid.*, p. 17.

94 Eberhard Aleff, *The Third Reich.* Hannover: Verlag Literatur und Zeitgeschehen, 1970.

95 Krause–Schmidt, p. 149.

96 Benjamin Ferencz, *Less Than Slaves.* Cambridge, Mass.: Harvard University Press, 1979.

97 Center of Federal Justice Bureaus for the Clarification of Nazi Crimes. Written communication of December 6, 1983. (Referred to hereafter as *Center.*)

98 *Population of Female Sub–Camps*, Weimar–Buchenwald, November 25, 1944. (Enclosure in written communication from *Center*).

99 *Publ. Pros. Ks.*, p. 6.

100 Female Sub–Camps of the Buchenwald Concentration Camp. Buchenwald Vol. 15/82. (Referred to hereafter as *Female Sub–Camps.*

101 *Archiv Auschwitz*, Document 54.

102 *Center*, p. 2.

103 Conversation with Mr. K., October 31, 1984.

104 *Ibid.*

105 *Publ. Pros. Ks.*, p. 354.

106 *Ibid.*, p. 244.

107 *Ibid.*, p. 335.

108 *Ibid.*, p. 349.

109 *Ibid.*, p. 350.

110 Davis and Turner, *German Uniforms of the Third Reich 1933–45.* Munich: Verlag Wilhelm Heyne, 1980, p. 194.

111 *Publ. Pros. Ks.*, p. 263.

112 *Ibid.*, p. 357.

113 *Ibid.*, p. 336.

114 *Ibid.*, pp. 336 and 351.

115 *Ibid.*, p. 159.

116 *Ibid.*, pp. 345 and 357.
117 Conversation with Mrs. H., October 26, 1983.
118 Written communication from Esther Fuchs, April 24, 1984.
119 See section titled *The Path to Work.*
120 *Center*, p. 2.
121 *Publ. Pros. Ks.*
122 *Center*, p. 2.
123 *Publ. Pros. Ks.*
124 *Ibid.*, p. 192.
125 *Ibid.*, p. 263f.
126 *Ibid.*, p. 119.
127 *Ibid.*, p. 333ff.
128 *Center*, p. 3. It is not clear whether a physician participated in the selection.
129 The *Archiv Auschwitz* informed me that they have no documents regarding the fate of the 206 women other than the transport list. Based on all previous knowledge, however, one must assume that they were murdered in the gas chambers.
130 *Archiv Auschwitz*, Document 20; also Documents 21–24.
131 *Female Sub–Camps*, p. 50f.
132 *Publ. Pros. Ks.*
133 *Ibid.*, p. 159f.
134 *Ibid.*, p. 75.
135 *Ibid.*, p. 152.
136 *Ibid.*, p. 191f.
137 *Ibid.*, p. 196f.
138 *Ibid.*, p. 202.
139 *Ibid.*, p. 281f.
140 *Ibid.*, p. 72f.
141 *Ibid.*, p. 121.
142 *Ibid.*, p. 264.
143 Susanne Hohlmann, *Pfaffenwald: Death and Birth Camp 1942–1945.* National Socialism in North Hesse, Studies in the Current History of the Region, Vol. 2, Kassel: Gesamthochschulbibliothek, 1984, pp. 86ff.
144 *Archiv Auschwitz*, Document 27.
145 Conversation with Mrs. A., February 13, 1984.
146 *Publ. Pros. Ks.*, p. 9.
147 *Ibid.*, p. 75f.
148 *Ibid.*, p. 160.

149 *Ibid.*, p. 283f.
150 *Ibid.*
151 *Ibid.*, p. 153.
152 Krause–Schmidt, p. 150.
153 Written explanation of a former concentration camp prisoner, April 8, 1945. (Property of Mr. Küllmer, Hessisch Lichtenau.)
154 *Register of Prison Locations*, p. 46. According to *Center*, p. 1, the camp was evacuated by March 23, 1945.
155 Conversation with Mrs. H., October 26, 1983.
156 *Publ. Pros. Ks.*, p. 76.
157 *Center*, pp. 1 and 3.
158 Kraus–Schmidt, p. 150.
159 *Publ. Pros. Ks.*, p. 119.
160 *Ibid.*, p. 284.
161 *Ibid.*, p. 122.
162 *Ibid.*, p. 197.
163 *Ibid.*, p. 76.
164 *Ibid.*, p. 248.
165 *Ibid.*, p. 155.
166 *Ibid.*, p. 284.
167 *Ibid.*, p. 145.
168 *Ibid.*, p. 197.
169 *Ibid.*, p. 76.
170 *Ibid.*, p. 192f.
171 *Ibid.*, p. 197f.
172 Werner Keller, *A Thousand Jewish Women in the Lichtenau Camp*, HNA, Werra–Meissner, November 26, 1983.
173 Conversation with Mrs. H., October 26, 1983.
174 *Register of Prison Locations*, p. 46.
175 *Publ. Pros. Ks.*, p. 20.
176 *Ibid.*, p. 244.
177 *Ibid.*
178 Conversation with Mrs. K., October 31, 1984.
179 Investigations of the Public Prosecutor's Office.
180 *Publ. Pros. Ks.*, p. 368.
181 Keller, *A Thousand Jewish Women in the Lichtenau Camp, op. cit.*.
182 *Were Jewish Women Shot and Killed in the Camp?* HNA, Werra–Meissner, January 1, 1984.
183 Article in the HNA/Werra–Meissner.

THE SECOND AND THE THIRD GENERATION HOLOCAUST SURVIVORS AND THEIR DESCENDANTS

Julia Szilágyi, István Cserne, Katalin Pető, and György Szöke

I. The Problem

In our everyday activity as psychiatrists and psychotherapists it has been our experience that for patients with various psychopathological disorders the experience of their parents concerning the persecution of Jews proved to be a traumatizing, pathological factor. This trauma became immediately evident only in a very small number of cases. In the process of psychotherapy, phenomena emerged that could be linked with the traumata suffered by the parents.

Our experiences were at first not very clear-cut. But as we began to collect more data about this phenomenon our conviction became ever deeper: the relationship between psychopathological symptoms and the sufferings of our patients' parents cannot be regarded as a chance and isolated coincidence; on the contrary it is an existing, what's more a rather regular, constellation. We therefore turned to the literature for help. Soon it became clear, however, that the early works on this subject themselves bring up several new and hitherto unsolved questions, primarily because of their deficiencies and the contradictory character of their data and conclusions. As for the special Hungarian circumstances, until now hardly any literature on this subject exists.

So the main question of the study is: are there special psychic consequences for the children if someone's parents are Holocaust survivors? As an anticipation of our results, we answer yes.

II. Some Remarks on the Relevant Literature

We can group the literature according to the date of publication, the subject matter chosen, and the conclusions arrived at by the authors. Instead of a detailed analysis let us only mention the most important thematic groups:

(A) The first group includes works dealing with severe psychic trauma and its early and late effects; these works range from Sándor Ferenczi (1918) through the Budapest psychoanalytic conference held in the Fall of 1987, where this topic was the main theme. Such traumata as the war neurosis, the "survivor syndrome" (well known from Holocaust literature), and the "post-traumatic stress disorder" (PTSD) diagnosis of clinical psychiatry have many things in common, but at the same time they contain extreme differences—both theoretically and as far as therapy is concerned. The study of István Székács (Schönberger) (1948) on the acute and fixated changes of the ego as a consequence of war traumata (e.g., the extreme modification of outer reality) deals with the problem from the point of view of modern psychoanalysis. Even Géza Róheim refers to this pioneer work. The contributions of a conference organized by Henry Krystal (*Severe Psychic Trauma*, 1968) contain much material on non-Holocaust themes, among them the psychological questions connected with recovery from severe somatic diseases, the traumatic states found in victims of natural catastrophies and the bombing of Hiroshima.

(B) The Holocaust as a trauma has been dealt with by psychoanalytically and non-psychoanalytically oriented authors since 1942 (see e.g., the works of Bettelheim, Kulcsár, Székács, Luchterhand, Eitinger, des Pres, Krell, Ludowyk-Gyömrői on the first generation). Several psychoanalytic studies discuss the treatment of more or less severe cases. There is an almost total agreement among the authors: the pathography of the Holocaust-survivors belongs to the "severe" class of psychopathological disorders. Their evaluations of these severe deviations, what they have to say about their mechanism and treatment seem to reflect the internal schisms and the development of psychiatric and psychoanalytical theory and practice. Characteristically, the authors cited are experts on other fields of severe psychopathology as well.

(C) Works dealing with psychological problems of Holocaust-survivors' children include those of Kestenberg (1972), Sonnenberg (1974), and Kogan (1987). The study of Rose and Garske (1987) contains abundant further literature. While we find some surveys (based on sampling and interviews) that were unable to find any psychopathological alteration, the overwhelming majority regard trauma among

Holocaust survivors' descendants as an independent entity. The theoretical views about the pathological mechanisms vary, of course, from author to author.

(D) The recent developments of psychiatry and psychoanalysis we used are contained in the works of O. F. Kernberg or in the literature dealing with post–traumatic stress and with personality disturbances in general.

Characteristically, the studies done immediately after the Holocaust were followed in nearly every country by a long pause. A new boom began in the mid–sixties. A more recent field of study has inevitably emerged: investigations are being made among not only children of Holocaust–survivors but also grandchildren.

We are not aware of any work dealing with the specifically Hungarian aspects of the issue. Which is very regrettable: as our knowledge in this area has deepened, the special features of the Hungarian situation have become ever more evident to us. The contradictory nature of the literature dealing with the psychological characteristics of survivors and their children is best demonstrated in how they evaluate the trauma that befall the survivors. In 1967–68 experts in the Federal Republic of Germany failed to discover any pathological symptoms that could have been linked to Holocaust traumata in persons who claimed compensation offered by the West German government as reparation. American experts, however, found several psychological symptoms caused by specific traumata in the very same persons. Beyond the different political views and atmosphere, the contradictory results of assessment are due to the scientific development of psychiatry: the deviations observed in connection with these traumata do not match the notions of classical psychiatry.

As far as the Hungarian situation is concerned it was and—it seems to us—has remained complicated. It was very difficult for more recent trends of psychopathology to take root in Hungary, and furthermore, the professional audience is almost totally indifferent to the specific traumata of Jewish survivors.

III. Sources and Methodology

Our original idea was to have interviewed Holocaust survivors' children, born under normal conditions between 1946 and 1950. It soon became obvious, however, that to accurately understand the transmittance mechanism we had to extend our scope, and interview the survivors themselves, and their children, too. Thus we became more "family-oriented." In some cases even this proved to be insufficient: the problems reappeared—though in somewhat modified form—in the third generation. In extending the range of our subjects, in any event, we followed primarily the aim of discovering the transmission process of the trauma.

One of our discoveries was that there is a universal tendency toward nearly total concealment of the Jewishness of the family and of the ordeals they underwent during the Holocaust. We speak here not only of those who were inmates of concentration camps, but also—in agreement with the relevant literature (see e.g., Kardiner (1965), Luchterhand (1970)—of traumatized survivors everywhere: the inhabitants of the ghetto, of the protected houses, those who were hiding, and those who took part in forced labor.

We by no means regard our study as completed. Our intention has been to lay the foundations of a longer study for practicing psychiatrists and psychotherapists that could help them in recognizing and treating hidden psychic defects. Our material also contains data referring to second generation consequences of other kinds of lasting severe threat and social isolation; the recent history of Hungary in the last decades unfortunately have brought several social strata into this situation. Our position is clearly psychoanalytical: to give a more precise definition it has to do with the personality traits of our subjects. The "questionnaire" method could have been, in principle, also possible; for several reasons, however, we regarded it as unsuitable for our purposes although the technique is simple and convenient (for the debates over methods based on "sampling" and case studies see, e.g., the works of Sonnenberg and also Rose and Garske). Questionnaires reflect at best the same information that the subject is already consciously aware of, but do not approach and discover subconscious contents. For such purposes we should apply clinical interviews (also in cases not requiring psychoanalytic treatment) or psychoanalytically interpreted projective tests.

Our practical experiences (like the relevant literature) have shown that the traumatizing factors have sunk into deeper levels of the psyche both in the case of survivors and the second and third generation. Moreover, the traumatic character, inelaborability, and pathogenic nature of the experience is dependent on the fact that the given experience is out of reach for consciousness and for the conscious ego.

The symptoms generally remained hidden, but nevertheless present, even if the subject's functioning was fairly normal (or seemingly so), while his or her family roles, social, and work achievements were intact. The disturbances, notwithstanding their hidden nature, are severe ones. It is precisely the failure in conscious elaboration of the traumata that stands in the background of severe disturbances. The social amnesia (the seeming insensibility, ignorance toward the problem of Jewishness and its connections with the Holocaust) aggravates the situation.

It is only in recent years that psychoanalytically oriented methods suitable for the treatment of (only indirectly pathologic) changes in the psychic character and of symptoms that are more difficult to identify have developed. Psychopathology has extended its field of competence to pathologies of origin in the early childhood: to traumatic effects caused by the disturbances and breaks in the mother–child relationship. We may mention in this connection the separation trauma and the accompanying normal and pathologic psychological crises, the (oral) traumata and functional disturbances related to nourishment. Among the mechanisms of pathogenesis a considerable role is played by the transmittance of the parents' pathogenic states and ways of reaction. There has recently been a vivid interest in psychiatry in this problem complex. Such transmittance mechanisms that are beyond the competence of traditional conceptions of mental illnesses were met in our investigations, too.

Decisive experiences with lasting negative effects sinking into the unconscious render them pathogenic for both parent and child. Traumatic contents will be suppressed, dealt with, or balanced by means of early psychic defensive mechanisms (see e.g., Kernberg (1976, 1984)). This is why only a minor and less characteristic part of these contents will be consciously accessible. The suppression or other forms of unconscious contents and the fact that our subjects cope with traumatic experiences by averting them is revealed in the form of characteristic family secrets: there are certain topics that the parent or grandparent doesn't speak of and that the child—seemingly—doesn't inquire about for a long time. (We shall return to the topic of secrets later.)

Our approach was clinical. Long interviews have been done with about forty subjects; the texts became the raw material of the case studies. In summarizing each interview, we based our conclusions on phenomena that varied in form from case to case yet somehow turned out to be constantly present. Our interviewing method was thus analytically oriented, although the aim of the study was not doing therapy. In spite of this the same phenomena emerged during the interviews that we meet in our every day psychotherapeutic work, (transference, resistance). Prior to each interview our subjects were informed about the aims and method of the investigation. No direct questions were posed; we asked the subjects to tell us everything they considered important about their life, their family, about their past and their present. During the conversation we constantly tried to promote the free flow of thoughts; the questions served only to reveal the pre–conscious content of what was said. Though we had no preconceptions and "ready made" questions, we of course tried to get acquainted with our subjects' physical and mental characteristics and their development, with their familial and other important relationships, as well as with their thoughts concerning Jewishness in general and their own Jewishness. The order of the contents, the place of eventual breaks in the dialogue, the themes that were evaded, were all taken into consideration as important evaluative points of view. To summarize briefly: our technique of interview–making and evaluation was nearer to the one used in the practice of psychotherapy than to that used in sociology. In interviewing the survivors we of course inquired about the events that befell them; we also asked their descendants how much they had heard about all this in the family. We tried to dig up personal experiences but instead of these we rather frequently got general evaluations, explanations, or "ideological" arguments. As one of our subjects, a third generation, high school student noted: "It is easier to list the names of concentration camps than to speak about our thoughts of them." In such cases we tried to lead the conversation in a more concrete way though we were quite aware of the fact that this spontaneous "ideologization" is also a kind of psychic defense mechanism.

Our subjects were recruited informally mainly through personal contacts. We tried to prevent any personal relationships between interviewer and subject: acquaintances were interviewed by other members of the team. The content of our interviews was treated according to the rules of medical secrecy even to the family members. It was instructive that in families where the problem complex of the Holocaust has been treated as a secret the children tried to dissuade us from contacting their parents, saying they would by no means agree to be interviewed. (In the majority of the cases this scruple of theirs proved to be unfounded.)

Whenever it was possible two or three generations were interviewed, for it was obvious to us that hidden traumata come into being and are transmitted first of all within the family and most specifically in the parent–child relationship.

The analysis of the completed interviews took the shape of a clinical case–presentation and –discussion. Apart from the written material we drew considerable attention to the seemingly concealed or inadequate moments, to sudden breaks in the flow of thoughts, and to those facts that were logically related to one another but were more or less consistently separated by the subject. It was during these discussions that the pattern of a final summary of the interviews became clear.

IV. Common Issues Extracted from the Interviews

During the elaboration the following characteristic features or symptoms proved to be generally valid and hence very instructive for fellow therapists dealing with character disturbances.

1. Clinical Symptoms

Anxiety, depressive disposition, frequent and severe psychosomatic symptom–formation are the symptoms (see Ferenczi, Kardiner, Krystal, and Breslau and Davis). They flow from the impossibility of emotionally working up the trauma and its verbalization. The material has completely verified the almost common–sense claim that Holocaust experiences were and remain largely unspeakable. "Normal reason is unable to understand it" is a current expression. The psychic apparatus, the human soul, by means of its functions (developed in normal circumstances) proved unable to elaborate experiences of such extremity. Mechanisms came into the foreground that are characteristic (on the level of fantasy) of only the earliest childhood—the period normally preceeding speech–formation (the systematic investigation of this field is based on the conceptions of Melanie Klein).

Frequent thematic groups that are not worked through are the separation trauma (the tearing away of the nearest relatives) and the oral trauma (the hunger that threatens even with dying), the complete physical and psychological defenselessness.

A striking phenomenon is an almost complete lack of the work of mourning. Mourning is a human means for making the death of relatives gradually explainable and acceptable. In the case of survivors this work of mourning was as a rule missing. The experiences of traumata became suppressed (or else were of such a kind that their objective elaboration proved to be completely impossible). The survivors wanted to protect their descendants, but this intention turned into its opposite: to the transmittal of an unbearable secret to their children. In each of the interviews the same secret referring to the trauma of Holocaust has been found but the mechanisms we discovered behind the same phenomenon were different.

The traumata the survivors had to suffer were so severe that their elementary aggressive contents and frustrations equal the dominant themes of the primary experiences in the first months of life in normal development. In the course of normal development the primary, so-called primitive defense mechanisms are followed by more mature ones. In our cases we saw just the contrary: the rational, conscious "explanation" given to the experienced trauma not only failed to complete psychic elaboration but actually made that completion even more difficult to accomplish: the conscious content has been "separated" from the experience of it. (This is the phenomenon of splitting: see below.)

In the Hungarian social atmosphere after 1945 the seeming necessity of forgetting the past and thus preserving the family secret became even more important, nearly institutionalized (see below among the social-psychological consequences).

Because the experience of the Holocaust remained thereby unelaborated the already existing (religious, racial and psychological) identity confusions were mobilized. There was hardly anyone among our subjects who somehow could have been able to cope completely successfully with this. In addition, let us note that the interest of our subjects in the investigation is in itself a proof of their openness toward identity-problems. On the other hand, it would be difficult to define the ideal, "normal" expectations in this respect.

2. Disorders in the Personality Structure of Survivors

Almost every subject's parents displayed, either actively or passively, one or more signs of the posttraumatic ("survivor") syndrome. In all these cases the ego-strength decreased considerably; the degree of ego-weakness, however, varies not only among the different subjects but also in various life-periods of the individual. Let us mention only one characteristic feature.

In spite of all the differences of character traits and life situations among different individuals a recurrent experience was the conspicuously strong disposition toward regression. Such primitive psychological defense mechanisms occur as negation, splitting, and projection. Characteristically, in all these mechanisms the past inadequately—or seemingly so—gets mixed with the present. The ego damages render the person incapable of using the otherwise intact higher-level defense mechanisms.

Let us illustrate with some examples the appearance of such a mechanism in the form of concrete symptoms. Separation anxiety turned up in one of our subjects (born in 1948) and in his surviving mother. The parents and their child spent their holidays abroad; the little girl lagged behind looking at shop windows. Her mother looked for her in terror, shouting in German "*zusammen, zusammen!*" thereby indicating that the family must hold together. This is how the state of mind during the persecutions becomes vivid for the mother and, projected on the realities of the present moment, contributes unintentionally and almost without notice to the "heritage" of the child.

The same thing occurred between another subject of ours (born in 1948) and her own children: the mother becomes very anxious if her children disappear from her field of vision even for a few seconds; the tension is not eased by the fact that she knows, in view of the present realities, that this anxiety is unfounded.

Another mother who also belongs to this age-group used to live on the eighth floor of a big apartment house. This, paradoxically, brought her reassurance for—as she says—"if something happens I can immediately jump out together with my daughter." Recently they moved to a house with a garden, which again reassured her because in some minutes' walk there was a foreign embassy and "if something happens I'll run there and hand over my child." (They have several relatives in that country.)

A special negation of one segment of reality (seemingly a simple one) and at the same time a characteristic example of splitting is expressed by another (now about forty years old) subject who—in his own words—"had no Jewish classmates in elementary school." If we contrast this statement with the next sentence, where it turned out that he had gone to school in Dob street—one of the typically Jewish districts in Budapest—we can't help feeling to have listened to a tragicomic joke.

The next example serves to demonstrate how suppressed memory reappears as a neurotic symptom. Our subject was a child in the period of persecutions: "I don't remember anything"—he says in agreement with the, for him, conscious reality. Once he traveled to East Germany and was falling asleep on the train; at the border, after he was nudged awake, and caught sight of the grey uniform of a GDR border guard, he fainted.

3. Social-Psychological Viewpoints

There are no sharp boundaries between these phenomena and the clinical symptoms mentioned above. They are mixed together and the "symptoms" have to be analyzed in their complexity.

In addition to the traumatic experiences of the Holocaust, the amnesia and the silence surrounding the persecution of Jews extend to almost the entire society and have, no doubt, social roots. The "secret" lies within the family aspect of the "amnesia" of the entire society. The secret comprises not only the experiences of the Holocaust but also the knowledge and open acceptance of being a Jew. (For a classical example of the pathogenic effects of the secret, see Freud's "Dora-case.")

Another theme that is closely connected with the phenomenon of secrets—and to some extent is a pathogenic factor too—is the irrational humiliation of the first generation. It is precisely owing to this irrationality that these experiences cannot be verbalized or elaborated. The ego of the Jewish victims was systematically destroyed by physical and psychic means, the victims were deprived of their identities, social roles, and relationships—indeed their entire past and future. The trauma is incredibly severe because the experiences are so immensely beyond everything that ordinary human beings could undergo in an ordinary life that the individual is incapable of integrating them into the ego (see Bettelheim, Szekacs, and des Pres).

Perhaps this gives us a clue to the seemingly illogical behavior of parents who survived the persecutions: being unable to express or explain their humiliations, they simply omit them in order to protect their children. Thus, the "secret" would be a depressing experience within the family even if it were not surrounded by social silence with some anti-Semitic tinge.

This is the point where social atmosphere plays a decisive role: it further enhances the necessity of keeping secrets in families and of a seemingly complete oblivion of everything that befell the individuals. The declaration (made after 1945 in Hungary) that the Jewish question (and the persecution of the Jews) has ceased forever could have been, on the rational level, an enticing perspective for both the humiliated Jews and the non-Jewish population (in a struggle with its guilty conscience). As a result, "if we don't speak of it, it doesn't exist" was added to the lack of mourning reaction, at least on the conscious level, of all that had happened. But something doesn't go away simply because we ignore it; what is regarded as a secret brings out unavoidably negative evaluations. What you conceal is wrong.

The post-1945 generation considers—in unconscious fantasies—both their own Jewishness and themselves and their families as something not quite "kosher." To put it more precisely: the criteria of good and evil are hopelessly entangled. This trait, usually characteristic of earliest childhood, here turns up in adulthood. As in early childhood, experiences are impossible to verbalize. (This mechanism is connected with the above mentioned phenomenon of splitting.)

We should make a distinction between two kinds of pathogenic factors under which the parents suffered. (1) Holocaust as a trauma that objectively cannot be verbalized, that is a necessary consequence of the persecutions that can only be brought to the surface by means of a long work of mourning, psychic elaboration; (2) the concealment of being a Jew. Thus a consequence of the "survivor syndrome" the descendants are threatened by a new trauma.

The first—directly or in a transmitted form—has been imposed on each of our subjects. The second is less general, although very frequent. According to our observations, when Jewishness was not concealed, the descendants could more easily elaborate the trauma and the process was connected with less pathogenic elements.

In each case secrecy means a strong tension, anxiety for the second generation. Very often it is a hidden book, a family photograph that it is forbidden to inquire about, a code phrase, the meaning of which is concealed from the child. Furthermore, this act is not ineluctably followed by relief because the child gets no explanation. The secret of Holocause is thus connected to the secret of being a Jew.

A characteristic feature of the phenomenon of splitting and of the special entanglement of good and evil is the almost tragic way in which the second (and frequently the third) generation is being informed about its Jewish origins. Most often, parents make the decision to reveal the facts because their children mock other children's Jewishness. In an extreme example, two brothers of the second generation mocked each other's Jewishness, so the parents felt obliged to instruct them. Though quarrels between the children were not rare, we cannot consider the antecedents of one of their most ferocious debates as quite accidental: it took place after the family had visited Auschwitz.

4. The Survivors and the Process of "Inheritance"

We are dealing here with the survivor syndrome only insofar as it played a decisive role in transmitting the trauma. The generalizations we try to arrive at may give our colleagues some clues to accomplish the task of discovering hidden symptoms.

The data have shown that psychic disturbances can be very severe in both sexes but passive–depressed character alterations are more frequent in men. What we (lacking a better expression) called "humiliation" had a more severe and lasting effect on them. Among women the survivor syndrome is most often expressed in the somatic and mental symptoms of constant anxiety, severe psychosomatic illness, or else in a characteristically "oversized" need to care for others—at the expense of treatment of their own diseases.

We have to take into consideraiton that survival itself meant something positive. The children born after 1945 at any rate inherited this "positivity"—the fact that their very existence was a proof of the parent's survival. In a more latent manner, however, they "inherited" something else too: namely that they were a means of survival, of a new and "clean" beginning for their psychologically injured parents who displayed manifest and latent symptoms (see Kestenberg, Freiberg).

The uniform and most conspicuous phenomenon of transmittance mechanisms is the "atmosphere of secrecy." Apart from the so–called character–level psychic symptoms an equally frequent phenomenon is the hidden "inheritance" of psychosomatic symptoms (a surviving mother mentioned, almost accidentally, toward the end of the interview, that she suffered from severe heart complaints, rheumatism, and a duodenal ulcer; she considered all these diseases incurable and they really proved to be so, because she neglected to have them treated). Two other subjects told us almost the same story about their mother: one of the mothers was a continuous "caretaker" in spite of her manyfold somatic diseases, the other made it impossible for anybody to provide tratment for her disease while she took care for the whole family until she suddenly died. (She used to say when discussions about family plans: "If we are still living then"— "we" being simultaneously, if ambiguously, as herself and the rest of the family.) An additional factor in the hidden nature of caretaking mothers' symptoms is that they stress the will to live, steadfastness, and if not mental health then at least its appearance.

5. Manifestation of the Inheritance of the "Secret"

Our first example stems from an interview made in 1987 with the representatives of three generations (the mother was born in 1917, her son in 1946, her grandson, born in 1972, was then a high–school student). The mother was in Mauthausen; she had lost almost her whole family, among them her two–year old daughter. She had never shared her memories with her son.

> We've never spoken about these things. It couldn't have been a constant theme, we had to live on; you couldn't forget all this, because you were constantly in it but to speak of it—would have been too much! Six of us remained alive from our 76–member family. You can't put that in words because if you lose one, that's something else but to meditate about whom I miss more, my child or my mother or all of them together. . . . We only felt [in 1945–46] that you would have something to eat and you must live. Whether it was correct or not, I cannot decide, you had to live, emotionally you couldn't have been more ruined you couldn't have ruined more. . . . I'm sorry I can't go on. . . . We weren't able to speak about this either then or afterwards. . . . If I'm going to speak about this what sort of education is it for my child? What will I teach him against my will? Vengeance or fear? No, thanks. We mustn't cry about the past, let's have a healthy family life.

That's how the story goes on: after forty years, at the age of seventy, she at last wrote down her Mauthausen memoirs. "I felt a sort of relief when I had finished. I had resolved something that society wasn't able to resolve."

And these are the words of her son born in 1946: "If I made a mistake in the class, me or Klári Klein, the teacher shouted: 'I shall bind you to each other!' I knew that Klári was a Jew but it was quite incomprehensible for me why it was precisely Klári the teacher wanted to bind with me."

The phenomenon of splitting can be very well observed here: to know and at the same time not to know something. He doesn't want to read his mother's memoirs either: "There is some subconscious self–defense in me against these disturbing experiences." He has never asked his mother: "I am against tearing wounds open."

Yet he learned something from his painful earlier experiences: when his own son went to nursery school he revealed the "secret" to him, but not to his younger sister: "She will not know it, although she has heard about it. . . . I have to carry on and not to speak about it."

And finally the grandson: "I've been given a clue, it entered my conscience. It is easy to learn from books about concentration camps but if my family hadn't been touched I wouldn't have thought it this way."

Here is another family, with two boys. The father: "We don't want to confuse their soul. In this new and free life why shouldn't we speak about the grandpa and grandma who were burnt?" The mother: "When I was liberated I had a nervous breakdown. . . . I would shout every night for months. . . . Night and day I thought my parents and brothers would return, though I knew that they couldn't." (The mechanism of the phenomenon is the defense based on splitting, an early form of the so–called denial.)

> We brought up our children to make them honest. . . . They quarreled and one of them said to the other: you dirty Jew. . . . Then we decided to tell them everything. To a five– and a six–year old child I couldn't tell that we had been in Auschwitz; what this means you can't tell. It wasn't a theme at home. I was thinking of this in 1956 because I saw a graffiti on a wall: "*Itzig*, we won't bring you until Auschwitz." [In Hungarian: "*Auschwitzig*": a mocking verse.]

The elder son:

> When I was nine, I saw on the wall of our house: "*Itzig*, we won't bring you until Auschwitz" . . . . I didn't understand the expression, that was the first time I met such things. It wasn't a taboo theme before. It simply didn't come up. My son plays soccer, one of the children, he was three years old, said that the MTK [a soccer team] is a Jewish team. Then I told him.

The younger son:

> I have read a book that was hidden at home, *The Death Factory*. . . . I was called a Jew and I knew it was an insult

and that was not good. . . . I have a brother, we had a big quarrel, I became nervous and called him a Jew.

VI. Summary

Is the vital threat (and its consequences) that was experienced by the parents a traumatizing factor for their descendants born after 1945? Our answer is yes. And we add: this trauma can be diagnosed, it needs to be recognized and treated by psychotherapy.

We have no doubt that the fundamentally traumatizing factor for the survivors' children (the external manifestations of which is the secret) cannot be easily recognized—precisely because of its hidden nature. And such is the case with the other symptoms. It's not very probable that our patients will call on us with such symptoms and complaints; during the process of psychotherapy, however, we should extend our free–floating attention to this eventuality.

As a result of further research we want to inform our colleagues about the possible focuses of this free–floating attention. In this respect our first generation subjects do not fundamentally differ from cases of the post–traumatic stress–syndrome. The second generation has been specifically touched by the change in the character of the parents and in the early and later parent–child relationship.

The severity of the distubance may of course vary; this is why we have to deal with individual varieties and attempt an explanation. The early ("primitive") psychic mechanisms making up the complex phenomenon of "secret" deserve a special attention; such is the denial based on splitting and some other mechanisms that are actually characteristic of borderline syndromes. In these cases we must make clear the degree of the narcissistic damage in the parent caused by persecutions and in the child as a consequence of disturbances in the parent–child relationship (the source of which is to be found in the parent's pathology).

All this has a double utility: a specific "disease entity" can be cleared up and our experiences may serve to aid in the discovery and treatment of other severe syndromes with few external signs and with rigidly defended appearances of outwardly normal functioning.

References

American Psychiatric Association, *Diagnostic and Statistical Manual of Psychiatric Disorders.* 3rd ed. Washington, DC: American Psychiatric Association, 1980.

Bergman, M. S. and M. E. Jucovy, "The Experience of Survivor Parents" in *Generations of the Holocaust.* New York: Basic Books, 1983, pp. 46–61.

Bettelheim, B., *Surviving the Holocaust.* London: Fontana, 1986.

Bettelheim, B., "Egyéni és tömegviselkedés szélsőséges helyzetekben" [Individual and Mass Behavior in Extreme Situations] in *A végső határ* [The Extreme Limit]. Budapest: Európa. Modern Könyvtár, 1987.

Breslau, N. and C. G. Davis, "Posttraumatic Stress Disorder: The Stressor Criterion." *Journal of Nervous and Mental Disease*, vol. 175, 1987, pp. 255–264. See also commentaries on pp. 256–276 by J. I. Escobar, *et al.*, J. D. Lindy, *et al.*, and R. J. Ursano.

Brown, J. A. C., *Techniques of Persuasion.* London: Pelican, 1981.

Des Pres, T., *The Survivor.* New York: Oxford University Press, 1976.

Eitinger, L., "Rehabilitation of Concentration Camp Survivors." *Psychotherapy and Psychsomatics*, vol. 17, 1969, pp. 42–49.

Erős, F. *et al.*, "Hogyan jöttem rá, hogy zsidó vagyok?" [How Did I Discover That I Was Jewish?] *Interjúk Medvetánc*, nos. 2–3, 1985, pp. 129–144.

Ferenczi, Sándor, "A háborús neurozisok pszichoanalizise (1918)" [The Psychoanalysis of War Neuroses] in *Lelki problémák a pszichoanalizis tükrében* [Psychic Problems in Light of Psychoanalysis]. Budapest: Magvető, 1982.

Frenkel–Brunswik, E. and R. N. Sanford, "The Anti–Semitic Personality" in *The Yearbook of Psychoanalysis.* New York: International Universites Press, 1949, vol. 3, pp. 243–264.

Freiberg, J. T., "Difficulties of Separation—Individuation as Experienced by Offspring of Nazi Holocaust Survivors." *American Journal of Orthopsychiatry*,. vol. 50, 1980, pp. 87–95.

Freud, S., "Fragment of an Analysis of a Case of Hysteria" ("Dora") in *Case Histories I.* London: Pelican Freud Library, vol. 8, 1977, pp. 31–166.

Kardiner, A., "Traumatic Neuroses of War." *American Handbook of Psychiatry.* S. Arieti, (ed.) New York: Basic Books, 1965, pp. 245–257.

Kernberg, O. F., "The Structural Interview" in *Severe Personality Disorders.* New Haven: Yale University Press, 1984.

———. "Technical Considerations in the Treatment of Borderline Personality Organization." *Journal of the American Psychoana-*

lytical Society, vol. 24, 1976, pp. 735–829.

Kestenberg, J., "Psychoanalytic Contributions to the Problem of Children of Survivors from Nazi Persecution." *Israel Annals of Psychiatry and Related Disciplines*, vol. 10, 1972, pp. 331–345.

———, and Y. Gampel, "Growing Up in the Holocaust Culture." *Israel Journal of Psychiatry and Related Sciences*, vol. 20, 1983, pp. 119–123.

Klein, H., "The Meaning of the Holocaust." *Israel Journal of Psychiatry and Related Sciences*, vol. 20, 1983, pp. 119–128.

Klein, M., "Notes on Some Schizoid Mechanisms (1946)" in *Envy and Gratitude*. London: Hogarth Press, 1975.

Kogan, I., "Working Through the Vicissitudes of Trauma in the Psychoanalysis of Holocaust Survivors' Offspring." Budapest, Nov. 1987. (A lecture delivered at the Conference of Psychoanalists on the Treatment of Trauma in Children and Adults.)

Kolb, L. C., "A Neuropsychological Hypothesis Explaining Posttraumatic Stress Disorders." *American Journal of Psychiatry*, vol. 144, 1987, pp. 989–995.

Krell, R., "Holocaust Survivors and Their Children: Comments on Psychiatric Consequences and Psychiatric Terminology." *Comprehensive Psychiatry*, vol. 25, 1984.

Krystal, H., (ed.) *Massive Psychic Trauma*. New York: International Universities Press, 1968.

Kulcsár, I., "A maradék zsidóság lelki keresztmetszete" [The Psychological Mosaic of Remnant Jewry] in *Maradék zsidóság* [Remnant Jewry] Benoschofsky, I., (ed.) Budapest: Budai Izraelita Aggok és Árvák Menházegyesületének Évkönyve, 1946, pp. 34–38.

Luchterhand, E., "Early and Late Effects of Nazi Imprisonment." *Social Psychiatry*, vol. 5, 1970, pp. 102–110.

———. "Prisoner Behavior and Social System in the Nazi Concentration Camps." *International Journal of Social Psychiatry*, vol. 13, 1964, pp. 245–264.

Ludowyk–Gyomroi, E., "The Analysis of a Young Concentration Camp Victim." *Psychoanalytic Study of the Child*, vol. 18. New York: International Universities Press, 1963.

Luel, S. S., and P. Marcus, (eds.) *Psychoanalytic Reflections on the Holocaust: Selected Essays*. Hoboken, NJ: KTAV, 1984.

Rose, S. L. and J. Garske, "Family Environment. Adjustment and Coping Among Children of Holocaust Survivors." *American Journal of Orthopsychiatry*, vol. 53, 1987, pp. 332–344.

Rosenfeld, D., "Identification and Its Vicissitudes in Relation to the Nazi Phenomenon." *International Journal of Psycho-Analysis*, vol. 67, 1986, pp. 53–64.

Solkoff, N., "Children of Survivors of the Nazi Holocaust: A Critical Review of the Literature." *American Journal of Orthopsychiatry*, vol. 51, 1981, pp. 29–42.

Sonnenberg, S. M., "Children of Survivors." *Journal of the American Psychoanalytic Association*, vol. 22, 1974, pp. 200–204.

Székács (Schönberger), I., "Disorders of the Ego in Wartime." *British Journal of Medical Psychology*, vol. 21, 1948, pp. 248–253.

Szilágyi, J., *Gondolatok egy zsidó származású beteg pszichoanalizise kapcsán (esettanulmány)* [Thoughts on the Psychoanalysis of a Patient of Jewish Origin. A Case Study], 1985 (manuscript).

Virág, T., "Elaboration of Trauma in the Psychotherapy of an 8–Year Old Boy." Esetbemutatás a Trauma–feldolgozás gyermek– és felnöttanalizisben c. konferencián. Budapest, Oct. 1987. (A case study presented at the Conference of Psychoanalists on the Treatment of Trauma in Children and Adults.)

THE LOSSES OF HUNGARIAN JEWRY
A Contribution to the Statistical Overview

László Varga

The Jews of Hungary Prior to the German Occupation

A scholarly inquiry into the demography of Hungarian Jewry is frought with many difficulties. This is due primarily to the lack of absolutely reliable statistical data. The problem is especially acute for the wartime and postwar periods. Relatively accurate data exist, however, with respect to the so-called Golden Era of Hungarian Jewry, the period of the Austro-Hungarian Compromise (*Ausgleich*), extending from the emancipation of 1867 to the end of World War I. The demographic evolution of Hungarian Jewry during this period is reflected in the following table:

Year	Total Population	Number of Jews	Percentage of Jews
1869	13,579,129	542,257	4.0
1880	13,728,622	624,737	4.5
1890	15,162,986	797,961	4.7
1900	16,838,255	831,162	4.9
1910	18,264,533	911,227	5.0

As these figures reveal,[1] the Compromise period was demographically characterized by a quickening of the process of assimilation and a leveling and later a marked weakening of immigration, contrary to the views—and accusations—traditionally advanced by anti-Semites.

The census data for the 40-year period of the Austro-Hungarian era do not show any rapid expansion of the Jews in the Hungarian part of the empire. However, as a result of defeat in World War I and the subsequent Trianon Treaty (1920), Hungary's demographic picture underwent a radical change. Under the terms of the treaty, Hungary lost over half of its total population with its Jewish population decreasing from 911,227 in 1910 to around 470,000. The proportion of the Jews in the total population, however, rose for a while at least, from 5 to 5.9 percent. The demographic evolution of Hungary during the interwar period is reflected in the following table:

Year	Total Population	Number of Jews	Percentage of Jews
1920	7,990,202	473,355	5.9
1930	8,688,319	444,567	5.1
1940	9,067,267	400,980	4.3

Within the new territory of Hungary the number of Jews first stagnated and then decreased remarkably. Their proportion actually fell below the prewar level. The chief reason for the decline was that Jews, once tolerated, were now being persecuted by the government. This fundamentally new tendency can only partly be explained by assimilation. In 1919, for instance, mostly after the triumph of the counterrevolution between August and December, approximately 7,000 Jews converted. The number itself can hardly be considered significant by standards of either the previous or the following "normal" periods. There were usually between 200 and 250 annually. The same goes for the mixed marriages, although in this respect a marked increase can be noted. Before the turn of the century there were a total of 400 mixed marriages. After the turn of the century there were a total of 400 mixed marriages. After 1920 the number averaged between 900 and 1,000 per year.

The abovementioned changes in the figures point to an increase of Jewish emigrations.[2] In spite of their decrease in number, the proportion of Jews should not be underrated, since in 1930s Europe, Hungary's proportion of Jews, 5.1 percent, stood out. The proportion of Jews was greater only in Poland (9.15 percent), Lithuania (6.55 percent), and Romania (5.54 percent). By contrast, the proportion of the German Jews was a mere 0.86 percent. It was hardlly an accident that, in his talks with Hitler, Horthy stressed that the German "solution" could hardly be applied to Hungary. Hungarian modernization had, in fact, been the work of Jewry for the most part—and assimilated Jewry at that.

The Hungarian Jewish population decreased even more dramatically in the decade after 1930, falling to 400,900, (4.3 percent) in 1941. This number, however, rose to 725,007 as a result of the territorial changes of 1938–1941. (Hungary acquired the *Felvidék* (Upper Province) and *Kárpátalja* (Carpatho-Ruthenia) from Czechoslovakia in 1938 and 1939, respectively; Northern Transylvania from Romania in 1940; and the Délvidék (the Bácska area) from Yugoslavia in 1941.)[3] According to the census of 1941, the number and percentage of Jews in Trianon Hungary and in the acquired territories were as follows:

Area	Number of Jews (by Religion)	Percent of Total Population
Trianon territory	401,000	4.3
Felvidék (Upper Province)	68,000	7.8
Kárpátalja (Carpatho-Ruthenia)	78,000	12.5
Northern Transylvania	164,000	7.5
Délvidék	14,000	1.4
Total	725,000	4.9

Source: 1941 Census

While the survey was relatively accurate, although hardly precise, it related only to that part of the population who belonged to the Jewish denomination. Those considered Jews only on the basis of the Nuremberg-type racial laws can only be guessed at. During the persecutions, the Third Anti-Jewish Law of 1941 was regarded as a legal basis, which meant that anyone was considered a Jew if at least two of his or her grandparents had been born in the Jewish religion. Accordingly, there was a certain difference in the German and the Hungarian interpretation and definition of Jewishness. The most important difference was that the Hungarian law did not acknowledge the concept of *Mischling*. Therefore, while in the Reich three categories were set up, in Hungary there were only two.

The 1941 census attempted to determine the exact number of those who declared themselves to be Jews. According to this, apart from those of Jewish religion there were 34,435 more people who confessed to being Jewish on the basis of Law No. IV:1939, the so-called Second Anti-Jewish Law. Experts in statistics, however, accepted these figures based on self-declaration only as a minimum. In this case such an evaluation seems obvious, since to declare oneself Jewish was to sentence oneself to discrimination. On the other hand, it is undisputable that the overwhelming majority of the population were very well aware of their origins. With all this taken into account, the number of Jews not identified by their faith could be put as high as 75,000–100,000.[5]

The 1941 census data can be applied to the conditions on March 19, 1944 only with modifications. The number of Jews kept declining. There were 5,250 fewer by the fatal day. On the other hand, the above figures were even more essentially altered by population migrations, which cannot be proven statistically but seem clearly supported by secondary sources. Thus, according to an estimate by the German Foreign Office, between 300 and 600 people departed each month before the occupation,[6] which establishes the number of Jewish emmigrants in the period between the last census and the German occupation between 16,000 and 17,000. As for immigration during this period, there are not even rough estimates. Immigration was almost completely illegal. Furthermore, one has to allow for the fact that the 1941 census did not extend to the illegal immigrants of previous years. That meant Jews of Hungarian nationality from Slovakia, Romania, and Austria, although in this latter case immigration was not confined to the Hungarian minority, and was accompanied by a certain amount of re-emigration as well. In comparison, the number of Jews immigrating into Hungary from the Reich was insignificant. Most of them were Polish. The number of Polish refugees has long been a disputed subject in the Hungarian historical literature, but there must have been at least 100,000. As to the Jews within this emigration, no attempt has yet been made to determine their proportion. From indirect sources—such as the reports of SS-*Obergruppenführer* Otto Winkelmann, leader of the SS in Hungary—and more specifically from the high proportion of Jews among the Poles arrested by the German authorities, one may conclude that the majority of Jews who fled to Hungary were Polish.

One must also allow for the losses suffered by Hungarian Jewry in the period between the 1941 census and the German occupation. Among these were the victims of the deportation of July–August 1941, of the 1942 massacre in Ujvidék, and of the labor service.[7] Therefore, the number of people considered to be Jews by the laws in effect at the time of the German occupation, can be stated only with order of magnitude accuracy. The demographic picture of Hungarian Jewry on March 19, 1944 is reflected in the following table:

Item	Number of Jews	Losses
Jews, by religion, according to census of 1941	725,000	
Identified as Jews under Law No. XV of 1941	100,000	
Natural increase/decrease in Jewish population, 1941–44		5,250
Immigration	50,000	
Emigration		16,000–17,000
Deportation to Kamenets–Podolsk*		14,000–16,000
Ujvidék massacres**		1,250
Victims of labor service system***		42,000
Total	875,000	78,500–81,500
Difference, approximately	795,000	

*Reference is to the deportation of the so–called "alien" Jews during the summer of 1941. Many sources identify the number of Jews deported as 20,000. According to currently available evidence, the actual number was between 16,000 and 18,500. Of these approximately 2,000 escaped; the others were massacred near Kamenets–Podolsk, together with the local Jewish population.
**The number of Jewish and non–Jewish victims of the so–called "anti–partisan" raids by the Hungarian military authorities in January–February 1942 in and around Ujvidék cannot be established with absolute certainty. The Nedic government of the wartime Serbian state spoke of 13,000 victims; the German Legation identified the number of Serbian casualties as 6,000 and that of the Jews as 4,000. The official postwar investigations, established the number of victims as 3,755. Of these, 1,250 were identified as Jews.
***The number of Jewish labor service casualties includes those who had fallen into Soviet captivity.

The German Occupation Era

The tragedy of Hungarian Jewry during the German occupation has been documented in numerous works.[8] It is difficult, if not impossible, to determine with any degree of exactness the share of responsibility that the Germans and Hungarians must bear for this tragedy. While it is not possible to hold the Germans accountable only for the Jews they destroyed outside Hungary's borders, it is equally impossible to blame only the Germans or the German occupation for the tragic fate that befell the Jews. Since one cannot regard Nazism as an exclusively German internal matter, it is pointless to classify the victims merely as victims of Germany.

The fate of Hungarian Jewry weighs heavily on both German and Hungarian history. Seeking a certain objectivity, several attempts have been made to round off the loss figures without doing any further investigations. However, it has been proved by research work carried out forty years later that the statistical findings of an earlier generation of demographers, although not always precise in details, were a true reflection of reality. These findings about the fate of Hungarian Jewry during the fateful years of 1944–45 are reflected in the table on the following page:[9]

By explaining the categories used in the following table, the fate of Hungarian Jewry is being reconstructed—very accurately in some parts, and in order-of-magnitude accuracy in others. The number of those deported needs explaining in the first place, with respect to the accuracy of the figure given here. This category consists of all of those who were forcibly transported and removed from the country and handed over to the German authorities. Thus, the number includes the deported Jews as well as the labor servicemen "lent" to the Reich. The number should be regarded as minimal insofar as it refers only to those documented in some way at the time. This means that even though far more labor servicemen are known to have been driven to the Reich in the final phase of the war, these are included in those "of uncertain fate," for lack of precise documentation.

Number of Jews on March 19, 1944		795,000	
Deported		508,861	
Of these returned by end of 1945	121,000		
Survived but not returned	5,000		
Died, approximately			382,500
Lived in Budapest at the end of the war	119,000		
In labor service at the end of the war	15,000		
Emigrated, approximately	5,000		
Of uncertain fate		147,000	
Of these died in Hungary			120,000
Survived	27,000		
Killed or died, total			502,500
Survived, total	293,000		

Although the number of survivors in Hungary—in contrast to the deported—can be stated only as an order-of-magnitude figure on the basis of the data at our disposal (a total of 134,000), this figure should also be considered minimal, since the number of the actual survivors is definitely higher. This can be attributed in part to the fact that whereas the number of Jews illegally in hiding in Budapest can be precisely stated, in the countryside only the more significant cases have been revealed. In addition, we have placed the foreign Jews in hiding into the category of those "of uncertain fate," for lack of precise figures. Some of these left the country illegally after the German occupation, but since the majority of those left behind stayed illegally either in or outside the Budapest ghetto, there is only fragmentary data concerning them. To the Budapest survivors are added those who lived to see the end of the war in labor service somewhere in wartime Hungary.

Apart from those mentioned above, we have included in the category "of uncertain fate" Jews who died in Hungary in the given period, for whom it is not clear whether their deaths are to be attributed to the German occupiers or Hungarian officialdom (or nonofficialdom for that matter) or are due simply to wartime activities, illness, and suicide. This number includes those killed on Hungarian territory—victims of the concentrations before the deportations and of the foot marches; those who were killed or died in labor service in their homeland; those killed in ghettos; massacred Jews who tried to escape or were discovered in hiding.

There is a separate class that consists of those Hungarian citizens who managed to escape deportation or labor service and to find refuge abroad. Their number is estimated at 5,000; the three main destinations of escape are Slovakia and Romania, Palestine, and the area controlled by the Yugoslav partisans. Nevertheless, these estimates are open to question, as there is no knowledge whatsoever as to how many of the Jewish escapees fell victim to the war activities in those areas.

On the basis of postwar censuses, the number of survivors with Hungarian citizenship in the 1944 territory of the country was estimated at 260,000. If we add to these the foreign Jews as well as those who managed to escape abroad or failed to return to Hungary after the deportations, and finally those who later returned from Soviet capitivity, the number of survivors could be put at around 300,000 in order of magnitude. Lastly, when making our final adjustment, the victims of the period preceding the German occupation must be added to the above 502,000 victims. Thus the Holocaust in Hungary claimed at least 550,000 Jewish lives.

Notes

1 The demographic figures are based on the statistics of the censuses made public by the Statistical Office of Budapest.

2 Whereas the decrease in the number of Jews of the Israelite faith between 1920 and 1930 can be explained by emigration (90 percent), the decrease that incurred during the next decade is explained by conversion (58 percent). The loss due to negative natural increase during this decade was also remarkabale (41 percent), for only 271 people emigrated during this period. Yehuda Don and George Magos, *Demographic Development of Hungarian*

Jewry. Department of Economics, Bar–Ilan University (Research Institute on the Economic Behavior of Jews.)

3 For demographic and other details relating to these territorial acquisitions, see Randolph L. Braham, *The Politics of Genocide. The Holocaust in Hungary*. New York: Columbia University Press, 1981.

4 Exempted from these provisions were those both of whose parents were born in the Christian faith. The law applied to marital legislation only; in all other cases, the definition of Jew was based on the provisions of the Second Anti–Jewish Law (Law No. IV of 1939). However, the emergency power granted to the government made it possible for it to apply the much harsher provisions incorporated in the so–called Third Anti–Jewish Law (Law No. XV of 1941), which was largely based on the Nuremberg Laws.

5 A contemporary statistician, identified as an "expert on the Jewish question," estimated that the number of the converted or Christian Jews was 100,000. Since this figure was also relied upon by the World Jewish Congress, it is also used here, especially since the assumption that there were only around 75,000 such Jews could not be verified either. It is a fact that between 1919 and 1941, 36,644 Jews converted in the area of Trianon Hungary. These were identified as Jews under the Second Anti–Jewish Law. At the time of the 1941 census, 30,731 Jews who did not belong to the Jewish faith regarded the anti–Jewish laws as binding on themselves. These data are really insufficient to determine the number of Christian and converted Jews with any degree of certainty. One may nevertheless assume that reality comes closer to the documented 58,320 than to the estimated 100,000. See also Jenő Lévai, *Zsidósors Magyarországon* [Jewish Fate in Hungary]. Budapest: Magyar Téka, 1948, pp. 463–469. See also Zeev Rotics, "Be–shulei ha–netunim ha–statistiím al ha–marat ha–dat be–kerev yehudei Hungaria be–shanim 1900–1941" [Jewish Conversion in Hungary. Remarks on the Statistical Data for 1900–1941] in *Dapim lecheker tekufat ha–shoah* [Studies on the Holocaust Period]. Tel Aviv: Hakibbutz Hameuchad, 1978, pp. 222–28.

6 *A Wilhelmstrasse és Magyarország. Német diplomáciai iratok Magyarországról, 1933–1944* [The Wilhelmstrasse and Hungary. German Diplomatic Papers Concerning Hungary, 1933–1944]. Compiled and edited by György Ránki, *et al.*. Budapest: Kos-

suth, 1968, Doc. No. 722.

7 For details on the pre–occupation losses of Hungarian Jewry, including the massacre of "alien" Jews near Kamenets–Podolsk, the Délvidék mass murders, the casualties of the labor service companies, see Randolph L. Braham, *The Politics of Genocide, op. cit.*

8 For bibliographical references, see Randolph L. Braham, *The Catastrophe of Hungarian Jewry, A Selected and Annotated Bibliography.* New York: Institute for Holocaust Studies of the City University of New York, 1984, 501 pp.

9 The statistics compiled for the World Jewish Congress, which was employing its own methods of computation, established the number of survivors at 260,500 and that of the victims during the German occupation at 501,500. These data have in part been corrected by Randolph L. Braham (see his *Politics of Genocide, op. cit.*, vol. 2, p. 1146), who reached, however, almost the same conclusions.

CONTRIBUTORS

Uri Asaf received a doctorate in chemistry from the Eötvös Loránd University of Budapest. On the research staff of the Racah Institute of Physics, Hebrew University of Jerusalem, Dr. Asaf is the author of numerous articles in professional journals.

István Cserne. A graduate of the Semmelweis Medical University of Budapest, Dr. Cserne is chief of the Drug Department of the National Public Health Council of Hungary.

Tamás Majsai is a Protestant Minister and a highly prolific author on a variety of subjects dealing with the Holocaust. He authored, among other things, several studies in the "Yearbook of the Ráday Collection" (*Ráday Gyüjtemény Évkönyve*).

Katalin Pető is a graduate of the Semmelweis Medical University of Budapest. A psychiatrist interested, among other things, in the trauma of children of Holocaust survivors, Dr. Pető is associated with an outpatient clinic in Budapest.

Maida Pollock. A former deportee from Szombathely, Ms. Pollock, a translator, served as Concert Manager of Princeton University from 1964 until her retirement in 1986.

Maria Schmidt received her doctorate in history from the Eötvös Loránd University of Budapest and is associated with the Institute of History of the Hungarian Academy of Science. A recognized expert on the Holocaust, Dr. Schmidt is the author and/or editor of several works, including *Kollaboráció vagy kooperáció? A Budapesti Zsidó Tanács* [Collaboration or Cooperation? The Jewish Council of Budapest].

Sándor Szenes is a writer and journalist formerly associated with *Népszabadsáq* [People's Freedom], a Budapest daily. He is the author of numerous works, including *Befejezetlen mult* [Unfinished Past].

Julia Szilágyi. A graduate of the Semmelweis Medical University of Budapest, Dr. Szilágyi is a psychiatrist associated with the National Institute for Nervous and Mental Diseases of Budapest. She is particularly interested in the psychotherapy of Holocaust survivors and of their families.

Szabolcs Szita is currently associated with the University of Pécs. He is the author of several scholarly works, including *Haláleröd. A munkaszolgálat és a hadimunka 1944–45. évi történetéhez* [Death Fort. Contributions to the History of Labor Service and Military Work in 1944–45] and *Holocaust az Alpok elött* [Holocaust in Front of the Alps].

György Szöke is a professor of Russian language and literature at the Eötvös Loránd University of Budapest. He also has a doctorate in psychology with specialization in psychoanalysis. He is the author of numerous essays on the psychology of artistic creativity.

László Varga is a sociologist associated with the Institute of History of the Hungarian Academy of Science. He is the author of several essays dealing with the history and sociology of the Jewish community of Hungary.

Dieter Vaupel has a doctorate in political science from the University of Kassel and is currently on the faculty of his *alma mater*. He is the author of *Das Aussenkommando Hess. Lichtenau des Konzentrationslagers Buchenwald 1944/45* and of a number of articles dealing with several aspects of National Socialism.